A CULTURAL HISTORY
OF EDUCATION

VOLUME 5

A Cultural History of Education
General Editor: Gary McCulloch

Volume 1
A Cultural History of Education in Antiquity
Edited by Christian Laes

Volume 2
A Cultural History of Education in the Medieval Age
Edited by Jo Ann H. Moran Cruz

Volume 3
A Cultural History of Education in the Renaissance
Edited by Jeroen J.H. Dekker

Volume 4
A Cultural History of Education in the Age of Enlightenment
Edited by Daniel Tröhler

Volume 5
A Cultural History of Education in the Age of Empire
Edited by Heather Ellis

Volume 6
A Cultural History of Education in the Modern Age
Edited by Judith Harford and Tom O'Donoghue

A CULTURAL HISTORY
OF EDUCATION

IN THE AGE
OF EMPIRE
VOLUME 5

Edited by Heather Ellis

BLOOMSBURY ACADEMIC
LONDON • NEW YORK • OXFORD • NEW DELHI • SYDNEY

BLOOMSBURY ACADEMIC
Bloomsbury Publishing Plc
50 Bedford Square, London, WC1B 3DP, UK
1385 Broadway, New York, NY 10018, USA

BLOOMSBURY, BLOOMSBURY ACADEMIC and the Diana logo are
trademarks of Bloomsbury Publishing Plc

First published in Great Britain 2020

Cover design: Rebecca Heselton
Cover image: Naughty little girl standing in the corner © whitemay / Getty Images

A catalogue record for this book is available from the British Library.

Library of Congress Cataloging-in-Publication Data
Names: Ellis, Heather, editor.
Title: A cultural history of education in the age of empire / edited by
Heather Ellis.
Description: London; New York: Bloomsbury Academic, 2020. | Series: A
cultural history of education; volume 5 | Includes bibliographical
references and index.
Identifiers: LCCN 2020030647 | ISBN 9781350035201 (hardback)
Subjects: LCSH: Education–History–19th century. |
Education–Europe–History–19th century. | Education,
Colonial–History–19th century. | Scholarship and
learning–Europe–History–19th century.
Classification: LCC LA126 .C85 2020 | DDC 370.94/09034–dc23
LC record available at https://lccn.loc.gov/2020030647

ISBN: HB: 978-1-3500-3520-1
        Set: 978-1-3500-3556-0

Series: The Cultural History Series, Volume 5

Typeset by Integra Software Services Pvt. Ltd.
Printed and bound in Great Britain

To find out more about our authors and books visit www.bloomsbury.com
and sign up for our newsletters.

CONTENTS

FIGURES

GENERAL EDITOR'S PREFACE

Bloomsbury *Cultural History of Education*

Education has not always been well recognized as being central to cultural history. Even the leading British cultural historian, Peter Burke, could omit education from his own list of the inner circle of neighboring forms of history and related disciplines, despite its importance in much of his own work. According to Burke, this inner circle of neighbors included intellectual history, social history, political history, history of science, history of art, history of literature, history of the book, history of language, history of religion, classics, archaeology, and cultural studies.[1] Yet education has a strong claim to be integrally involved in all of these areas. The anthropologist Clifford Geertz was perhaps more alert to this when he noted in *The Interpretation of Cultures* that education was indeed fundamental when attempting to match "assumed universals" with "postulated underlying necessities." On a social level, Geertz continued, this was because "all societies, in order to persist, must reproduce their membership." In psychological terms, moreover, "recourse is had to basic needs like personal growth—hence the ubiquity of educational institutions."[2] Even earlier, Raymond Williams in *The Long Revolution* pointed out the "organic relation" between the cultural choices involved in the selection of educational content and the social choices involved in its practical organization, and demonstrated how these links could be traced and analyzed historically.[3] This six-volume series, the Bloomsbury *Cultural History of Education*, seeks to build expansively on these essential insights.

After the Second World War, there were a number of historical texts that sought to explain educational changes since Greek and Roman times.[4] Since the 1970s, such a broad chronological sweep has become increasingly rare. An international infrastructure has grown for research into the history of education, with its own societies, journals, and conferences now well established.[5] Internationally, for example, the International Standing Conference for the History of Education (ISCHE) supports an annual conference and a journal, *Paedagogica Historica*. There are national societies around the world with their own conferences and journals, including the USA, the UK, France, Australia, and many others. However, these have often tended to promote specialist research in particular areas rather than broad synthesis.

Indeed, this process of increased specialization has tended to be both horizontal and vertical in nature. Horizontally or laterally, as it were, journal articles often are only able to engage with relatively narrow aspects or historical contexts in a detailed manner. They have tended also to be largely confined to study of the local or national picture, although recent "transnational" research has provided a significant corrective to this.[6] Vertically, they largely eschew a longer-term framework for the field conceptualizing continuity and change since ancient times. They have also increasingly concentrated on the most recent periods, the nineteenth and twentieth centuries, rather than on earlier ages.

The current project offers a form of coherence and indeed synthesis in the history of education. Perspectives based on the cultural history of education promise to highlight continuity over time, and the resilience of practices, values, and ideas. As one collection of articles based on an international historical conference has concluded, "there may be remarkable periods of stability for cultural and educational formations and the role they play in the making of particular ethno-national-religious communities," even though there is also "seemingly inevitable challenge, reform, sometimes regression—always change."[7] In this respect, the Bloomsbury *Cultural History of Education* series offers both a general synthesis of recent international research and an overall conceptual framework linking together different epochs, to inform and stimulate further work in the field.

Early work in the cultural history of education arose from a new approach to the history of education that fought against its traditional preoccupation with the growth of national systems of modern schooling, while embarking on a wholesale revision of its key aims and aspirations.[8] In a landmark publication in 1960, *Education in the Forming of American Society*, Bernard Bailyn called for a widening of the scope and definition of "education" in educational history. According to Bailyn, it should be concerned rather less with the rise of modern schooling and much more with educational processes as they have occurred in many different kinds of institutions and milieux, pervading individual lives and collective social experiences. Topics and problems in a "new" educational history would not be restricted to "those bearing on schools, teachers and formal instruction," and it would consider nothing less than the "process and content of cultural transfer."[9] Bailyn hoped, indeed, that education itself might be reappraised "not only as a formal pedagogy but as the entire process by which a culture transmits itself across the generations."[10]

Following the earlier works of R. Freeman Butts,[11] it was Lawrence Cremin who did the most to define and explore the cultural history of education. Cremin proposed that "education" should not be regarded either as age-related or as being confined to schools, but that it constitutes, far more broadly, "the deliberate, systematic, and sustained effort to transmit, evoke, or acquire knowledge, attitudes, values, skills, or sensibilities, as well as any outcomes of that effort."[12] This was a set of processes more limited than terms such as "socialization" or "enculturation" might imply.

Nevertheless, it undoubtedly takes the idea and practice of education, in Cremin's words, "beyond schools and colleges to the multiplicity of individuals and institutions that educate—parents, peers, siblings, and friends, as well as families, churches, synagogues, libraries, museums, summer camps, benevolent societies, agricultural fairs, settlement houses, factories, radio stations, and television networks."[13] Cremin himself embarked on a three-volume history of American education based on this central premiss.[14] The organization of chapters in the current serial production owes more than a little to Cremin's classic design.

Cremin's approach to the cultural history of education has often been criticized, both for its practical limitations and for its extensive vision. For some, he appeared so preoccupied with the many informal educational institutions of modern society that he allowed too little space to accommodate the growth of modern schooling.[15] For others, such as Harold Silver, the project was itself a perilous pursuit:

> The attraction and importance of extending the history of education into such fields as the history of the press and the modern media, church activities and popular culture, are obvious. So are the dangers, with the possibility of the emergence of an amorphous history which fails to locate discrete educational institutions in a clear relationship with other processes, and also fails to establish acceptable and understandable definitions of wider educational territories.[16]

Its application to the United States since the late eighteenth century was itself an ambitious undertaking. In the current volumes, such a project must be scrutinized against the widest possible canvas of time and space, from ancient times to the present.

The past generation has witnessed the rise of cultural history in its many forms and variations.[17] At the same time, an extensive literature has developed the cultural history of education further in a number of areas, including the emergence of a "new" cultural history of education.[18] Lynn Fendler emphasizes language as the "material stuff" of new cultural history and insists that such history is generally oriented to be critical of "mainstream histories," but concludes that "new cultural history opens up many more possibilities for history of education: more topics, more perspectives, more analytical possibilities, more directions, and more interdisciplinary collaborations."[19]

Key examples of research on the cultural history of education in the past two decades include that of Harvey Graff and others, who have understood the history of literacy in terms of its social and cultural practices.[20] Peter Burke has produced a detailed social history of knowledge, including changes in media and communications, in two volumes.[21] Other work has explored religion and morality in society, with the church as a key defining educative agency alongside the family that has also attracted extensive interest.[22] Children and childhood have been the focus of much historical interest since the early work of Philippe Ariès.[23] Teaching and learning have been widely discussed for their longer term historical characteristics, not only in schools and other formal educational institutions but throughout life and society.[24] The notion of learning lives, or of learning throughout the lifespan, also introduces the aspect of individual agency that can be examined through case studies of life histories.[25] In more global terms, cases of cross-cultural encounters and their consequences have been documented in depth and detail.[26]

These key themes are explored in depth in the six volumes of the Bloomsbury *Cultural History of Education* series. My warmest thanks go to the volume editors who have each produced excellent collections of original essays by leading researchers in this burgeoning field, to the contributors of these essays that navigate and interpret such broad areas of territory, and to the publishers for their patience and support as this project has developed.

Gary McCulloch
Brian Simon Professor of History of Education
UCL Institute of Education London
December 2019

Introduction

Education in the Age of Empire 1800–1920

HEATHER ELLIS

INTRODUCTION

The nineteenth century is remembered in a variety of ways in the history of education, but whether long or short, the age of nationalism or of empire, it is always important. Other periods are frequently defined in relation to it; the eighteenth century has been described as a "reservoir of educational strategies" for the nineteenth century and the twentieth century is often viewed as dominated by its legacy.[1]

The Cultural History of Education series has given the title "Age of Empire" to the nineteenth-century volume, which covers the period 1800–1920. It is worth pausing to think about this for a moment. The phrase, "age of empire" has most famously been deployed by Eric Hobsbawm in his tripartite series covering the modern history of Europe.[2] Specifically, he characterized the final third of the "long" nineteenth century, the years from 1875 until 1914, as the "age of empire." This period certainly corresponds to the highpoint of Western imperialism; but despite Hobsbawm using other metaphors to describe earlier parts of the nineteenth century, namely the Age of Revolutions (1789–1848) and the Age of Capital (1848–75), there are, I would argue, good reasons to consider the entirety of the long nineteenth century (defined here as 1800–1920) as the "age of empire."

Firstly, it is important to consider the term "empire" critically. Its most familiar definition is that given by Catherine Hall and Sonya Rose: "a large, diverse, geographically dispersed and expansionist political entity" that reproduces "differentiation and inequality among people it incorporates."[3] "At its heart, empire is about power."[4] Such a definition would characterize accurately the far-flung colonial empires that cast a long shadow over much of the nineteenth century including those of Britain, France, Germany, Italy, Belgium, and Japan. Some distinction needs to be made, however, between these "empires overseas," as Joyce Goodman, Gary McCulloch, and William Richardson have termed them,[5] and the large, contiguous land-based empires that were equally significant in power and influence, which included Russia, China, the Ottoman Empire, and Brazil. There is a strong case to be made for including the USA in this group as well, which expanded post-independence to dominate much of the continent of North America.

As Marc Depaepe has noted, the useful split which Goodman, McCulloch, and Richardson make between "empires overseas" and "empires at home" makes most sense for those Western European colonial empires in which considerable geographical distances separated metropole and colonies, and in which the involvement of the colonial power in educational matters was a relatively new and sudden development.[6] For land-based, continental empires such as Russia, Austria, and the Ottoman Empire, although large in geographic terms and diverse in cultures, their territorial contiguity and centuries-long social, political, and economic entanglements rendered the distinction between "home" and "away" far less clear.

This distinction is also important when we reflect on how to use the terms "nation" and "empire," which are crucial to understanding the educational history of this period. While much good work has been done in recent years by historians to argue for the abolition of a dichotomy, which is still widely used in sociological and international relations literature,[7] some differences in how we use the two terms remain important. Daniel Tröhler argues convincingly for the need to retain a respect for national differences in the study of the emergence of mass education systems in Western and Central Europe in the nineteenth century.[8] He criticizes sociologists of education for identifying "myriad international similarities, despite the fact that the national educational systems were instituted on national agendas."[9] Instead of a history of "European standardization" in education, he argues for a "European history of education, reconstructing a striking educationalized nation-building in its diversity and transnational flows."[10]

In Western European states including Britain, France, Germany, and Italy that all developed mass education systems over the course of the nineteenth century,[11] although linked, the discourses of nation and empire remained distinct, largely because of the usually substantial geographic separation between the imperial metropole and its colonies. Hence the possibility of describing "empires overseas" and "empires at home" in relation to them. The same would also apply to the Japanese Empire. In the case of contiguous land-based empires, however, the link between nation and empire was much closer. Many such empires including Russia, the Ottoman Empire, China, Austria, and arguably the USA as well sought with varying degrees of success to make the geographically contiguous imperial territory coextensive with a Western-style version of the nation-state; and the attempted introduction of state-sponsored mass education systems was a crucial part of this.

This was something never attempted by Western colonial powers with regard to their territories overseas with the possible exception of the French in Algeria, which was officially incorporated into metropolitan France in 1848. As a result, we tend to see much weaker state-sponsored educational initiatives in the colonial empires of European states. While there are differences, in general, large-scale formal education for the masses was primarily left to local political elites and religious movements—in particular, missionary groups and charities—to establish and organize. Hence the great variety in the nature, extent, and effectiveness of formal education in the colonies of Western empires.

This also cautions us not to restrict our understandings of education to formal state-sponsored schooling or, for that matter, to formal schools sponsored by any organization or body. In the vast majority of cases, these were restricted to initiatives offering elementary education. With the partial exception of the USA, access to secondary and higher education remained limited to the most well-off in society and, for the most part, to men. In addition, as much recent work has shown, the effectiveness of formal educational initiatives, whether sponsored by states, religious organizations, or charities, was substantially limited by a range of actors with their own agency and agendas. These included most obviously parents, teachers, and the children themselves but also religious groups (where the state or a particular religious group was the sponsor), local elites, and traditional educators.[12] Following the suggestions of Lawrence Cremin, we should be expansive in our understanding of what education is and where it takes place.[13] For Cremin, we should focus on "the multiplicity of individuals and institutions that educate," which include parents, siblings and wider family, churches, synagogues, mosques, libraries, and museums.[14] There are many stories to be told of the development of informal educational spaces as well as counter initiatives developed by indigenous peoples in the long nineteenth century which intersect and interact with the more familiar narratives of the development of state and missionary-sponsored education.

Finally, in this introduction I want to point to recent work in transnational history and historical geography that emphasizes "empire" as a complex, networked space rather than a political and cultural entity or actor.[15] I am keen to consider the long nineteenth century from the point of view of "empires" as spaces in and across which a wide variety of educational actors, objects, and ideas traveled, driven by an equally wide range of motivations and purposes.

EMPIRES OVERSEAS

Following Hobsbawm's sense above, the best-known story of "empire" in the long nineteenth century is that of the ongoing overseas expansion of a number of Western European countries including Britain, France, and Germany, joined later by powers such as Japan. Yet even here there are important distinctions to draw. While many Western and Central European states laid claim to large parts of North America, Africa, Asia, and Oceania, only Britain exported considerable numbers of its own population to "settle" some of its overseas colonies, notably Canada, Australia, New Zealand, and South Africa. As Laurence Brockliss and Nicola Sheldon explain, these were "settlement colonies where wave after wave of white immigration had quickly overwhelmed the small indigenous populations and eventually led to the establishment of self-governing but dependent clones of the mother country."[16] Elsewhere in the world—"in India, South-East Asia, Africa and the Caribbean—European immigration had generally been very limited, and a minuscule colonial elite, ultimately taking orders from the metropolitan government, was in charge of large swathes of territory occupied by native peoples who were seldom ethnically or linguistically homogeneous."[17]

The development of formal education in Britain's settler colonies was of necessity affected by discussions about state-sponsored schooling in Britain. In the early nineteenth century, it sometimes happened that land was reserved to build an elementary school when new settlements were established; what was more common, however, was the decision of the colonial administrations to allow inhabitants to set up schools of their own. Few of these institutions, however, had a significant educational impact with the majority of successful schools in the mid-nineteenth century being organized, as in Britain, by church groups and charities. By mid-century there were growing calls for the colonial authorities to provide greater levels of financial support and practical intervention. The majority of the settler population in Australia and New Zealand, for example, were farmers and people were concerned that most schools were located in urban areas.[18] A major driver of popular schooling in Canada was wide-scale social unrest. In the 1830s the colonial government in both Lower and Upper Canada witnessed significant opposition and uprisings; in these conditions, mass education was introduced in an attempt to avoid further social breakdown and unrest. A system of public schools sharing a curriculum and staffed by qualified teachers was set up designed to educate all the children of settler families.[19] Interestingly, the system's architects based their design on the school system in Ireland which had been established over the course of the 1830s. It even recommended that textbooks printed by the National Board of Commissioners in Ireland be used in Canadian schools.[20]

While Britain's settler colonies saw free, compulsory mass schooling established, the same cannot be said for the other colonies of European empires, particularly where European settlers were in the minority. This was not for want of trying. For most colonial powers, state-sponsored education still represented what they considered the most effective way to instil loyalty and imperial patriotism. Algeria's governor-general declared in 1847 that "one school will replace two battalions."[21] Both France and Britain also liked to make much of the "noble" and "improving" function that their colonial projects were, they said, designed to effect and education was central to this project. In their own words, mass elementary schooling was intended to spread Christianity, morality, discipline, self-control, hygiene, and basic practical skills in manufacturing and farming.[22]

Despite this, however, the British state was decidedly hands-off when it came to setting up education in its colonies. In large part it relied on voluntary efforts, in particular, those of missionary societies with international networks, to provide basic education as part of their missionary work. Direct involvement on the part of colonial governments in the British Empire would only take place if there was seen to be an urgent need. This is in somewhat stark contrast with the French, who, given their secularist outlook where education was concerned, chose rather to found colonial schools that were funded and run by the state. In Algeria, for example, despite low initial levels of state involvement—by the end of the 1870s there was only a small number of state schools catering for children who spoke French or Arabic—by 1883 a much grander plan had been put in place, based directly on changes that had already been implemented in France. Following the 1883 change in policy, all communes in Algeria were to benefit from a compulsory state-funded school that was free to attend, offering a comprehensive education in French to all girls and boys of school age.[23]

Among a number of other factors, Antonio Nóvoa called in 1995 for the history of colonial education to focus much more on rediscovering the experience, identities, and political actions of educational actors in colonial spaces.[24] One of the ways this call has been most effectively answered has been in the many examples of recent work by historians investigating the agency, experiences, and resistance of indigenous peoples who were subjected to the colonial education initiatives of Western imperial powers. Particular attention has been drawn recently to scholarship that employs notions of "frontiers" and "contact zones," which operate not simply as geographical concepts but also as metaphors for "processes of interaction between indigenous peoples and Europeans."[25] Such concepts challenge and disrupt the established chronologies and geographies through which the history of colonial education and the history of indigenous peoples and their agency has been understood. This focus on the agency of the colonized has also received much support from subaltern and postcolonial studies, which collectively have stressed the need to rediscover previously hidden or suppressed narratives, representations, understandings, practices, and cultural values.[26]

Historians have traditionally pointed to the huge financial burden of directly funding mass education in colonial settings by the metropolitan state when trying to account for the relative failure of these initiatives.[27] However, historical scholarship is now increasingly recognizing the extent to which the agency and resistance of indigenous peoples limited the effectiveness of the efforts of colonial states to introduce formal education—both directly and indirectly through missionary societies, charities, and other voluntary groups. In particular, research is highlighting the extent to which communities in parts of the globe with long-standing indigenous literate cultures, including large parts of North Africa and Southeast Asia, continued to favor existing schools, particularly religious schools, in an effort to resist the attempts of colonial education to convert their children to Christianity and to the language of their colonizers.[28]

In some cases, agents of colonial governments actively worked to undermine state-sponsored education for indigenous people, especially in areas where there were large numbers of European settlers. Historians have recently highlighted examples where settler families pressured colonial governments to spend the majority of the funding available on setting up schools for their own children rather than children of the indigenous population. As Harik and Schilling have shown, in 1908 the Algerian *colon* congress demanded that elementary education be suspended for the children of indigenous people, prompted by fears that an education in French chiefly provided by teaching staff drawn from France could promote social unrest and protests against colonial rule.[29] There were similar tensions developing in the Belgian Congo. Despite building large numbers of state-funded and state-run elementary schools for the children of the black indigenous population, it remained the firm aim of the Belgian colonial authorities to separate and reinforce the perception of fundamental difference and inferiority between the Congolese black students and their white European counterparts. Key to this was to restrict the education offered to the native languages of the black Congolese peoples. As Marc Depaepe shows, there were systematic attempts in Belgium in the early twentieth century to develop a specific tailored pedagogy appropriate to the "psychology" of the Congo's black peoples, which was ultimately designed to ensure the continuing subordinate status of black children and of the colony as a whole.[30]

In British India, the colonial state concerned itself primarily with educating a relatively small elite who would assist in governing the subcontinent. Missionary activity in India focused its efforts chiefly on the children of relatively wealthy parents. As the work of Nita Kumar shows, the vast majority of Indian children, if they received any formal education, were schooled in one of the traditional Hindu schools that were dotted throughout the subcontinent.[31] In recent years, historians of education have been revealing the complex array of indigenous individuals, groups, and networks who strove to offer alternative educational initiatives and pathways for children and young people in colonial India. The work of historians such as Barnita Bagchi who has studied the lives and activism of Indian women in promoting women's and girl's education in colonial Bengal, refocuses scholarly attention on the agency and resistance of actors previously cut out of traditional accounts of educational development.[32]

EMPIRES AT HOME

However, as many historians have pointed out, the experience and impact of possessing an overseas "empire" was also very much felt "at home."[33] At the start of the period covered in this volume, this impact was not significant. Writing for a middle- and upper-class audience, James Mill gives a good impression of the state of affairs in Britain in the opening paragraphs of his 1817 *History of British India*: "On other subjects, of any magnitude and importance, I generally found, that there was some one book, or small number of books, containing the material part of the requisite information [...]. In regard to India, the case was exceedingly different. The knowledge, requisite for attaining an adequate conception of that great scene of British action, was collected no where." "Hitherto," he continued,

> the knowledge of India, enjoyed by the British community, has been singularly defective. Not only among the uneducated, and those who are regardless of knowledge, but among those who are solicitous to obtain a competent share of information with respect to every other great branch of the national interests, nothing is so rare as to meet with a man who can with propriety be said to know any thing of India, and its affairs. A man who has any considerable acquaintance with them, without having been forced to acquire it by the offices he has filled, is scarcely to be found.[34]

This is broadly representative of the situation in France as well at the start of the nineteenth century. While it is true that, in a sense, imperialism was taking on a more popular form with Napoleon declaring himself "first consul" in 1799 and then "emperor" in 1804 with all the trappings of ancient Rome, this did not involve a substantive engagement with France's overseas territories, the so-called "first colonial empire," most of which had been lost by the turn of the century. The same can be said of Napoleon's attempts to conquer and subdue much of Western and Central Europe. Despite the imperial rhetoric, which was particularly strong around his legal and educational interventions in other European countries, the extent to which the general public in France were involved in this has been debated by historians.[35] Few other European states had substantial colonial empires at the start of the nineteenth century. The most important "empire" for inhabitants of the various German states in this period was the Holy Roman Empire.

Yet by 1920, in Britain, France, and Germany, the promotion of a popular imperialism had become the focus of intense effort in the respective state-sponsored education systems. This has been most comprehensively studied in the British case. Historians of Britain such as Linda Colley have highlighted the "tightening grip of empire on Britain's culture and self-image" and the fundamentally entangled nature of Britain's domestic and imperial endeavors.[36] "The history of Britain and the histories of its various overseas ventures cannot be adequately approached separately," writes Colley. "For good or ill, they were interlinked."[37] Historians such as Stephen Heathorn have shown convincingly how the discourse of "empire" and imperial citizenship came to infiltrate state-funded education in Britain through textbooks, pageants, wall charts, poems, songs, and annual commemorative events such as Empire Day.[38] As their work reveals, there were concerted efforts to cultivate an overarching imperial loyalty and identity as an imperial "race" in an effort to bind the increasingly powerful working classes to the traditional elites. Imperialism, in this sense, was designed to lessen a sense of cleavage between rich and poor, those Benjamin Disraeli famously likened to "two nations,"

> between whom there is no intercourse and no sympathy; who are as ignorant of each other's habits, thoughts, and feelings, as if they were dwellers in different zones, or inhabitants of different planets; who are formed by a different breeding, are fed by a different food, are ordered by different manners, and are not governed by the same laws.[39]

While members of the working classes in European nations were taught to believe themselves members of a predestined "imperial race," distinguished against the many indigenous peoples living under colonial rule, there were similarly intense efforts to train up elite young men to think of themselves as leaders of the imperial race. This for the most part took place in expensive and exclusive private boarding schools. In Britain, this enterprise was dominated by a network of long-established and more recently founded private schools (confusingly known as "public schools") that criss-crossed the country. Several aspects of this education for imperial leadership have been examined in detail by historians, in particular, the emphasis on a classical education, which encouraged parallels with ancient Rome, and a growing cult of athleticism, which peaked around the turn of the twentieth century;[40] in the British case, there were also important links between the elite private schools and the newly founded elementary schools following the 1870 Education Act, which helped to ensure a similar emphasis on the importance of empire in elementary classrooms.[41] Recently, the other European colonial powers have come under greater historical scrutiny in this regard. John M. Mackenzie's edited volume

European Empires and the People: Popular Responses to Imperialism in France, Britain, the Netherlands, Belgium, Germany and Italy examines what Mackenzie terms the "colonisation of consciousness" in a series of six case studies that urge the comparative study of the transmission of ideas about empire within the colonizing states themselves in the nineteenth and twentieth centuries.[42]

Yet we have to look beyond the Western European states. "Empire at home" had a meaning outside Europe and this is perhaps most clearly demonstrated in Japan during the later years of the nineteenth century when it was expanding its overseas territories. At the outbreak of the First World War almost all school-age children in Japan were attending state-run schools and the cultivation of a shared sense of imperial citizenship and destiny was as prominent here as anywhere in Europe. Inculcated through a focus on neo-Confucian ethics, fealty to Japan's Imperial House alongside traditional virtues of deference and duty were placed at the heart of the Japanese domestic education system.[43] The intended effect was clear to see from the Imperial Rescript on Education of 1890, which was issued to all schools in Japan along with a portrait of Emperor Meiji. It contained the following injunction: "Should emergency arise, offer yourselves courageously to the State; and thus guard and maintain the prosperity of Our Imperial Throne coeval with heaven and earth."[44] All Japanese children were required to memorize and repeat the Rescript in their classrooms on special occasions. As in Britain, growing significance was attached to physical activity and development. The importance of education to the development of the individual, which had been stressed in Japan earlier in the nineteenth century, was significantly downplayed in later years. In the words of the Law of Educational Administration promulgated in 1900: "Education is not simply the development of the individual's abilities […] the primary aim is to cultivate imperial subjects for the benefit of the state, citizens who will contribute to its existence and survival."[45]

Outside the imperial powers themselves, however, the experience of being part of an "imperial people" also impacted on the educational experience of children and young people from settler families in the overseas territories. Across the British Empire, for example, by the end of the nineteenth century, many schoolchildren in Canada, South Africa, Australia, and New Zealand were using the same textbooks and commemorating the empire in the same way as their metropolitan British counterparts;[46] this shared "imperial" discourse continued outside of school as well with popular children's literature such as boys' and girls' annuals being produced in one-size-fits-all varieties across the empire.[47] Similar efforts were made by other European colonial powers to promote a shared "imperial" identity among their citizens resident in the colonies. Daniel Walther, for example, has explored the attempts of the German colonial government and social and political elites to inculcate a sense of imperial identity in German citizens resident in German West Africa at the end of the nineteenth century and the beginning of the twentieth.[48]

NATION-EMPIRES

Joyce Goodman, Gary McCulloch, and William Richardson make the important point that the long-standing focus of historians of education on the interaction between education and Western imperialism in the long nineteenth century derives from the very specific postwar milieu of decolonization and the corresponding rise of postcolonial studies.[49] "Reassessment of education and empire," they write, "has taken place within a rapidly changing post-colonial intellectual and cultural milieu in 'the West,' a *zeitgeist* given momentum and space by the long withdrawal from empire of European states after 1945." "But," they continue,

> if this is the main arena which has influenced post-colonial ways of thought [...] it is by no means the only theatre of relevance. Beyond Africa and the region labelled by the British in the nineteenth century as "the Middle East", the subjugation of indigenous peoples by ascendant powers in North America, South America, Asia and Oceania all fall within this ambit.[50]

In these types of land-based contiguous empires, a considerably different and more blurred relationship between "nation" and "empire" persisted. Tomoko Akami puts it well when she argues for the need to view the two terms as an "integral unit."[51] In these land-based empires, nation-building processes, including, crucially, the establishment of education systems, took place coextensively with the imperial territory. With varying degrees of success these states attempted to turn large, culturally and ethnically diverse territories into something resembling a Western-style nation-state.

Until the final decades of the nineteenth century, the Russian Empire had a large, ethnically diverse population but was one of the least industrialized states compared with Central and Western Europe. The years leading up to the First World War saw both significant levels of economic expansion and an unprecedented drive by the Russian state to create a mass elementary education system designed to further the process of urbanization and the creation of new literate workers by concentrating new schools in towns. As part of the emancipation of the serfs in 1864, Tsar Alexander I instituted a School Statute in which plans were laid for a national network of "terminal schools" where school-age children would receive at least three years of free education. These were to be constructed and paid for by municipal *duma* but overseen by a centralized state inspectorate. Army recruits were encouraged to obtain school leaving certificates and a new statewide curriculum was launched in 1897 with more legislative reforms in 1908. Ultimately, however, the impact of these reforms was considerably less than was hoped for. As Ben Eklof has shown, on the eve of the First World War, there was little, if any, mobility between primary and secondary levels of education, with the latter remaining very patchy and dominated by the social elite.[52]

More impactful in terms of social mobility and economic growth were the popular education reforms in the United States. As soon as independence from Britain had been achieved, one of the first reforms to be demanded was a state-funded elementary system with the primary aim of constructing a shared national identity for the white inhabitants of the former British colonies. However, despite Thomas Jefferson proposing bills on several occasions between 1779 and 1817 that called for the establishment of such a system these were not put into effect. Only later in the nineteenth century, following significant social, cultural, and political changes including the introduction of universal manhood suffrage, increasing industrialization, and the beginnings of mass immigration did the scheme gain favor with elected representatives. By the start of the American Civil War, in the northeastern and western states a comprehensive, state-funded system of "common schools" had been established under the oversight of a superintendent of education. Even so, black and indigenous Americans were pushed to the margins of this new system. As Ellen Berg argues, "Although the early public schools were known as common schools, children's experiences were often not common at all, depending on their race [...] Non-whites, whether Native Americans, Asians, or African Americans, had vastly different educational experiences from their white counterparts."[53] As the work of Christine Renée Cavalier, B.S. Chapman, and others are showing, there were many different responses by African Americans and Native Americans to state-funded educational initiatives, ranging from covert resistance to prominent public counter-initiatives focused on promoting indigenous and African American writing.[54]

Demonstrating the true complexity of the term "empire," the Brazilian Empire founded in 1822 developed out of the former Portuguese colony and, as with the United States, struggled with the task of building a new sense of common identity across vast swathes of territory following independence. Just as in the USA, education was central to the debate about how to do this. Yet, despite considerable government rhetoric and many promises, no statewide system was established. Instead, the task of building and running schools was given to local councils who lacked both the money and manpower to successfully set up a new education system. Long-standing racial and social class prejudices impeded progress with black and indigenous peoples having little access to formal education.[55]

Beyond Europe and the Americas, even in societies with established literate cultures there had been few attempts to set up nationwide government-funded education systems before the final decades of the nineteenth century. In many places, including the Ottoman Empire, Burma (Myanmar), and Thailand as well as large parts of India before the establishment of the British Raj, education was chiefly organized and funded by local religious authorities. To avoid precisely this fate of being incorporated within the domain of European empires, many within the ruling classes of the Ottoman Empire, China, Thailand, Iran, and other large countries took the decision that in order to survive they had to begin their own nation-building efforts in earnest; and education initiatives understandably featured prominently in these plans.

In the Ottoman Empire, universal elementary education—the teaching of reading, writing, and basic maths—through curricula emphasizing a common Ottoman identity, sense of pride, and history was considered most important and key to its survival as an independent state. In reality, however, very little was accomplished by the end of the Ottoman Empire in 1918. The religious and ethnic diversity of the empire was reflected in a number of distinct school systems organized by the different communities. The state simply found itself unable to replace or incorporate this complex network of different schools into a nationwide secular education system. As well as a lack of engagement and take-up among the inhabitants of the empire, the would-be founders of a national state-sponsored system of schooling were significantly under-resourced.[56]

In China too, the Ch'ing government promoted state schooling with the aim of countering dissension and unrest among its huge and diverse population.[57] Yet, it provided no coherent funding to support the establishment of such a system and what schools there were continued to be funded and organized by local elites or overseas missionary groups. As a result, long-standing social divisions remained entrenched. The children of the elite were taught in their homes by private tutors while their less well-off counterparts received education either at charity schools set up by provincial governors or at the traditional *sushu* schools, which provided instruction to pupils belonging to particular clans or lineage groups. The education across these different types of schools was similar: children would learn to read and write Chinese characters, some history and science, as well as Confucian philosophy and traditional moral values. While the system was patchy and the majority of the population remained illiterate, it did succeed in providing a form of education to a significant number of children in China as well as an avenue for some boys from poor backgrounds to obtain a place in the state bureaucracy through the open competitive examination system. Variation across China was immense. As Sally Borthwick has shown, some provinces such as Zhili had by 1906 established as many as twenty elementary schools per county.[58] However, even here, this was far too few to provide anything close to universal coverage. With some 30 million inhabitants and 2.5 million children of school age, Zhili could offer only 209,668 elementary school places in 1909.[59] Indeed, the realization of a national system of state-sponsored education would have to wait until the advent of the communist state in 1949.

EMPIRES AS SPACE AND PLACE

In the final section, I take a step back from "empires" as political entities. Instead, I want to think of them as networked spaces, which, although shaped by political ideologies and power differentials, were made use of and traveled through by a wide range of (more or less) mobile actors frequently pursuing purposes and driven by motivations not directly connected with any national or imperial cause. It is with this in mind that Isabella Löhr and Roland Wenzlhuemer have called for the development of a "new analytical framework" that replaces the traditional analytical categories of "nations" and "empires" with a focus on "interaction and flows, transfers and exchanges as core categories in the study of history."[60] In the introduction to their 2014 edited volume *Connecting Histories of Education: Transnational and Cross-Cultural Exchanges in (Post)Colonial Education*, Barnita Bagchi, Eckhardt Fuchs, and Kate Rousmaniere highlight the "ways in which a transnational perspective deepens and complicates our understanding of colonialism, the nation state and the responses of local communities, institutions and individuals."[61]

Scholars including Steve Ballantyne and Antoinette Burton, and David Lambert and Alan Lester have argued that empires should be viewed as complex networks in which a wide range of commercial interactions, knowledge transfers, migrations, and other forms of contact and exchange took place in addition to more widely studied geopolitical and strategic military activities.[62] Moreover, they call for a focus not simply on interactions taking place within the spaces of empire but also on those that took place across imperial borders. Power relations linked to categories of "race," religion, gender, and class still conditioned those interactions; yet, it is important to recognize that individuals and groups making use of imperial networks did not operate exclusively within the spaces of empire.

Scholars working on the history of universities, for example, have tended to assume that the travel of scholars and students within the British Empire implied a positive view or promotion of imperial ideology.[63] This has been particularly the case with the way in which the scholarly fields of geography, ethnology, and anthropology have been seen in the nineteenth and early twentieth centuries.[64] This is itself, I suspect, closely related to another tendency within the historiography of universities in Britain (and across the world), namely, to assume a close relationship between the flourishing of universities and the growth of the nation-state and nationalism.[65] If we consider the close links (discussed earlier) between national and imperial identity, then, it comes as little surprise that many historians have assumed that Oxford, Cambridge, and to a lesser extent also the Scottish and provincial English universities extolled the idea of empire as they were also perceived to have been enthusiastic promoters of national identities over the course of the nineteenth century.[66]

If, however, we follow the example of David Lambert and Alan Lester in their 2006 study of imperial "careering" and conceive of "empire" in purely spatial terms, we decouple the term from an automatic association with imperial sentiment and allow the possibility that many different motivations drove groups and individuals who traveled within the borders of empires and made use of their networks. It is with this in mind that Lambert and Lester stress "the complexity, varied scale, constitutions and compositions of personal imperial spaces and networks."[67] Another advantage of conceptualizing empires in spatial terms, rather than simply as idea or ideology, is that it encourages us to treat it in a comparative light, alongside other spatial frames of reference such as the local, the regional, the national, and the global, which may also have shaped people's educational experiences and identities in the long nineteenth century. As Frederick Cooper has expressed it with regard to university scholars, "The spatial imagination of intellectuals [...] from the early nineteenth century to the mid-twentieth century was [...] varied. It was neither global nor local but was built out of specific lines of connection and posited regional, continental and transnational affinities."[68] In other words, the challenge is to ask how important (relative to other spatial frames) empires were to those who traversed their networks and under what specific conditions they emerged as especially relevant. Here, we should heed the call of Robin Butlin to pay more attention to "the dynamics and spatial scales of cultural circuits" in the nineteenth and early twentieth centuries.[69]

I began this introduction with the reflection that while the nineteenth century can and has been characterized in many different ways, it is always considered pivotal in accounts of educational developments taking place in earlier and later periods. The eighteenth century is frequently portrayed as preparing the ground for it; and much of the twentieth century (at least until 1945) is considered to have unfolded in its shadow. The period between 1800 and 1920 witnessed many of the key developments that still shape the aims, context, and lived experience of education today. Empire, as the title of this volume indicates, was a key organizing principle through which major educational developments across the globe were filtered in this period and without reference to which they cannot be properly understood: the spread of state-sponsored mass elementary education; the efforts of missionary societies and other voluntary movements; and the resistance, agency, and counter-initiatives developed by indigenous and other colonized peoples as well as the increasingly complex cross-border encounters and movements that characterized much educational activity by the end of this period.

However, it is vital that we also reflect critically on the meaning of "empire" and its relationship to other key nineteenth-century ideas, in particular, the "nation" and how this has varied over time and across space. The relationship between education and empire has too frequently been explored only with regard to the relationship between European colonial powers and their overseas territories. Yet, as recent scholarship in the history of education has shown, the impact of empire "at home" was just as significant. Nor should we only think of "empires overseas"; some of the most important "imperial" educational projects took place within and were initiated by central governments in large land-based contiguous empires such as the Ottoman Empire, Russia, and China. Historical research on education and empire has also traditionally tended to limit itself to considering empires as geopolitical entities and actors. In the final section, I pointed to one of the most significant trends in recent historiography—the move to conceive of empires as networked spaces in and through which many different actors, both individuals and groups, moved and exchanged ideas driven by diverse motives and agendas.

CHAPTER ONE

Church, Religion, and Morality

MARIA PATRICIA WILLIAMS

INTRODUCTION

Morality remained central to education in the period 1800–1920. To promote understanding of a good life and the means to live such a life a variety of educational practice was used in a range of formal and informal settings. The major development, however, was moral education and formation of children in the elementary schools of the evolving national education systems in Western Europe and North America. These were part of the response to modernity in these Christian-majority countries.[1] Muslim-, Hindu-, and Buddhist-majority countries did not experience the establishment of national education systems until later.

Expanding urban areas were a particular focus of concern in relation to moral stability. The emergence of the nation-state resulted in a new focus on civic virtue and the moral formation of citizens. The period saw the expansion of educational provision for the laboring classes, variously referred to as popular education, public education, and the common or public school.[2] The relationship between religion and morality had been challenged during the Enlightenment. Owen Chadwick points out, however, that at the beginning of the nineteenth century "nearly everyone was persuaded that religion and morality were inseparable."[3] Debate ensued, initially on the kind of Christianity appropriate to popular education and later on whether religion had a place at all. Churches and Christian organizations built on their established base and were the major providers of education until the 1870s. From that point, secular provision, which separated religion and morality, increased. The economic purpose of education in a competitive world, with the need for intellectual and technical knowledge and skills, became more important. The political and cultural conflict over the place of religion in the modern state, central to European "culture wars" of the period, also had an impact.[4] Church–state conflict and religious intolerance were seen as barriers to national unity and stability and contributed to increased support for secular education.

In exploring church, religion, and morality, examples will be taken from a range of national and transnational contexts. France, Italy, the United States, and England provide examples from two broad models of state intervention, one centralized, the other decentralized. Margaret Archer refers to the centralized model, where the state restricted provision, as a "concessionary" one.[5] It was adopted in France, Italy, and the United States. She describes the decentralized model, which incorporated existing provision, as a "competitive conflict" model—England is the best-known example. Church–state relations impacted on provision and practice in all four nations. In Italy, however, the presence of the papacy and the condemnation of Modernism made the church–state relationship there unique.[6] Whilst these four nations allow for comparison, they also provide opportunities to consider transnational issues. Many of the educational providers in all four nations were transnational organizations working in several or all of the nations as well as empires and diasporas. The largest provider, the Catholic Church, became more global in an age of nationalism and the nation-state.[7] Organizations promoting secular education were often part of transnational networks. Mass immigration had a profound impact on the relationship between education and religion in the United States and, on a smaller scale, in England. Three interrelated perspectives will be considered: the purpose, the provision, and the practice of education. The purpose will set out the desired outcomes of state legislation. The provision will identify the range of schools established by churches and Christian and secular organizations to achieve these desired outcomes in ways informed by their beliefs. The practice will explore pedagogies employed in schools, giving some indication of the experience of pupils and their teachers.

THE PURPOSE OF NATIONAL EDUCATION

Stability and unity 1800–70

The Enlightenment ideal of citizenship, enshrined in the United States' Declaration of Independence, referred to "the pursuit of happiness." The happiness of the individual was not, however, a major concern in the establishment of national education.[8] The purpose of a national education system was to meet the needs of the nation. Margaret Archer explains, in relation to France, that "the individual had no right to education if the state had no need of it."[9] Richard Aldrich noted that the term "national education" could mean "national as opposed to local and national as opposed to foreign."[10] Local loyalties in terms of class, religion, and geographical location were evident in divisions and disturbances during the nineteenth century. Contemporary observers focused on the violence and threat to order rather than the grievances and objectives of the protesters.[11] Popular education offered a means to promote a common morality that would contribute to stability and national unity.

Napoleon sought to unite the French to work and fight for the nation after the divisions of the revolutionary period (1789–1804). This remained the aim of successive French regimes: the Bourbon monarchy (1816–30), the July monarchy (1830–48), the Second Empire (1850–70), and the Third Republic (1870–1940). In building the United States following the War of Independence (1776–83) education was seen as "crucial to the vitality of the Republic."[12] Horace Mann (1796–1859), the best-known supporter of the common school, believed that "it would promote what he took to be the moral character required for democratic citizens."[13] National unity continued to be important in reconstruction following the Civil War (1860–5). Whilst England did not experience the upheaval of France, the years of Spa Fields (1816), Peterloo (1819), and Cato Street (1820) were not stable ones. M.J.D. Roberts has argued that "most members of the opinion-forming classes sensed a society adrift from precedent and past societies."[14] The demands and actions of the Chartist movement of 1838 to 1848 raised further concerns. Urban areas were viewed as in particular need of moral regeneration. As Brown observes, "The heathen city became an official discourse of the British state."[15] Immorality and poverty were seen as closely linked.

The unification of most of the Italian states in 1861 brought to the fore the need to "make Italians." Uniting those from different regions with common values and a commitment to the new nation was important. Silvana Patriarca, in *Italian Vices: Nation and Character from the Risorgimento to the Republic*, has also shown that concern with the character of the laboring classes featured significantly in national discourse.[16] For the Liberal leaders, "making Italians" was also about addressing vices, particularly sloth. The patriotism of Catholics was brought into question as Pius IX (1846–78) condemned the separation of church and state, a foundational principle of the united Italy. After the fall of Rome in 1870, he declared that Catholics should not participate in national politics. Attempts at reconciliation by both sides under Leo XIII (1878–1903) failed and there was no settlement until the Lateran Treaty of 1929.

The matter of "national not foreign" was important in relation to concerns regarding the loyalty and assimilation of immigrants. Between 1820 and 1920, 33.6 million migrants entered the United States.[17] Large numbers of Catholic migrants from Ireland and continental Europe entered England and the United

States, Protestant majority countries, fleeing oppression, poverty, and famine. Between 1851 and 1920, 3.3 million Irish entered the United States.[18] In 1886, 80,000 Italians entered. That figure doubled by 1891 and in both 1906 and 1913 the total was half a million.[19] Lawrence Cremin refers to American "urban situations in which high concentrations of impoverished immigrant families struck the fear of social disorder in the hearts of city fathers."[20] There were also high concentrations in England. The 1851 census showed that in Liverpool 83,813 or 22.3 percent of the population were born in Ireland. In Manchester it was 52,504 forming 13.1 percent of the population.

These were the contexts in which the churches and Christian organizations found opportunities to become major providers of elementary schooling at a time when morality and religion were deemed inseparable. The cost in terms of physical and human resources is another important reason. Christian organizations had structures in place and access to resources to build on their established base in popular education. Religious freedom, enshrined in the first amendment to the United States Constitution in 1791, spread to France, England, and later Italy during the nineteenth century. Religious tolerance, however, did not always feature in the morality of the period, particularly the relations between different providers of education. Owen Chadwick points out that early in the nineteenth century "the division was not between secular and religious education but between two different notions of religious education."[21] Both understood morality as derived from Divine Revelation. For Catholics and Anglicans denominational explanations of beliefs evident in Scripture, developed by theologians dating back to the early Christians were important. Their tradition was based on both faith and reason. They therefore supported the establishment of denominational schools. Other denominations argued that teaching morality did not require reference to denominational doctrines that should be explained in places of worship and within the family. These included many nonconformist Christian denominations, for example, Methodists, Baptists, Congregationalists, and Presbyterians. Separation of morality from theology also reflected their tradition referred to as "sola scriptura" (only Scripture). They supported the establishment of nondenominational Christian schools. The work of Christian organizations in education was, however, restricted with regulatory legislation allowing for increased monitoring and control by the state. This laid the foundations for secular provision that separated religion and morality.

By the mid-nineteenth century the basis of a national education system was in place in France, Italy, England, and the United States. This included the allocation of public funds to contribute to the cost of school buildings, teachers' salaries, fees for the poorest, and systems for central administration and monitoring. In the United States the state of Massachusetts was a leading promoter of the common school. In 1827 state legislation permitted the establishment of school districts permitted to raise taxes for school provision. As Lawrence Cremin points out, "it was more carrot than stick" as the state provided incentives in the form of subsidies rather than punitive fines.[22] Other states followed. The common school was conceived as a nondenominational Protestant school based on the idea of a common Christianity. Initially some Catholic schools that provided for the poorest children were allocated public funding as they were perceived as common schools, in the sense of serving the needy of the neighborhood. In the France of the July monarchy, the 1833 Guizot Law required each commune to establish a school. All teachers in public and private school were required to have a teaching qualification known as a *brevet de capacité* (certificate of capability). In 1859 in the Kingdom of Sardinia the Casati Law made similar requirements, which were extended to the rest of Italy following unification. These laws put in place the framework to decrease the influence of the Catholic Church in education. In England the matter of state financial aid for elementary schools had been raised as early as 1807. In 1833 the first public grant aid was allocated to two religious organizations, the National Society for Promoting the Education of the Poor in the Principles of the Church of England and the British and Foreign Bible Society representing other English Protestant denominations. In 1847 public funding was also allocated to the Catholic Poor School Committee.

National uniformity 1870–1920

From 1870 in England, France, and Italy legislation to extend schooling contributed to the separation of religion and morality in schools. In the United States the conception of the common school, now referred to as the public school, was reviewed and became more secular. The term "secular" has a variety of meanings in relation to education depending on the context in which it is used. It was in use to refer to the subjects of the curriculum which were not religious. James Arthur has identified a number of other understandings: "'secular' could mean an education independent of religion or it could mean the advocacy of an outlook that was hostile to religion, depending on the context and who was using the term. Many liberal Christians understood the term 'secular' to mean 'non-denominational', as opposed to 'non-religious'."[23] It was also understood as relating to popular education. The French term for "secular," "laïque," comes from the Greek word "laikos," meaning "of or belonging to the people."[24] The historiography reflects these different understandings. English scholars' use of the term "popular education" is usually understood broadly as educational provision for the laboring classes or national systems of education. French historians have used the term "popular education" in relation to "laïque" or non-religious education for these groups.[25]

In England there was a focus on the promotion of economic efficiency, commercial and technological development, requiring secular subjects. England had become a leading industrial nation in spite of very little investment in education.[26] At the Paris World Fair of 1867 advances of other nations were demonstrated. At the fair of 1851 England had won most of the prizes but performed badly in Paris in 1867. In 1870 the Forster Act established local school boards to set up secular rate-supported elementary schools in areas that had no school.

Elementary education was made free and compulsory in Italy with the Coppino Law in 1877 and in France with the Jules Ferry Laws of 1881 and 1882. These laws also allowed for the separation of morality and religion. Coppino proposed a new norm, the "duties of man," with reference to no particular religion. In England it became compulsory in 1880 and free in 1891. The term "moral Instruction" appeared in the Board of Education's 1904 and 1906 *Codes of Regulations for Elementary Schools* and 1905 *Suggestions for the Consideration of Teachers.* In both England and Italy details were to be decided locally. In France, however, Ferry replaced religious education with "moral and civic instruction." These developments in moral education arose from concerns common to England, Italy, and France.[27] Supporters of secular education argued that provision based on religion had failed to cover content needed for citizenship. They also considered that interdenominational conflict distracted religious organizations from developing the required approaches. Intolerance had also resulted in a failure to communicate. Zeldin explains in relation to France: "What the ecclesiastical history of this century shows above all is a crisis of communication: churchmen and free-thinkers were so carried away by the bitterness of their disagreements that they became incapable of understanding each other, and hopelessly confused as to what their quarrels were about."[28] Bruneau argues that stability was needed "to keep the country from falling apart and to make it a secure home for property owners and those aspiring to that status."[29] The nation had experienced successive changes of regime, popular protest in 1830, 1848, and the 1870 Paris Commune. From 1871 the Republicans in France sought to establish "a program of moral instruction whose broad principles would apply everywhere and at all times in the education system."[30] It was hoped that such a program could establish unity through uniformity.

The United States saw increased urbanization from the 1870s. Active "national" Catholic parishes embraced the customs of the migrant groups they served, including the Polish and Italians. From mid-century an alliance of European immigrant radicals with Protestant reformers fueled anti-Catholic feeling.[31] The public school was viewed by Catholics as "a new form of Protestant religious establishment."[32] As a result, "the 'common Christianity' consensus broke down."[33] Cremin refers to the quest for an American "paideia," inviting comparison with the ancient Greek *paideia* or education for the ideal member of the *polis* (ancient Greek city state).[34] Catholics argued that there was no single model as "Americanism came in plural forms not in the single pattern of a Protestant *paideia*."[35] In 1870 a group of Catholics, Jews, and Freethinkers in Cincinnati proposed that because of the religious pluralism of the city the schools should be devoid of all religion.[36] The proposal was adopted by the Cincinnati School Board and supported by the Ohio Supreme Court. There was a widespread fierce reaction, with Catholics labeled as "un-American." In 1875 Congressman Blaine tabled an amendment, initiated by President Grant, to prohibit the use of state funds for religious schools. Rejected by Congress, it was later adopted in thirty-seven states. Religion and the public school was the major focus of the presidential campaign of 1876. Republican Rutherford B. Hayes defeated Democrat Samuel J. Tilden with what he saw as "a winning combination of anti-Catholicism and a pro-pan-American public school ideology."[37]

SCHOOL PROVISION

By the start of the twentieth century national educational systems encompassed three broad traditions: the denominational Christian, the nondenominational Christian, and the secular.

DENOMINATIONAL

Catholic

The reestablishment and significant extension of Catholic educational provision during this period was in large part due to the foundation of many institutes of Catholic female and male religious. They provided a massive unpaid workforce. The female congregations made the major contribution. During the nineteenth century over 400 were founded in France and 185 in Italy.[38] Most were teaching congregations. Members took a vow of poverty, which meant that they were not waged. Congregations were self-funding, often led by sister entrepreneurs. Their fee-paying schools, established to meet the demand from the emerging middle classes, funded free schools. They had other benefits. Many pupils became sisters and benefactors. Politicians in France and Italy did little to provide post-elementary education for girls.[39] A convent education was viewed as a good preparation for middle-class wives and mothers who were seen as having a particular responsibility for the transmission of morality. In France the number rose from 14,100 in 1837 to 27,300 in 1863.[40] In Italy in 1884, there were 1,584 fee-paying convent schools, with almost 50,000 pupils between ages six and seventeen.[41]

The increase in Catholic educational establishments outside of continental Europe benefited from waves of anti-Catholicism in Europe. Members of the Society of Jesus were forced to leave a number of European countries with the rise of liberalism in the first half of the nineteenth century. As a result, they "made modern Catholicism global."[42] Many priests and sisters fled the *Kulturkampf,* the conflict between the government and the majority of Catholic bishops in Germany during the 1870s. Between 1906 and 1909 many left France due to the legislative restrictions. The Society of the Sacred Heart closed 47 houses and 2,500 sisters migrated. Many European Catholic congregations developed as transnational organizations sending missionaries to colonies and diasporic communities. During the nineteenth century the Presentation Sisters, founded by Nano Nagle in Cork, Ireland, in 1775, spread to Newfoundland, India, England, Tasmania, Australia, and continental North America.[43] The Missionary Sisters of the Sacred Heart of Jesus founded in Codogno, Italy, in 1880, by Saint Frances Xavier Cabrini, expanded transnationally to work with Italian migrants. They had schools in the United States, Argentina, Brazil, Nicaragua, Panama, France, Spain, and England.[44]

Following Catholic Emancipation in 1829 the Catholic population of England and Wales rose from an estimated 80,000 in 1767 to over 700,000 in 1851 to 1.5 million in 1886.[45] Catholic schools expanded rapidly in urban areas, primarily to meet the needs of the many Irish immigrants. The 1850 Synod of Westminster decided to build schools before parish churches. The number of schools rose from 350 in 1870 to 1,045 in 1900. In 1870 the average number of children attending was 66,066, rising to 255,036 by 1900.[46]

In the United States, Catholic elementary schools were established by parishes and religious congregations. Initially some Catholic bishops had reservations, viewing education as the responsibility of the family and parish. Others were keen to support the public school system, regarding American liberalism as distinct from that of Europe. They developed the idea of "American exceptionalism." This rested on two premises: the first that European liberals were violent revolutionaries and the second that the American Founding Fathers had been orthodox Christians.[47] The expansion of the public schools as a "national" Protestant system, however, led the bishops to establish a system of parish schools. Many of the schools were bilingual, described by Cremin as "oases in the desert of Protestant hostility."[48] There was also a rapid growth in the number of teaching sisters. The School Sisters of Notre Dame, a German foundation, had 1,344 sisters in 1850 and 40,340 in 1900.[49] Provision did, however, vary across the country. New York benefited from the commitment of Bishop John Hughes from 1838. He adopted the policy of building schools before churches.[50] By 1865 there were schools in 75 percent of parishes. In Boston diocese, which built churches before schools, the figure was never more than 40 percent throughout the nineteenth century. Nevertheless, by 1920 the Catholic parochial school system was "second only in size and scope to the public school system."[51]

Anglican

In England and Wales, the Anglican Church provided the majority of elementary schools throughout the nineteenth century. Anglican education was also established in British colonies in Asia, the Pacific, and Africa through the work of the Anglican Missionary Society established in 1799. In 1811 the National Society for Promoting the Education of the Poor in the Principles of the Church of England was founded by Andrew Bell, an Anglican clergyman. It aimed to extend parish school provision, building on the legacy of parish schools and Sunday schools. Richard Aldrich pointed out that in 1812 some members of the Society "hoped that the National Society might provide the basis, if not the whole of national education. By the end of the century such a prospect had much diminished."[52] Traditional means of funding Anglican schools continued alongside the state grant. These included endowment, benevolence of individuals, including clergymen, collections on "sacrament Sundays," and prominent local families facilitating school building.[53] In 1859 the National Society was allocated two-thirds of the total state grant for education. Marjorie Cruickshank's *Church and State in English Education 1870 to the Present Day* provides a statistical overview.[54] By 1870, 77 percent (6,382 of 8,281) of grant-aided schools were Anglican. By 1900 this had fallen to 58 percent (11,777 of 20,117). Similarly, in 1870 pupils attending Anglican schools constituted 73 percent of the total recorded in aided schools (844,334 of 1,152,389). By 1900 it had fallen to 40 percent (1,885,802 of 4,687,646). This was the result of the growth of Catholic schools and the introduction of board schools. Most village schools, however, were Anglican.[55] Anglican clergymen played a key role in overseeing the work of the teacher, visiting and sometimes teaching. Teachers in the national schools were viewed as servants of the church and often expected to act as the vicar's assistant.[56] This changed during the century as teaching developed as a profession.[57]

NONDENOMINATIONAL

In continental Europe, England, and the United States, Protestant denominations put aside differences to work together to establish nondenominational Christian educational provision as an alternative to that of the established church. In France the educational interests of Protestants were promoted by the Société pour l'encouragement de l'instruction primaire parmi les Protestants de France (SEIPF) (Society for the Promotion of Elementary Schooling Among French Protestants), founded in 1829.[58] Well-known members were the politician François Guizot, and Benjamin and François Delessert, brothers from the Protestant banking family. In some regions of France, for example, parts of Gard and l'Hérault, 50 percent or more of the population were Protestants.[59] Protestant schools could become the commune school and gain funding under the Guizot Law of 1833, therefore numbers increased. After 1833 a number of Protestant evangelical societies opened schools. The Société évangélique (Evangelical Society) had opened 80 schools, employing 275 teachers by 1883, and the Société centrale (Central Society) had opened 60 by 1882.[60] In England from 1814 the British and Foreign Bible Society developed from the work of the Quaker schoolmaster Joseph Lancaster. It represented a range of nonconformist Christian denominations and was also active in the colonies. The society was also supported by some liberal Anglicans.[61] By 1870, 1,549 nondenominational schools received grant aid with 241,989 pupils. By 1900 the number of schools had decreased slightly to 1,537 but pupil numbers had increased to 345,759.[62]

In the United States the growth of the public school system was hindered by the concerns of several Protestant denominations.[63] Presbyterians, concerned to teach doctrine, built parish schools from the 1840s until the 1870s. The success of the public schools and their clear Protestant American identity won the Presbyterians over. The situation of Lutherans was different. They wished to provide religious, cultural, and linguistic integration in education. Sects such as the Amish and Mennonites did not send their children to public schools, fearing they might be corrupted. Lawrence Cremin refers to growth of the public school system as substantial in the North and North Atlantic states, moderate in the South, and spectacular in the Midwest.[64] The latter may have been influenced by Protestants seeking to dominate the west.[65] Following the election of President Hayes in 1876, Republicans sought to increase the role of the federal government in "standardizing education for blacks and whites and Northerners and Southerners."[66] Whilst public funding for Catholic schools for white immigrants was refused on grounds of promoting sectarianism and division, it was allocated to schools in the South, which segregated black pupils. In the early twentieth century "two centuries of racism towards blacks and Indians expanded to include early Asian immigrants" with separate schools for Chinese and Japanese children.[67] Whilst denominational schools did not receive public funding, the federal government had a different policy for Native Americans. Reservation schools were placed in the hands of Christian missionary organizations to "civilize" their pupils.[68]

SECULAR

Provision of secular schools did not necessarily mean there would be no religious teaching and supporters were not predominantly atheist. The "Destra" (historical right), which governed Piedmont and then the Kingdom of Italy until 1876, was made up of property owners and moderates, the majority of whom were Catholics, who wanted to see the church reformed and revitalized.[69] The requirement for "rights and duties," in the Coppino Law of the *Sinistra Storica* (Historical Left) government, was influenced by the ideas of Mazzini, a Protestant freemason. François Guizot was also a Protestant freemason. Isabelle Olekhnovitch points out that, "for Guizot, secular (*laïc*) was not opposed to Christianity, quite the contrary."[70] Guizot understood secular education as linked to freedom of religion and saw no role for the state in religious education. A petition in favor of popular education organized by the *Ligue de l'enseignement*

(Teaching League) indicated divided opinion. The *Ligue*, founded in 1869 by Jean Macé (1815–94) a deist teacher, was influenced by the movement of the same name in Belgium. It spread rapidly across France due to Macé's links with the Freemasons.[71] Of the signatories 383,381 favored free and compulsory instruction and 348,765 free, compulsory, and secular instruction.

In England the Central Society of Education was formed to lobby the state for an educational system that excluded religion from schools in 1836 but gained little support. The climate had changed by 1897 when the Moral Instruction League was founded. Susannah Wright argues that the influence of the organization far outweighed the membership.[72] The supporters included liberal Christians who "found themselves campaigning with committed secularists, freethinkers, positivists, socialists, eugenicists and atheists."[73] Eugenics prompted a new direction in the thinking of some members. The November 1907 meeting of the league led to the establishment of the Eugenics Education Society.[74] Eugenics, described by Brian Simon as the "triumph of Darwinism with its emphasis on heredity,"[75] was based on the work of Francis Galton, a professor at University College London (UCL). Known for influencing thinking on innate intelligence and the rise of selective education, it also impacted on ideas about moral formation through a new "scientific" understanding of the human person. Arthur explains that the Eugenics Education Society "held that low moral character was something predominantly inherited, and one solution was to sterilize the morally inferior and restrict marriage for the poor. The logic was clear: biological inferiority = social inferiority = inferior moral character."[76] In a paper given at the London School of Economics in 1904, Galton proposed eugenics as a "new religion," explaining that "It must be introduced into the national conscience, like a new religion. It has, indeed, strong claims to become an orthodox religious, tenet of the future, for eugenics co-operate with the workings of nature by securing that humanity shall be represented by the fittest races."[77]

Supporters of secular education usually lobbied the government to establish secular schools administered by the state rather than establishing their own schools. Secular schooling varied, however, according to the local context and agency of individuals. In England, 5,758 board schools had been established by 1900, comprising 29 percent of the total state-funded schools. They were large, however, with an average of 2,201,049 pupils attending or 47 percent of the national total.[78] In France the 1,535 Protestant schools became secular (*laïques*) following the Ferry Law.[79] In Italy and England local bodies were responsible for implementing legislation on moral instruction. Catholics were elected as representatives on the Italian communal (municipal) and provincial councils.[80] In England, Anglican clergymen and Catholic priests were elected to school boards.[81] There were fewer Wesleyan ministers due to their frequent movement. Clergymen could not, however, serve as teachers. In France, the Ferry Law did not allow Catholic clergy or male and female religious as teachers. Legislation of 1904 to close all private schools, the majority of which were administered by religious congregations, was not fully implemented due to the First World War.

The attitude of the French and Italian governments to the role of Catholic congregations in schools abroad was different, mirroring that of the United States government to the education of Native Americans. They saw the possibility of "civilizing" provision. In the French colonies, Catholic congregations were welcomed due to a concern regarding the immorality of the French population there, as Rebecca Rogers has shown with regard to Algeria.[82] It was similar in the Italian diaspora where the Italian government used the expatriate network of "Italians Abroad" to create what Mark Choate describes as a "supranational global nation."[83] Bilingual Catholic schools, like those of Frances Cabrini, received financial support from the Commission for Emigration alongside their secular counterparts.[84] The failure of communication between Catholic and secular organizations identified by Zeldin in France was also found in international settings. The Fourth International Conference on Popular Education, to be held in Madrid in 1913, was canceled due to the registration of a high number of representatives of Spanish Catholic educational organizations. This was seen as a strategy to frustrate the organization: "a clear statement that ideas and activities to educate the people were not necessarily laic by nature. Catholic attempts to educate the poor and needy, they considered, should also be included in the definition of popular education."[85]

EDUCATIONAL PRACTICE

There was wide agreement that Christianity was essential to the moral formation of pupils. There was less agreement, however, on the kind of educational practice required to achieve this. Three broad pedagogical approaches will be considered: pedagogies of fear, scientific pedagogies, and pedagogies of love.

PEDAGOGIES OF FEAR

Pedagogies of fear aimed to engender fear of the consequences of unacceptable behavior in order to prevent it. The Bible includes many stories showing the consequences of failure to observe the Ten Commandments. The nondenominational approach excluded interpretation by the teacher. Priscilla Chadwick points out, however, that without this interpretation the stories "were not necessarily edifying or productive of the kind of morality that would help the government to keep down the crime rate."[86] Promoters of secular approaches also questioned the impact of the threat of future rewards and punishments.[87] In practice, as Susannah Wright has shown in the case of the Moral Instruction League in England, they "did not deviate far from standard Judeo-Christian morality."[88] In France, theorists hoped to see moral reasoning in the school curriculum but in practice indoctrination to engender fear was common:

> young girls were offered frightening pictures of the consequences that awaited if they dispensed their sexual favors to any but a future husband. And the hell of alcoholism, the horrors of unemployment, and the degradation that followed on hedonistic life as the night the day – all were vividly portrayed in picture, text, and object lesson, and in every public school of the land.[89]

Harsh punishments administered by the teacher were part of this pedagogy. In a historiography of religions and the history of education Deirdre Raftery highlights a significant body of literature documenting them in both Protestant and Catholic schools managed by male clergy.[90] In England, an inspection report by Reverend F. Watkins HMI in 1845 referred to the "discipline of fear rather than of love," which he encountered in 145 (89 percent) of the 163 schools that he visited.[91] In those schools, corporal punishment was used for misdemeanors including talking or laughing in class, inattention, disobedience, and lateness. It was, however, ineffective. Behavior was worse than in schools not using it. He explained: "20 of them are notoriously lacking in discipline some of the worst, if not the very worst in the Northern district." Mary Clare Martin's 2013 case study of the London hinterland, however, challenges the view that brutal discipline was the norm in schools managed by religious bodies and decreased in the board schools after 1880. Her case study schools operated systems of rewards rather than corporal punishment. The latter was only used for serious offenses such as "throwing stones or candlesticks about the classroom."[92] Violence increased after 1880 with the board school recording canings for "offences such as talking, or idleness." For some Christians rewards and punishments were understood as essential to Christian educational practice.[93] They rejected approaches that excluded them, including that of the Italian educationalist Maria Montessori (1870–1952). Father Casulleras, a Spanish promoter of her Method, noted in a 1917 report that a priest friend considered it contrary to Catholicism "because it eliminates rewards and punishments and our religion is founded on rewards and punishments in the afterlife."[94] Casulleras on the contrary, like Reverend Watkins, thought that punishments were not an effective means of improving pupil behavior and forming good Christians. He observed that they produced inequality and pupil resentment toward the teacher. The Montessori Method, on the other hand, provided an environment suited to the development of Christian virtues in the child: "The Montessori system places the child in a special environment, of order, peace and activity, he can be seen to spontaneously help his companions and he admires and praises what others have done without pride or envy; so nobody is superior or inferior."[95]

Constant surveillance of pupils was another means of trying to ensure both high standards of behavior and achievement. Peter Gordon draws attention to Edmund Holmes's (1850–1936) observations on this issue.[96] Holmes, Chief Inspector for Elementary Schools in England, wrote in 1908 that "the child is bored to yawning-point by the teacher's insane distrust of him."[97] He considered this "seriously detrimental to his character as well as to his mind." Writing in 1912, Dorothy Canfield Fisher described a similar attitude in the United States, referring to "the lion-tamers' instinct to keep an hypnotic eye on the little animals which is so marked in our instructors."[98] Both Holmes and Canfield Fisher became promoters of the Montessori Method. During her visit to the Montessori school in Rome, Canfield Fisher observed that the pupils were given responsibility and that the teacher "happened to stand all the time with her back to the children."[99] Surveillance was understood to be an appropriate Christian approach by those influenced by Christian traditions with negative understandings of the human person including Jansenism and Rigorism. Jansenism developed under the influence of Cornelius Jansen (1585–1638). The Jansenists promoted the belief that Christ suffered and died to save a predestined few. Jansenist beliefs were condemned as heresy by successive popes between 1653 and 1713. Nevertheless, they remained influential in parts of France and Northern Italy during the nineteenth century. Wendy Wright refers to a sister from the Visitation Congregation sent as superior to a convent in Troyes, France, in the early nineteenth century, which was under diocesan supervision due to Jansenistic tendencies.[100] Rigorism, an extreme form of Augustinianism, was influential in Saint Patrick's Seminary in Maynooth, Ireland. It stressed the sinfulness of human beings and influenced priests who worked both in Ireland and in many other parts of the world.[101] Catholic teachers who were members of congregations could experience harsh treatment from superiors informed by this type of theology. Barry Coldrey has shown that teachers often reproduced the relationships that they experienced themselves.[102]

Priscilla Chadwick also points out that some of the Dissenting Protestant bodies had "a darker conception of the effects of original sin in producing 'total depravity' in unredeemed human nature."[103] Christians believe that baptism removes the taint of original sin with which all Christians are born. Unlike Catholics, Anglicans and many Protestant denominations who believed in infant baptism, Dissenting Protestant bodies practiced adult baptism. Priscilla Chadwick argues that an understanding of infant baptism informed nurturing approaches in Christian education. *The Education of Catholic Girls* (1911) provides an example.[104] The author Janet Erskine Stuart was the General Superior of the Society of the Sacred Heart, which had a global network of schools. She wrote of "the grace of baptism in the soul and later the Sacrament of penance" giving "a steady impulse towards the better things."[105]

SCIENTIFIC PEDAGOGIES

Brian Simon identifies understandings of child development resulting from scientific pedagogy informed by research in continental Europe.[106] He highlights the lack of such a pedagogical tradition in England. From 1870, however, the school boards in the industrial cities of England encouraged their teachers in the use of this kind of positive pedagogy. The success or failure of the child was due to the skill of the teacher, not the fault of the child. He argues that knowledge of scientific pedagogy provided the means for the teacher to address both the intellectual and moral development of the child. He cites helpful pedagogical work that emerged in the latter part of the nineteenth century, such as that of Alexander Bain and A.H. Garlick.[107] Alexander Bain (1818–1903), Professor of Philosophy at the University of Aberdeen, was influenced by the work of John Stuart Mill. He produced a number of works on education. His *Education as a Science* (1879) had been reprinted sixteen times by 1900. He presented associationism as "extend[ing] beyond the formation of the intellect and acquisition of knowledge to the formation of character and the acquisition of attitudes and habits."[108] Garlick was head of the Woolwich pupil teacher center. His *New Manual of Method* (1896) was another popular book, reaching the fifth edition by 1901. For Garlick, poor pupil behavior such as inattention, laziness, stupidity, or truancy was "remedial provided the teacher knows how to tackle the problem."[109]

Simon makes no reference to the work of Catholic teaching sisters. European scientific pedagogical traditions would, however, have been familiar to teacher members of Catholic congregations in Europe, many of whom moved to England. They were required to study and gain a certificate if they were to teach in schools in France from 1833 and Italy from 1859. Whilst these measures were initially viewed as government restrictions, Catholic congregations subsequently embraced pedagogical study and examinations.[110] One factor may have been that some of the best-known pedagogical theories of the period were child-centered, nurturing approaches, informed by the Christian faith of their creators, for example, Pestalozzi's Pietism, Fröbel's Lutheran Protestantism, and Montessori's Catholicism. Many Catholic sisters gained Fröbel diplomas, for example, 123 women religious studying at the Saint Catherine Institute in Rome in 1890.[111] Montessori's 1910 and 1911 training courses were held in her Casa dei Bambini (Children's House) in Via Giusti, Rome. It was housed within the convent of the Franciscan Missionaries of Mary, a French congregation and early adopters of her Method. Sisters from a number of different congregations attended these courses with fifty-three passing the end of course exam in 1911.[112] As many belonged to transnational congregations, Catholic sisters were significant in mobilizing these methods. The Sisters of the Assumption, another French foundation, hosted Montessori training in England at their convent in Kensington and subsequently established a Montessori school there.[113]

PEDAGOGIES OF LOVE

Pedagogies of love were based on the understanding that pupils developed the virtues as a result of experiencing loving kindness in the process of teaching and learning. Moral education in this tradition was as dependent on invisible as visible pedagogy. Mary Clare Martin points out that in England the early annual reports of the National Society "stressed the need to treat children with kindness."[114] Founders of religious congregations wrote of the need for loving, respectful approaches and advised against the use of humiliating punishments. This did not always work as hoped. An incident at Frances Cabrini's school in New Orleans is a good example. A clock and some money were stolen in 1893. The sisters' action was recorded in the House Annals as follows: "we encouraged them to return the stolen goods and put them back in their place without us even knowing who had done it."[115] This worked for the money but not the clock. An appeal to the consciences of the pupils brought no result. Finally, two sisters visited the families of the suspects and told them that they would have to replace the stolen clock. A mother returned it the following day. Everyone knew the culprit and the sisters' attempt to prevent her humiliation had failed. Respecting the potential of children was also important. At the Montessori course in Rome, Dorothy Canfield Fisher observed children taking responsibility for the meal hour.[116] This can be seen in Figure 1.1.

She came to understand that the soup might be cold but it was more important for the children to experience trust and respect. In *Dio e il bambino* (God and the Child) Montessori explained this trust and respect with reference to the Child Jesus: "the son of God who preferred to come into the world as a *Child* and to pass through all the phases of infant life. Now whoever scorns little ones because they are 'only children' should be aware of their lack of respect because in scorning the child as a child they are scorning the child Jesus."[117]

Other participative activities, such as performing arts and sport, also contributed to pedagogies of love. Frances Cabrini's schools all had music and drama performances as they made children happy. She believed that children were more likely to grow in virtue if they developed a happy disposition.[118] Saint John Bosco (1815–88), the Italian priest who founded the Salesian Congregation of teaching priests and brothers, also made happiness a priority, with a "pedagogy of joy and festivals."[119] The Salesians were best known for organizing festive oratories on feast days where poor boys could receive religious instruction and play games. In France the sport offered in Catholic schools distinguished them from the public schools. Zeldin points out that "the Catholics were keenest to develop sport among young people because they laid so much stress on 'moral' qualities."[120] In his 1845 report Reverend Watkins suggested that recreation periods could provide opportunities for "cheerful

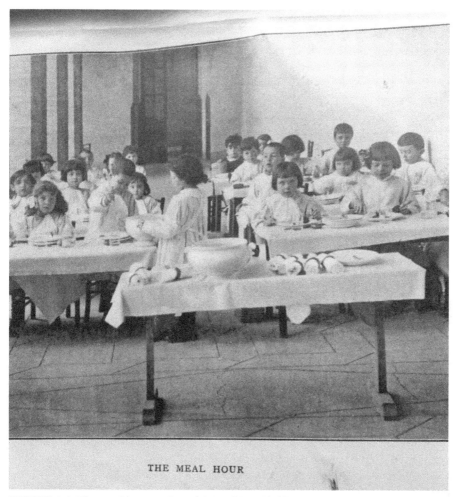

THE MEAL HOUR

FIGURE 1.1 The meal hour at Casa dei Bambini (Children's House), Rome, 1911.
Source: Dorothy Canfield Fisher, *A Montessori Mother* (New York: Henry Holt and Co., 1912), p. 23.

companionship of the teachers and pupils."[121] By the end of the century, teachers and pupils in England prepared contributions to the historical pageants that were popular at the time and often included religious content and themes of good and evil.[122]

Pedagogies of love made significant demands on the teachers. Reverend Watkins wrote of the need for "improvement in the character of teachers."[123] Father Casulleras believed that few teachers would "know how to interpret" the Montessori Method. Yet Montessori wrote that he had told her that it appeared to be inspired by Catholicism:

The humility and patience of the teachers, deeds worth more than words, the sensory environment as the beginning of psychic life, the silence and recollection obtained from little children, the freedom to perfect itself left to the infant soul, the meticulous care in preventing and correcting everything that is bad or any simple error or small imperfections, the prevention of error itself with development materials and the respect for the interior life of the children shown with the cultivation of charity, were all principles of pedagogy which seemed to emanate from and be inspired by Catholicism.[124]

Casulleras may have envisaged difficulties for teachers because the tradition of Christian moral theology that informed pedagogies of love was not the dominant one in the nineteenth century. Servais Pinckaers argues that a "morality of obligation" prevailed.[125] This was very focused on the Ten Commandments and law and duty. He identifies a second tradition, a "morality of happiness."[126] This presents the Ten Commandments "as a preparation for the exercise of the virtues, especially the love of God and neighbor."[127] Dating back to early Christian thinkers this tradition was consolidated in the writings of Saint Thomas Aquinas (1225–74). Aquinas, following the Catholic tradition of faith and reason, drew on the work of the ancient Greek philosopher Aristotle (384–322 BC) to explain Christian virtues. Unlike the morality of obligation, that of happiness did not separate morality and spirituality. Whilst the morality of happiness may not have been the dominant Christian theology in the nineteenth century there were, nevertheless, those who promoted this approach. The writings of Saint Francis de Sales (1567–1622) became popular in nineteenth-century Italy and France. They were promoted by clergy and bishops to counter Jansenism.[128] Saint Francis de Sales wrote of the goodness and love of God and each person's potential for holiness. He advised gentleness in teaching. In the United States, the Protestant theologian Horace Bushnell (1802–76) argued for a "gentle growth into faith" in his 1847 work, *Christian Nurture*.[129] He also favored infant baptism and countered "a theology in which a wrathful God condemned helpless human beings to eternal damnation."[130]

A loving God was also presented in the most popular images of Christ. *The Light of the World* (Figure 1.2), a painting by the English Pre-Raphaelite William Holman-Hunt (1827–1910), was reproduced on an enormous scale and taken on a world tour.[131] The image is a visual representation of a verse in the book of Revelation: "Behold, I stand at the door, and knock: if any man hear my voice, and open the door, I will come in to him, and will sup with him, and he with me."[132] Christ is waiting for the person on the other side of the door to open it so that he can enter and befriend and help them. Similarly, the Sacred Heart image presents Christ pointing to or holding his heart, symbolizing his love for each person (see Figure 1.3). The image and related devotional activities were promoted globally by the Jesuits. Both images were found in homes, churches,

FIGURE 1.2 William Holman-Hunt, *The Light of the World*, c. 1900–4.
Source: https://www.stpauls.co.uk/history-collections/the-collections/collections-highlights/the-light-of-the-world.

FIGURE 1.3 Frances Cabrini with the Missionary Sisters of the Sacred Heart of Jesus,
New York, photograph by A.F. Sozio, 1890, Cabriniana Collection, Cabrini University.
Courtesy of the Missionary Sisters of the Sacred Heart of Jesus.
Source: https://cdm17305.contentdm.oclc.org/digital/collection/p17305coll11/id/27/rec/3

and schools. These teachings and images all encouraged the experience of a
close personal relationship with Christ as a response to his love.

Figure 1.3 is a photograph of Frances Cabrini with a group of her Italian
Missionary Sisters of the Sacred Heart of Jesus in the United States. They include
the statue of the Sacred Heart as a symbol of their relationship with Christ. It was
not a sentimental gesture but a visual representation of a spiritual relationship.
It was this relationship that Christian teachers, who adopted pedagogies of love,
hoped to reproduce in their relationships with their pupils. This would facilitate
their growth in virtue. As good Christians, they would be good citizens.

CONCLUSION

The major role of churches and Christian organizations in the establishment
of national education systems was due both to morality being deemed to be
Christian and the reluctance of governments to fund education. Morality was,
however, separated from theology in the nondenominational Christian schools

that constituted the provision in the United States and formed a significant part of it in England. The desire of governments for standardization and uniformity of moral education was a key consideration in the establishment of secular provision, which separated religion and morality in theory if not always in practice. Pedagogies of fear were evident in the denominational, nondenominational, and secular provision of moral education. In Christian provision they were informed by a morality of obligation. Secular moral education was also informed by obligation and duty. In an age when science and religion were separated, scientific pedagogies based on religious principles did not overtly present their theological foundations. Montessori, for example, made no reference to Christianity in her volume on Method. Pedagogies of love were informed by a morality of happiness that brought together the spiritual and moral aspects of Christian theology. They were also indirectly informed by Aristotle's secular concepts of the virtues developed by Saint Thomas Aquinas. Aristotle's secular approach had more impact on Christian than secular approaches in which "there were few appeals to the ethical theories of the ancient Greeks as possible sources of moral authority."[133] Although not adopted widely, pedagogies of love were, nevertheless, a distinctly Christian feature of the provision of moral education and formation in the age of empire.

CHAPTER TWO

Knowledge, Media, and Communication

JANA TSCHURENEV

INTRODUCTION: GLOBAL CIVIL SOCIETY NETWORKS AND TRAVELING PEDAGOGICAL KNOWLEDGE IN THE "AGE OF EMPIRE"

This chapter explores the travels and transformations of pedagogical knowledge in the age of empire. The fundamental changes in education that occurred in many parts of the world throughout the long nineteenth century were, from the beginning, shaped by the global proliferation of Protestant missions. The evangelical enthusiasm for reaching out to the "heathens" inhabiting distant lands was closely entwined with the geographical trajectories of imperial expansion. Moreover, it overlapped with the cultural ideology of colonialism as a project to bring "moral and material progress" to the new subject populations in Asia and Africa, and the indigenous people incorporated into settler colonies.[1] The hegemonic ambitions of imperial educators, the unequal dynamics of colonial knowledge production, and the deeply Eurocentric definitions of what was worth teaching were core features of the cultural history of education in the age of empire.[2] The nineteenth-century processes of educational expansion and reform were embedded in the cultural politics of empire, and the renegotiation of class, gender, racial, and other structural inequalities that these entailed.[3]

At the same time, the spread of modern schooling was motivated by ideas of liberalism, enlightenment, and secular progress. There was a strong belief in education as the panacea for improving both individual humans and the societies they formed. The nineteenth century was also a period characterized by the dynamics of nation-building, state-formation, and territorialization.[4] While British colonial rule was consolidated in India, and European colonial expansion continued in the East, a first wave of postcolonial nation-formation already took place in the former Spanish and Portuguese territories in the west. In this context, schooling emerged as the central means for raising republican citizens.[5]

This chapter locates the long nineteenth century's educational transformations in both these political constellations. On the one hand, it stresses communication within "imperial social formations,"[6] with a major focus on Britain, and the central part of its eastern empire, British India. In the early nineteenth century, the British Empire became an important "transnational educational space."[7] It provided a space for educational expansion, pedagogical innovation, and fundamental educational change. Educational policy decisions made in London left a major impact on the development of schooling in colonial lands. New pedagogical ideas were easily communicated through the reporting and corresponding system of colonial administrative structures. This was not a one-way exchange: colonial educational experiments were closely observed in Britain and critically evaluated, both by imperial administrators and the wider public. On the other hand, the chapter links the expansion of schooling to the ideology of secular national progress, which marked the new republics of Latin America, but also emerged in eastern and southeastern Europe, where new nation-states were carved out from the multiethnic Ottoman and Habsburg empires.[8] Finally, we must consider the international, cosmopolitan educational reform movements of the early twentieth century, which promoted pedagogical innovation to further human development globally. With its stress on science, progress, and child development, the New Education movement can be considered as part of a "new era";[9] but it still built on and critically responded to the culture of schooling that characterized the age of empire.

The nineteenth century was a period in which school systems were assembled under modern, centralized government institutions.[10] Indeed, the role of education in the process of modern state-formation can hardly be overestimated.[11] However, as this chapter shows, modern nongovernmental, nonprofit organizations created important channels for pedagogical communication within the British Empire and beyond.[12] The expansion of civil society has been hailed as an important element of globalization processes in this period. It entailed the formation of global communication networks and the emergence of a cosmopolitan mindset.[13] But the expansion of civil society also overlapped with colonial expansion. Scottish Enlightenment moral philosophy developed a concept of civil society that rested on notions of social progress, or "progress of civilisation," which informed the ideology of the colonial civilizing mission.[14] This chapter shows that the paradigmatic civil society actors—voluntary associations—pursued diverse sociopolitical agendas of educational reform: they actively participated in civilizing missions, were agents of national integration, and at times were a democratic force.

The chapter discusses the activities of four major educational movements. First, it looks at the collaboration of educational societies and Protestant missionaries in the monitorial movement, which, as the chapter shows, was highly relevant for the global spread of a modern culture of schooling (1800s–30s). Second, it discusses the case of the Fröbel kindergarten movement to show how reformers aimed to improve the established pedagogical culture (1840s–1900s). Thirdly, it focuses on social movements, which aimed to reform not the pedagogical culture but the curricular content, namely, the knowledge imparted to children in public schools (1880s–1920). Finally, the chapter discusses the push toward a scientization of childhood and education (1890s–1920). Looking at the emergence and interaction of these movements and their organizations and networks, the chapter argues, provides us with a unique lens to explore shifting geographical patterns of global pedagogical communication, and shifting notions of what and how to teach children.

"THE CAUSE OF UNIVERSAL EDUCATION": THE MONITORIAL MOVEMENT

In the early nineteenth century, the monitorial system of education emerged as a "universal method" for the proliferation of modern elementary schooling.[15] Based on the principle of more advanced students teaching their peers (as "monitors"), the monitorial system seemed well adapted to further the cause of educational expansion, under conditions of shortage of funds, and a lack of trained teachers. Several transregional communication circuits took part in the spread and translation of the new pedagogical method. The major ones were a British imperial circuit and a transatlantic liberal circuit, both intersecting in the imperial metropole of London.[16] But pedagogical debate in continental Europe was an important part of the monitorial movement as well as the emergence of regional centers of further knowledge transmission.[17]

The global proliferation of the monitorial system of education depended on the close collaboration of nongovernmental, nonprofit organizations dedicated to the cause of educational reform and the early nineteenth-century Protestant mission movement. The British and Foreign School Society (BFSS) was founded in 1808 by an alliance of dissenters and utilitarians. Its rival, the National Education Society (NES), was set up in 1811, supported by the subscriptions of the Anglican Church faction.[18] Popular schooling, both parties hoped, would counteract pauperism and political unrest, and help to reestablish social order.[19] In a politically and economically fast-changing society, public elementary schools appeared as a means of "civilizing the masterless poor."[20]

In the context of the mushrooming of Protestant missionary societies, the BFSS and NES formed close ties with the early nineteenth-century foreign mission movement: "for if the world were full of Bibles," Andrew Fuller of the Baptist Missionary Society preached on behalf of the BFSS, "it would be of little avail if the people were not taught to read them."[21] The BFSS's expressed aim was to provide inexpensive schools for the poor "throughout the whole habitable globe."[22] Missionary publications, such as the Church Missionary Society's (CMS's) *Missionary Register*, gathered and publicized information on the global spread of the monitorial system, through the agency of missionaries.[23] Education societies like the BFSS and NES were formed in India's colonial centers. As collaborative ventures between the new urban intellectual elites, missionaries, and colonial officials, organizations such as the Calcutta School Book Society (CSBS) and the Bombay Native Education Society (BNES) became important agents in the introduction of colonial schooling in India.[24] An imperial civil society network emerged that connected London with the colonial centers of India and promoted elementary schooling for both the poor of the imperial metropole and the colonial subjects abroad.

At the same time, the BFSS became involved in liberal networks across the Atlantic.[25] Joseph Lancaster (1778–1838), one of the "inventors" of monitorial schooling, promoted his innovation in the USA.[26] In Canada, the monitorial movement furthered educational system-building and the emergence of modern educational governance.[27] In newly independent Spanish America, monitorial schools were set up to establish universal education for republican citizenship.[28] Finally, foreign missionary movements and early efforts toward nation-building intersected at the European periphery, in the Balkans. Even before their independence from the Ottoman Empire, monitorial schools, or schools of mutual instruction, supported national movements in Greece and Bulgaria. They were part and parcel of the building of "national education" in Bulgaria, and the standardization and reform of the modern Bulgarian language.[29]

In the second half of the nineteenth century, the monitorial system of education gave way to new pedagogical innovations, some of which had grown out of the earlier monitorial experiments. Teaching became increasingly professionalized, at first through the so-called "pupil-teacher system," which the BFSS and NES shifted to.[30] While government agencies took over the institutions created by the monitorial movement, pedagogically, the classroom system became the chief characteristic of modern schooling.[31] However, in the first half of the nineteenth century, the monitorial movement was remarkably successful in paving the way for mass education and a new pedagogical culture suited to teaching large groups of children.

Several factors contributed to this success. First, the BFSS and the NES developed a communication strategy that greatly facilitated the adoption of their innovations in other contexts.[32] They described the new system of

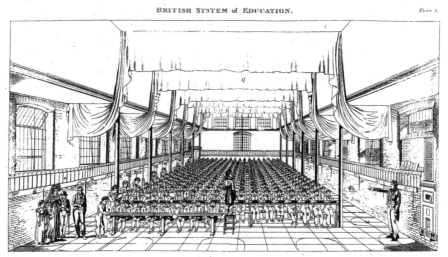

FIGURE 2.1 "Interior of the Central School of the British & Foreign School Society, Borough Road." In the *Manual of the System of Primary Instruction pursued in the Model Schools of the British and Foreign School Society* (London: Printed for the Society, 1834).

instruction in handy manuals, which gave teachers and school providers concrete guidance on how to set up and run a monitorial school, how to organize the classroom communication, and how to structure teaching and learning processes (Figure 2.1).

These manuals combined the suggestion of a standardized course of elementary studies (or school knowledge) with the *savoir faire* necessary for school providers. They were particularly appropriate media for transferring knowledge around a wide-reaching transregional communication system. The BFSS's and NES's manuals were translated into many languages, and adaptations of them were used by missionaries and educational societies throughout the world.[33] They were combined with standardized packages of teaching materials, such as board lessons for the initial alphabetization processes. Moreover, the manuals advertised the various advantages of the new method. They were well illustrated. The BFSS and NES, in short, pursued an active strategy of "non-profit marketing,"[34] which fit the demands of their various partners around the globe.

A second factor was that the monitorial system of education not only resonated with the new values of rationality and efficiency, which were characteristic of modern market societies, but also with emerging notions of liberal governance.[35] The age of empire was also the period in which modern techniques of governance were experimented with, not only in Britain but also in the sites of colonial encounters.[36] The monitorial system of education applied and reaffirmed liberal notions of subjectivity. Monitorial schools aimed to instil capacities of self-regulation and moral conduct among the general population.[37] They introduced "the principle of *self-tuition*" under the watchful eye of the schoolmaster with elements of student "*self-government*."[38] At the same time, carefully limited curricula and the emphasis of discipline and subordination allowed monitorial schools to be adjusted to conservative social agendas as well as to the production of new social hierarchies in colonial contexts.[39] Cost-efficient monitorial schools could thus be incorporated into different, even contradictory, agendas of nineteenth-century social reform.

The monitorial movement, which often helped set up the initial infrastructure for centralized education systems, facilitated the global spread of a modern culture of schooling. Monitorial schools entailed strong elements of standardization, of curricular content, and institutional models. However, their proliferation produced different local variations, corresponding not only to educational reformers' sociopolitical agendas but also to resilient local pedagogical traditions and persisting educational semantics.[40] There was a broad range of local variety within the emerging modern culture of schooling.

The history of the monitorial movement is not a story of "westernization." Its development in India is an important case in point (Figure 2.2). Missionaries and educational societies did indeed introduce new pedagogical knowledge and contributed to a radical alteration of the educational landscape. They initiated a process in which indigenous forms of knowledge transmission gave way to a modern-colonial education system and a pedagogical culture centered on the textbook and the rote learning of standardized content.[41]

FIGURE 2.2 "A Hindoo Village School." In the *Missionary Register* (1822), p. 543.

FIGURE 2.3 "Native School at Lakoody, near Burdwan, with part of the village." In the *Missionary Register* (1819), p. 102.

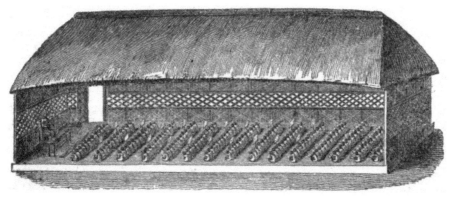

FIGURE 2.4 "Interior of the Native School at Lakoody." In the *Missionary Register* (1819), p. 102.

However, the promoters of monitorial schools in India emphasized the need to "adapt" the new system to local circumstances.[42] This ranged from children sitting on the ground, as they were used to at home, to the adjustment to parents' demands for skilled penmanship (Figures 2.3 and 2.4).

Even more importantly, the monitorial system itself rested on knowledge produced by the colonial encounter. Andrew Bell (1753–1832), whose version of the monitorial system of education was globally marketed by the NES, had conducted his initial "experiment" with the new pedagogy in a colonial orphanage in Madras (present-day Chennai), in South India.[43] Bell observed South Indian pedagogical practices, interpreted them according to his own upbringing in the intellectual ferment of the Scottish Enlightenment, and incorporated them into his own "system." Elements foreign to European pedagogical knowledge traditions were thus adopted into the monitorial system, which was used for the modernization and universalization of elementary schooling in Britain. This included initial alphabetization by means of writing instead of reading exercises and specific forms of peer-to-peer instruction.[44]

Different knowledge traditions thus came together in the development of monitorial schooling in its various local forms. Multiple feedback loops connected the BFSS and NES in London with the knowledge produced in colonial encounters and in wider global spaces of interaction.[45]

LEARNING THROUGH PLAY: THE KINDERGARTEN MOVEMENT

The global movement involving the proliferation of monitorial schools, the previous section has shown, was a moment of educational expansion and initial institution building. It was about reaching "the poor," the "heathens," the hitherto unschooled. Although the pedagogical theory of Andrew Bell and Joseph Lancaster referred to Enlightenment notions of education—notions such as the perfectibility and educability of each human being—the pedagogical practice was one based on rote learning. The colonial versions of this movement, in particular, introduced a reduced empiricist understanding of knowledge and learning.[46] Although such practices remained characteristic of many schooling cultures throughout the nineteenth century and beyond, they were challenged by pedagogical reform movements, which aimed to improve classroom practices and set up better, more child-friendly learning environments.

The field of early childhood education was a fertile ground for pedagogical experimentation with observation, touch, and play. Already the infant school movement, which almost immediately followed the paths set by the monitorial movement throughout the British Empire, aimed to incorporate object lessons, playgrounds, and physical activity into the realm of formal education.[47] Even more influential was the Fröbel kindergarten movement, which aimed to replace the "3Rs" with children's active engagement with their natural and social worlds.[48] Kindergartens aimed "to foster moral and intellectual development by making the paraphernalia of childhood—plays, toys, constructive games, nursery songs, etc.—symbols of metaphysical truths and designs intuitively comprehensible to the child."[49]

The idea of the kindergarten was first developed by the Thuringian schoolmaster Friedrich Fröbel (1782–1852), drawing from the educational theories of the Swiss educator Johann Heinrich Pestalozzi (1747–1826) and the German idealist philosophy of Johann Gottlieb Fichte (1862–1914). Distancing himself from the provision of mere day care, Fröbel conceived of his "children's garden" as a place where children could flourish. The concept of the "garden" invoked notions of natural growth, or the unfolding of an inner potential, and the necessity of carefully tending to the young minds and bodies. The job of caring for and teaching children was equated to the job of a gardener—hence the term kindergartner (children's gardener). Fröbel envisioned his kindergarten as an institution for all German children aged three to six, before they would enter the stage of primary schooling.[50] In the German States, Fröbel's suggestions were enthusiastically taken up by the liberal reformers of 1848.[51] Women's rights activist Bertha von Mahrenholtz-Bülow (1810–93) became a crucial figure in the proliferation of Fröbelian ideas in the German states and abroad. Since the Prussian government banned kindergartens in 1851 as part of the reaction to the liberal movement, Mahrenholtz suggested seeking "to gain over foreign countries, so that we may open the way from them for the cause in Germany."[52]

The first stage of Mahrenholtz's international lecture tour led her to London, where the Fröbel Society for the Promotion of the Kindergarten System was formed in 1874. The country, however, where the new educational model proved most successful was the United States. In the first decade of the twentieth century, kindergartens were incorporated into the US public school system, though on a non-compulsory basis.[53] Moreover, the United States became a center for the further international proliferation of what was now termed "the kindergarten system." By 1900, the International Kindergarten Union (IKU), which had been founded in 1892,[54] was the third largest educational organization in the world.[55]

American missionaries became important actors in promoting kindergarten education abroad. In some places, they even initiated processes of state-institution building, as the case of missionary Elisabeth Clarke in Bulgaria—one of the regional centers of American missionary activity—shows.[56] Having studied the system at the National Kindergarten and Elementary College, Chicago, Clarke founded the first kindergarten (1898) and kindergarten teacher training centre (1900) in Bulgaria, where by 1923 state-funded kindergartens existed in all towns with more than 20,000 inhabitants.[57]

Two features of the global kindergarten movement deserve to be highlighted. First, the cause of the Fröbel kindergarten movement was closely entwined with the history of transregional women's activism. From its very beginnings "the kindergarten movement was a feminist cause, and its development was linked to that of feminist movements in both Germany and the United States."[58] Fröbel's dictum that the ideal teacher of young children was like "a mother made conscious" was further elaborated on by German feminists, who argued that women's nurturing qualities could benefit society at large.[59] As professional educators, women could exert a "spiritual motherhood." This, however, necessitated a scientific training. The (paradigmatically female) kindergartner was expected to combine loving care with an expert knowledge about children's development and their learning patterns. The kindergarten movement thus followed a dual objective: the provision of nurturing environments, where young children could grow and flourish, and the expansion of educational and professional options for the women to whom their care was entrusted.[60]

The second feature was the increased complexity of transnational knowledge exchange and the multiplicity of actors and movements who supported the Fröbel kindergarten movement. The original pedagogical innovation occurred in a German-speaking context, embedded in European exchanges. However, both the British Empire and, particularly toward the end of the nineteenth century, US-American civil society networks provided important channels of global pedagogical knowledge circulation. American civil society, thereby, often followed the pathways of the imperial mission movements.[61] Both features, the close intersection with women's activism and the increased geographical complexity of transregional knowledge circulation, can be illustrated by again turning to India as a case in point.

In the early nineteenth century, it was missionary women, and BFSS-trained teachers, who were pioneers of both girls' schools and infant schools in colonial Bengal.[62] The Fröbel kindergarten was promoted by American missionaries and female kindergarten experts from Britain alike.[63] Moreover, British imperial activists such as social reformer Mary Carpenter (1807–77) and her National Indian Association (NAI) pushed the cause of the kindergarten in India.[64] The British National Fröbel Union, which was founded in 1887, not only oversaw the standards of the Fröbel teacher's certificate in the UK but throughout the empire.[65] At the same time, however—and this is noteworthy—Indian women reformers joined the movement. It was no longer British and American activists alone who aimed to improve Indian education and Indian society with the help of new pedagogical knowledge. From the 1870s onwards, Indian educators such as Francina Sorabji (1833–1910), her daughter Susie Sorabji (1860–1931), and Pandita Ramabai (1858–1922) promoted kindergarten methods, and actively sought new knowledge abroad. They became local partners of the IKU and of various transregional women's networks.[66] This marks an important shift in agency and initiative in pedagogical communication, already under imperial conditions.

Indian Christian feminist Pandita Ramabai, whose remarkable life history has been well researched by pioneering women's historians,[67] founded a school for high-caste Hindu widows in 1889, which included a training program for kindergartners. The school was named Sharada Sadan, or house of learning. While traveling through the United States—fundraising for her educational endeavors in India[68]—Ramabai took the chance to enroll herself in a kindergarten training course in Philadelphia and to meet with kindergarten experts.[69] Thus, it was not the communicational infrastructure of the British Empire but her contacts with US-American women activists—educationalists and moral reformers—that enabled her to gain the expert knowledge she found useful for her own projects. Back in Bombay (present-day Mumbai), Ramabai promoted kindergarten teaching, elementary school teaching, and nursing as professional options for Hindu widows, who were prevented by caste and custom from remarriage.[70] At the same time, she found kindergarten methods highly useful for stimulating her students' learning capacities and interests—for many of the girls and young women attending the Sharada Sadan this was their first experience with formal schooling.[71]

The global spread of kindergarten methods shows a remarkable connection with diverse social and political movements. Kindergartens were also adaptable to a variety of cultural contexts.[72] One of the factors behind this was that the media of instruction, Fröbel's toy sets, or "gifts," were material objects. Although their approach to learning environments and processes was radically different, both monitorial and kindergarten methods proved immensely flexible. Both transcended the Christian-Protestant context, from which they had originally emerged. While the monitorial system was linked to institution building, the kindergarten movement's outcomes were more mixed. In the United States, and Germany, kindergartens became distinct preschool and social-welfare institutions, which supplemented public school systems. In India, in contrast, kindergarten methods were also incorporated into the existing teacher training institutions and implemented in preexisting school settings.[73]

In the early twentieth century, kindergarten methods were often superceded by new innovations, but the pedagogical knowledge the kindergarten movement created remained important for twentieth-century pedagogical reform and "alternative education" movements. Several of its trajectories were taken up in early twentieth-century educational reform efforts. The role of women's organizations and women's transregional networks in promoting and enabling pedagogical communication intensified.[74] This also provided a new push toward the professionalization of care and teaching for young children.[75]

EDUCATION AND MORAL REFORM: THE WCTU AND SCIENTIFIC TEMPERANCE INSTRUCTION

Toward the end of the nineteenth century, we can observe a wave of curriculum reform movements, which aimed to use public schools as platforms for the spread of moral lessons among the population.[76] Public schools appeared as an apt entry point for the establishment of middle-class cultural hegemony, for national mobilization, or for the cultural assimilation of immigrant groups.[77] Schoolchildren were, after all, a captive audience.[78] The early nineteenth-century monitorial movement had already suggested the use of schooling for the spread of useful knowledge among the poor, the working classes, and colonial subjects. The major difference was that now, more than half a century later, the basic educational infrastructure was already in place, in many parts of the world, even in colonial India. The increasingly centralized state education systems became "a ready target for lobbies that claimed to represent moral majorities and that wished to write laws to inculcate their version of truth and virtues in the rising generation."[79] Mass schooling seemed to provide social reformers with an effective machinery of knowledge transmission, since it enabled them to reach all the children and, through them, the parents and local communities.

Examples of such curriculum reform movements taking place from the 1880s to the 1920s in different parts of the world include the campaign for civic education in the United States, for Eugenics education in Australia, or hygiene instruction in Uruguay.[80] Another case, which will be discussed further, was the movement toward the introduction of "scientific temperance instruction" (STI) as a compulsory subject in public schools, which accompanied the intensive political anti-alcohol campaigns of the late nineteenth century.[81]

In 1882, the US-American Woman's Christian Temperance Union (WCTU) started a campaign for the compulsory teaching of the negative physical and psychological effects of alcohol in schools under the name of "scientific temperance instruction" (STI).[82] The WCTU had been formed in 1873, as part of the "women's crusade" against saloons and liquor shops. Under the leadership of Frances Willard (1839–98), its so-called "do-everything" policy included "social purity" and campaigning for Anglo-Saxon women's right to vote.[83] The WCTU, which for several decades was the USA's most important women's organization, became an active agent of educational reform. This comprised advocacy for the kindergarten movement. The founding of fee-free kindergartens for lower-class children became one of the WCTU's formal "departments" of work.[84] Frances Willard termed kindergarten work "the greatest theme, next to salvation by faith, that can engage a woman's heart and brain."[85] The WCTU also supported the professionalization of kindergarten work. Advising local activists on how to set up a kindergarten, the WCTU's *Union Signal* explained: "Do not employ 'Miss So and So' as your kindergartner because she is charming and loves children [...], for, while the love for children is very necessary, it does not fit one to teach them. Select a student from some kindergarten college where the standard is kept high."[86]

Guided by a belief in American women's providential mission to take care of their "enslaved sisters" abroad, the WCTU's international umbrella organization, the World's WCTU, started in 1883 to work internationally for temperance and social reform.[87] The World's WCTU's networks closely overlapped with the American foreign mission movement, and they participated in the making of what Ian Tyrrell has called "America's moral empire."[88] The stronghold of this network was an "imperial community" of Anglo-Saxon women missionaries and reformers in former British settler colonies and British colonial territories, with the remarkable exception of Japan.[89] An interesting case of transcultural cooperation was the WCTU's support for the setting up of the Ramabai Association, which funded Pandita Ramabai's Sharada Sadan in Bombay. The saving of India's unfortunate child widows, for them, was a worthy cause for American women's global "moral" mission. Ramabai, in turn, reported that the Sharada Sadan's students had formed a temperance union, a measure which she hoped would "encourage the development of public spirit among our girls, and [...] teach them to conduct their own meetings."[90]

In the USA, the WCTU's STI campaign was a highly effectual curriculum reform movement. Former chemistry teacher Mary Hunt (1830–1906) and her fellow WCTU activists had, by 1901, managed to enforce legislative compulsion to introduce regular STI school lessons "in every state and territory in America."[91] In the 1901/2 school year over 22 million children received scientific temperance instruction.[92] The WCTU was "perhaps the most influential lay lobby ever to shape what was taught in public schools. Though it was a voluntary association, it acquired a quasi-public power as a censor of textbooks, trainer of teachers, and arbiter of morality."[93]

In the first two decades of the twentieth century, STI became a global current. The global WCTU's network played an active part in this. Soon, however, various models, originating from different places, were in circulation. The first countries (besides the United States) to make STI a compulsory subject in the public schools were Sweden (1892) and France (1902). The Board of Education in England issued standardized syllabi on health and hygiene, including STI, in 1909, which were adapted by educational authorities in Australia, South Africa, and India.[94] In Germany, Austria, and Switzerland, STI lessons were officially recognized and permitted, but not compulsory. The Deutsche Zentrale für Nüchternheitsunterricht (German Centre for Temperance Instruction), founded in 1914, explicitly followed the institutional example of Sweden. It promoted a model of itinerant teaching, namely, of full-time temperance teachers providing standardized model lessons to schools and seeking to convince teachers to systematically include them in the curriculum.[95]

The founder and chairperson of Austria's Verein Abstinenter Frauen (Women's Temperance Union), Julie Schall-Kassowitz (1854–1938), found the American efforts of pressure groups to enforce "parliamentary intervention" into the domain of public schooling astonishing, since this was "indisputably" the domain of "experts."[96] In German-speaking countries, she argued, the way of implementing STI must necessarily differ from the United States. It had to concentrate on winning teachers' support and consent. As Schall-Kassowitz argued, this was due to the fact that the Anglo-Saxon pedagogical tradition centered on the textbook, not on the authority of the teacher.[97] Indeed, the differences between German- and British-based pedagogical trajectories had already been highlighted in the early nineteenth-century's contestation over the suitability of the monitorial system of education for the German *Volksschule*.[98] The relevance of persistent pedagogical semantics and institutional trajectories thus comes again to the fore. What we also see in the global history of STI is a combined effect of powerful civil society campaigning, and transregional networks, with state legislation.

Despite the rhetoric of "science" in the WCTU's campaign, the priority of STI was to impart moral lessons on the evils of alcohol consumption.

The objective of moralizing children had already been at the heart of the project of mass education in the context of the monitorial movement. For the NES and some of its partners, a knowledge of the Anglican catechism was the foundation of all morality. Now, Christian temperance women sought to ground moral instruction in a knowledge of "facts" about health, hygiene, and the human body and biopolitical arguments about public health. An educational booklet prepared by Dr. Maud Allen, the Indian WCTU's "Superintendent of Scientific Temperance Instruction", illustrates this.[99] The section on alcohol contained the following statements:

1. Alcohol is a poison.
2. Alcohol is not a food, because it does not strengthen or nourish the body.
3. Alcohol when given to children retards their physical and mental development.
4. Alcohol endangers the moral nature of the child. [...]
5. The greater part of feeble-minded [...] children are the offspring of alcoholic parents.

In the United States, STI was subjected to a strong contemporary critique, particularly for its *lack* of grounding in scientific findings. The so-called "Committee of Fifty," which had been tasked with scientifically assessing the USA's "liquor problem," came to the devastating conclusion that "under the name of Scientific Temperance Instruction there has been grafted upon the public school system of nearly all our States an educational scheme relating to alcohol which is neither scientific, nor temperate, nor instructive."[100] Unable to enlist prominent scientists for STI's advisory board, Mary Hunt recruited the support of clergymen and educators instead.[101]

Another radical critique was expressed from the perspective of pedagogy. Within the global temperance movement, youth organizations deployed song, play, and sociability to stimulate emotional responses and social learning.[102] The US-American STI, in contrast, adhered to a pedagogical culture that centered on standardized textbook lessons and rote learning. Children were given "facts" to recite and memorize whether they were particularly "interesting" or not.[103] The textbooks, approved by the WCTU, presented "a lurid world of virtue and vice."[104] Temperance women "translated the Calvinists' separation of the saved and the damned into physiology. The physical condition of the saved was testimony to their moral health. The damned choose to poison themselves."[105] Mary Hunt adhered to old puritan notions of "child depravity," the need to correct children's inclinations toward evil. This kind of pedagogy and its underlying religious assumptions were no longer found adequate by educational experts at the turn of the twentieth century. It was thus not only medical doctors and scientists who opposed STI. In the United States, the movement also stood in direct opposition to the advances in child study and the emerging expert culture in pedagogy and educational administration.[106]

FIGURE 2.5 "Scientific Temperance Instruction." *Union Signal*, June 13, 1918, front page.

THE SCIENTIZATION OF PEDAGOGY: THE CHILD STUDY MOVEMENT AND NEW EDUCATION

In contrast to the STI movement, which deployed a superficial rhetoric of science but adhered to religious-based philosophies and practices of moral education, there was a strong tendency, from the 1890s onwards, toward a scientization of pedagogy. Two influential transnational movements aimed to reestablish pedagogy as a positivist science and to ground children's education in scientific methods of observation and quantitative measurement.[107] The first was the child study movement, "STI's key academic antagonist."[108] The second was the proliferation of Maria Montessori's (1870–1952) ideas and methods of a "scientific pedagogy."[109] Both currents, in different ways, built on the new field of experimental psychology, which first flourished in Germany before it reached the United States in the 1870s, and particularly on the research done in Wilhelm Wundt's (1832–1920) pioneering psychological laboratory in Leipzig.[110]

Psychologist G. Stanley Hall became the central figure of the US-American child study movement, which emerged at the intersection of transnational academic networks in the fields of psychology and psychiatry and various social movements invested in "child welfare." He was joined by Earl Barnes, Professor of Education at Stanford University, who "saw formal, quantitative child study as the cornerstone of a scientific pedagogy."[111] The works of both were widely received among educationalists in other countries, such as the UK, who in turn founded national child study associations and networks.[112] The objectives that the British Child Study Association formulated in 1902 clearly illustrate the movement's motivation: "it is only by a more precise knowledge of the natural process of unfolding of the human mind, and of the way in which this can be modified by the environment, that further advance can be made in education."[113]

The positivist approach to pedagogy corresponded to a wider ideology of science and progress at the turn of the twentieth century. It was linked to tendencies toward the professionalization of teaching, social work, and educational administration, the growth of expert knowledge, and a technological approach toward social problems. Mass schooling, social work, institutions for juvenile "delinquents" and for children with disabilities created a whole new institutional complex that produced large amounts of data about children. At the same time, public-funded measures to guarantee the social welfare of children needed expert guidance. How to cater best to children's needs? Which patterns of physical and mental development were "normal," and which required professional intervention and "correction"? Particularly in the US-American context, the academic child study movement was allied with the professional social workers, parent organizations, and teachers, even if all these groups pursued their own interests as well.[114]

Experimental psychology was G. Stanley Hall's starting point when it came to the scientization of pedagogy. For Maria Montessori, it was medicine and psychiatry, or more precisely, a combination of practical feminism with the Italian fin-de-siècle social medicine approach.[115] In the last decades of the nineteenth century, women in Europe, Asia, and Latin America used the study of medicine as an entrance point into higher education, professionalism, and social activism.[116] It was a period of widespread belief in the "redemptive capacities of science," and its crucial role in moral and social "regeneration."[117] At the same time, there were fears of "degeneration," which were articulated in medical, social, and educational debates about mental illness. Disability, addiction, and early childhood development were at the heart of biopolitical concerns about the health and strength of national populations.[118]

Montessori combined her early interests in women's social work, psychiatry, disability, and positivist science in her Casa dei Bambini (Children's House). The work with disabled children, for her, was the experimental ground on which she formulated her "scientific pedagogy."[119] In 1913, Montessori offered an international training course in Rome—one of many to come. It was attended by visitors from the Americas, India, Africa, and Australia, some of whom became "proselytes," who joined in the global proliferation of the "Montessori Method." "The immense number of studies dedicated to the Montessori phenomenon bears witness to her appeal: between 1909 and 1914, some two hundred books and articles inspired by her work were published in the United States and England."[120]

These new movements working for the establishment of education as a positivist science "entered a field that was already occupied by Froebelians."[121] The child study movement rejected Fröbel's philosophical approach to education. Theological or metaphysical conceptions, they found, had to give way to scientific explanation. A biological-developmental model came to dominate the view of the child. Moreover, there was a gender dimension in the small regard that male experts in academia had for female kindergartners and Fröbelians. Some proponents of a scientific pedagogy, however, credited Fröbel for having appreciated the value of play and for thinking in terms of growth and development.[122] Moreover, the child study movement built practically in many ways on the kindergarten movement. In Hall's first empirical study—which followed up three previous German studies on what children knew, when they were about to enter primary school—400 children were examined in Boston. As examiners, he relied on experienced kindergarten teachers.[123] However, revisionist Fröbelians, who rejected the standardized kindergarten apparatus in favor of free play, also drew support from the new insights produced by the child study movement.[124] All three movements, child study, the proliferation of Montessori's ideas, and the Fröbel kindergarten movement, were primarily concerned with young children. In their confrontation, pedagogy was transformed, education became institutionalized as an academic discipline, and the new education movement began to take shape.

KNOWLEDGE, MEDIA, AND COMMUNICATION

This chapter has discussed several transregional movements in the age of empire that aimed to expand the reach of schooling, improve education, or make use of public schools as instruments of social reform. These educational and social reform movements were concerned with two kinds of *knowledge*. On the one hand, there was the question of curricular content, of what children learn. In the context of the monitorial movement (1800s–30s), this was a combination of basic literacy and numeracy, locally defined "useful knowledge," and what could be summarized as the capacity for moral self-regulation.[125] "From their inception, formal schools in Western capitalist societies have been designed to discipline bodies as well as to regulate minds." Mass schooling aimed at both, the formation of rightful conduct and "the acquisition of prescribed knowledge."[126] This is also true for colonial contexts, where schooling became linked to the competing projects of social differentiation, cultural hegemony, social reform, and nation-building.[127] In contrast to the monitorial movement, which often had to set up the schools it aimed to use for the transmission of knowledge, late nineteenth-century curriculum reform movements could build on the already established institutional structure. Movements such as STI reaffirmed a conceptualization of public schools as machineries of knowledge transmission, among the students, and their families and communities.

On the other hand, educators and school reformers were concerned with the questions of how children learn and how best to teach them. This refers to the domain of pedagogical knowledge and educational theory. Andrew Bell and Joseph Lancaster shared a belief, inspired by Enlightenment philosophy, that educational methods had to be devised in accordance with the nature of students as learners. Monitorial schools aimed to make use of students' feelings of sympathy and emulation, instead of simply repressing the vivacity of children.[128] The practices used in them, however, in hindsight appeared as drill and discipline, and the mindless repetition of textbook lessons. In India, monitorial schools marked the beginning of a colonial pedagogical culture in which "the textbook is the curriculum."[129] It was this kind of pedagogical culture that the Fröbel kindergarten movement, and later the new education movement, wanted to replace with play, sensory experience, and experiential and practical learning. Moreover, the child study movement and proponents of new education aimed to build a positivist-scientific knowledge of children's development, behavior, and learning patterns. Only on this basis, they thought, could pedagogical practice be improved.

The transregional communication of pedagogical and educational knowledge was also linked to the production, circulation, and adaptation of different *media* of instruction. The organizations involved in the monitorial movement created, marketed, and proliferated various materials for classroom usage, including card boards, or wall tables, from which students would transcribe letters, syllables, and short lessons. Educational associations produced textbooks, which were distributed to school providers in their surroundings. The STI movement made sure to disseminate standardized textbooks on the evils of alcohol, which students would have to remember. The kindergarten movement, and the Montessori Method, in contrast, developed and distributed material objects for learning and play.

Throughout the nineteenth century, the British Empire remained an important transnational educational space. Knowledge did not only flow from the metropole to the colonies but colonial knowledge produced important repercussions for British society. Moreover, there were many other transregional knowledge circuits for the circulation and translation of pedagogical knowledge, which included "America's moral empire" and continental European expert cultures.

Looking at such far-reaching networks of pedagogical *communication*, several shifts can be observed. In the early nineteenth century, it was a strong alliance of educational associations in Britain and its empire, with the Protestant missionary movement, which had provided the communicational infrastructure for the spread of pedagogical knowledge. This included the monitorial system of education as well as the infant school system. Educational associations, and missionaries, now most importantly American missionaries, remained important in the proliferation of the Fröbel kindergarten; however, they were now supplemented by transregional women's movements and other social movements. Women's movements continued to play a major role in the late nineteenth-century curriculum reform movements and in new education. The child study movement, finally, marks an important tendency toward the secularization of pedagogical knowledge and educational expertise. It was now an alliance of social movements with transnational scientific expert cultures, which sought to establish a new ground for educational reform.

CHAPTER THREE

Children and Childhood

STEPHANIE OLSEN

INTRODUCTION

If one looks at a photograph of the inside of a classroom in late nineteenth-century London (see Figure 3.1), and compare it with a similar photograph depicting a Canadian residential school (see Figure 3.2), we might easily be fooled into thinking that the educational experience of children across national, colonial, and racial divides had much in common. But any apparent similarities belie radical differences in the experience of childhood in educational settings, according to the expression of colonialist power, ideologies of race, class, and gender that reflected or otherwise more tightly defined concepts of childhood in the period covered by this volume. Guiding questions here concern how children derived their childhood, if they did at all. Were they bestowed it by those in authority? Were children complicit in their education or were they forced to participate in it? Was their education viewed as a means to achieve full adult participation in citizenry or as a means of control? To address such questions is to reveal the historical interplay among concepts of childhood, different visions of education, and the experiences of children.

The main focus of this chapter is on the link between a nineteenth-century "discovery" of childhood, requiring a certain set of rights and roles for children, and the development and spread of organized and legislated formal education institutions. This puts the onus on schools as "important sites of contact and exchange between different groups of people, and their ideologies."[1] In addition to classrooms in formal schooling situations, in residential settings, and in religious settings, the consideration of less formal environments such as playgrounds and exchanges among peers is crucial to form a more complete understanding of the concept of childhood and its intersections with race, gender, class, age, and geographic location. It should be noted here that childhood was not really "discovered" in the nineteenth century, but rather a certain set of meanings, prescriptions, and proscriptions—a certain concept of childhood—became entrenched in this period. Nor, of course, was this the only concept of childhood in the nineteenth century: competing and sometimes clashing older and indigenous views of childhood were certainly present. The "modern" concept of childhood, still prevalent in many contemporary societies and enshrined in the United Nations Convention on the Rights of the Child (1990), is an ideal that reserves for children a period protected from adult concerns, and allows them to develop through education and play. While the emergence of this concept might be thought to have unburdened children and to have provided scope for more agency, many real harms were done to children under its guise and not least through educational policies and practices, implemented in the interests of spreading an idea and ideal of childhood, which could serve broader political interests.

Changing definitions of childhood became associated with concepts of modernity and civilization. And conversely, as Bengt Sandin pointed out, "schooling in the West emerged as one of the main influences on the definition of childhood and on the lives of children and their families."[2] In other places in the world, education increasingly became one of the most important markers of childhood, whether children were "entitled" to it or not. As James Marten explained, "access to education became one of the hallmarks of a 'modern' childhood"; though he adds that "education is also one of the most variable elements of the development of modern sensibilities about children."[3]

It is precisely this nexus that forms the core of this chapter. The survey offered here cannot hope for complete coverage or do justice to global differences and distinctions over time and place in a comprehensive manner. Instead, the aim is to offer an overarching appraisal of the ways in which apparently progressive or "modern" conceptualizations of childhood have been deployed to different ends according to differing political and ideological contexts, and the ways in which children's experiences have been affected by the educational settings in which they were caught, more or less. The chapter begins, therefore, with a brief account of the conceptual history of "childhood" in this period, and the perceived potential for the education of children accordingly. Thereafter, it surveys the metropolitan education of children, with a focus on the ways in which class and gender influenced notions of what children were and how they should be taught. These lines of distinction receive much greater emphasis in imperial settings, an analysis of which follows, where in complicated and contradictory ways, racial ideology trumped the concept of "childhood" as being intrinsic to children and young people. This section is followed by a closer case study of Canadian residential schools, exemplifying the vicissitudes of a concept of childhood that was made to serve a corrupt notion of civilization.

CONCEPTUAL HISTORY

Childhood has a definite history: its meanings, applications, and the experiences associated with it change over time. This history is central to understanding the history of education in the nineteenth century. The terms children and childhood cannot be understood neutrally. Who was included and excluded, and what made up their definitions, are an integral part of the political, social, and cultural history of education and of young people. Who was considered a child and why? This is especially important because in the nineteenth century, at an ever-increasing pace, the only acceptable place for "children" was in school. Laws increasingly enshrined certain chronological age ranges as protected in formal schooling and from adult responsibilities. Yet many young people in the same age range were left out. Why was this? The multifaceted explanation comes from looking at fundamental categories of the history of childhood: class, race, ethnicity, gender, and location.

Over several decades now, historians have problematized the seemingly neat categories of the child and of childhood. Although his periodization of the "discovery" of childhood is now viewed as problematic, Philippe Ariès's *L'Enfant et la vie familiale sous l'ancien régime* (1960; Eng. *Centuries of Childhood,* 1962) is often still acknowledged as the seminal text in this field. Persuasive reasons why historians should stop relying on Ariès have been supplied by, among others, Colin Heywood.[4] Significant shifts have taken place in what it means to be a child, an adolescent, and a young adult. Changes have come about through government legislation, education, private initiatives, scientific expertise, and mass media, and have significantly affected the meaning of childhood at the level of society as a whole. Educators (as well as reformers more generally) looked to childhood as an important stage in the life cycle, informed by Enlightenment ideas, especially John Locke (1632–1704) and Jean-Jacques Rousseau (1712–78) and their followers, who saw children as in need of nurture and development. According to Elizabeth Foyster and James Marten, parents in this period began to strive to "instill love and mold the child's mind."[5] Moreover, these Enlightenment ideas led to increased attention to education and to child development with an emphasis on providing settings that would allow children's mental processes to flourish. In many places during the long nineteenth century, a particular concept of childhood was distilled down from its Enlightenment origins and, as it became culturally entrenched and dominant, it was politically or legislatively codified. Increasing emphasis on childhood as a time of protection and education led to the creation of national programs of schooling with increased funding. These formal educational initiatives were complemented by a rise in efforts informally to educate the young. Of course, this trend did not occur universally at the same rate or level of effectiveness in all places. Nor were all children deemed worthy of having a childhood, with the rights and privileges that entailed. As Satadru Sen has stated, for example, "British experts in India [...] generally saw native children as distorted mirror images of the children they imagined at 'home.'"[6] Understandings of children as innocent and malleable became increasingly dominant in the nineteenth century, yet not all children were perceived to have these qualities equally. The judgment of colonial policy-makers and the effect of colonial practices in general created a hierarchy of childhood, embedded within complex schemes of class, race, gender, sexuality, and geography that determined and naturalized lines of inclusion and exclusion, within discourses of docility, plasticity, and potential. Furthermore, as Rebecca Swartz points out in her book on education, empire, and race in the nineteenth-century British settler colonies of the Caribbean, Australia, and South Africa, in its structure, content, and increasingly racist logic, "education was pivotal to the construction of racial difference in the colonies of settlement," impacting Indigenous children and their families even when it was not directly available to them.[7] In many parts of the colonized world there was a perceived need for more governmental intervention in education in the last quarter of the nineteenth century, with debates as to whether the aims were mainly humanitarian or whether children were to be tools in the mechanisms of the colonial settler project. Either way, the conceptual delimitation of "childhood" had the effect of instrumentalizing children for ideological ends. This is not, however, to say that children were mere pawns. Children (and their families) used education as a means to their own ends where they could.

The modern concept of childhood, still largely familiar today, is clear: childhood is a distinct time in the life cycle set aside for developing, learning, and playing, free from paid work, responsibility, and burden. A modern childhood is one that is protected, healthy, and well provided for, both physically and emotionally. This, of course, is an ideal definition and did not represent the lives of many children in the nineteenth century (or later). Moreover, the ideal was rhetorically plastic, serving a variety of ends in different places. It was used as a way to enact legislation, to invest financially in children, and to muster up support for nongovernmental organizations. It was used by missionaries to fundraise and to convert youngsters. It was used to grant children more say in their own lives and education, but also to limit, to coerce, and to cajole. The concept of childhood could be deployed without regard for the implications for real children and, as such, fostered mixed results in its influence on educational policies and practices. The extent to which actual children were captured by a working concept of "childhood" or, conversely, the extent to which their lived experience fell outside of it, should be a guiding question for historians of childhood and youth, and of education. As detailed below, the first education systems in the German states demonstrate the prevalence of this concept as does educational policy and practice in nineteenth-century Britain and its settler colonies.

DEVELOPING AND SPREADING CONCEPTS OF CHILDHOOD

In Western Europe and North America, narrowing definitions of childhood were often associated with increasing efforts to shape young people in the "best" way. Children's social and cultural upbringing, which had previously taken place primarily within families, communities, and religious institutions— and for lower-class children also in workplaces—was increasingly assumed by educational authorities and states, and conversely by peer groups. In the eighteenth century and well into the nineteenth century, a male elite was the main focus of education for children. As the nineteenth century progressed, gender became less of a factor in determining which children deserved a childhood. Girls, however, were mainly not entitled to the same education as boys, both in duration and in subject matter. The target of basic literacy for children, however, began to permeate class and gender boundaries, especially in areas where Christian belief required children to cultivate a personal relationship with God by reading the Bible and religious tracts. Learning to read gradually became more systematic and there was a significant rise in literacy rates in the late nineteenth century in many parts of the world.[8]

The push for universal literacy coincided with a substantial increase in mass education, often conducted first by religious or other nongovernmental institutions. Yet education remained a piecemeal affair in most of the world. Prussia established a series of educational reforms in the late eighteenth century, which were built upon in the early nineteenth century and subsequently became influential in other educational systems. In Britain at the start of the century, patchwork efforts by Sunday School promoters to create and expand day schools and the creation in 1811 of the (Church of England) National Society for Promoting the Education of the Poor contributed to the provision of schooling opportunities in industrial towns. The 1833 Factory Act restricted children's employment in factories while the Children Act of 1908 (also named the "Children's Charter") extended state responsibility to cover all children in England and Wales, ended child imprisonment, restricted corporal punishment, instituted the first national system of juvenile courts, and supported temperance efforts.[9]

Education, mostly compulsory and free by the end of the nineteenth century in many places in the world, increasingly came under the purview of the state. The establishment of compulsory, universal education is an important result of the desire to shelter modern childhood from the world of adults. In England and Wales, a series of Education Acts, starting in 1870, consolidated educational efforts throughout the country, with compulsory education starting in 1880. The 1891 Elementary Education Act established that elementary education was to be free. The Education (Scotland) Act 1872 required compulsory attendance from the start. In British settler colonies and dominions, most provinces and states had instituted compulsory elementary education between the last decades of the nineteenth and the first decade of the twentieth century. South Africa was the exception.[10] During the British Raj (1858–1947) there was no system of universal education in India, despite some attempts to establish compulsory primary education in some provinces.[11]

As many scholars have pointed out, childhood in the nineteenth century was "bestowed" or not, based on gender, race, class, or political expediency and the means of bestowing it often took the form of access to education or forced attendance in school. David Pomfret has shown how Britain as a colonial power had a different relationship to the childhood of its subjects than did France, based not on the well-being of the colonial young people involved but rather on the different exigencies of maintaining and expanding their empires. As Pomfret explains, unlike in Britain where sentimental views of the potential of Indigenous children increasingly dissolved, especially after the establishment of the British Raj in 1858, late nineteenth-century French colonial expansion "encouraged explicit appeals to sentimental ideals of childhood and the modern family."[12] Nevertheless, ideas of racial superiority and the infantilization of subject peoples colored understandings of children and childhood in both these and other imperial settings. In British, French, Dutch, and German colonies these ideas were translated into apparatuses of coercion and control through informal means but also most visibly through formal sites of power such as penal institutions and schools. As Ann Laura Stoler's seminal work reminds us, "colonial powers created institutions, both penal and pedagogic [...] that were often indistinguishable" in order to "rescue young citizens in the making."[13]

Education systems that might be framed as emancipatory, therefore, had the potential to be experienced as such or as threatening to a similar degree. Education framed as "training," a commonplace in the first part of the nineteenth century, could be critiqued and experienced as a means of control. The interplay between these varied views of education, between the changing meanings of childhood, and the vicissitudes of experience within educational systems is important. Children were shaped by, and contributed to shaping, this interplay. Together with Karen Vallgårda and Kristine Alexander, I have elaborated the concepts of "emotional frontiers" where various "emotional formations" negotiate and clash.[14] Schools and other sites of children's education are contact zones where children confront gender, class, race, and other categories of difference as well as negotiate the politics of belonging and potential.

As urbanization, mass culture, and other potentially negative influences developed in the course of the nineteenth century, policy-makers increasingly asked how to prevent degeneracy and educate the next generation to be useful citizens with "correct" political, social, imperial, and nationalist outlooks.[15] Useful citizenship was at the core of new views on education in both Britain and in Prussia. In order to shape the "right" kinds of children and to guide youthful energies and impulses, several reform movements took hold of educational thinking in the late nineteenth century. As Bowersox details, Germany was the originator and major proponent of many such movements, such as *Reformpädagogik* (reform pedagogy), *Kunsterziehungsbewegung* (the art education movement), *Jugendbewegung* (the youth movement), and *Lebensreform* (the life reform movement).[16] Broadly, together these influential movements promoted experience, observation, discovery, exploration of nature, and outdoor activity, and eschewed rote learning and practices associated with it. Prussia instituted educational reforms early on. As Jeff Bowersox explains,

> An influential, international circle of educators collected under the umbrella of "reform pedagogy" (Reformpädagogik) directed their attention to reshaping the practice of classroom instruction. They condemned mechanistic teaching methods, which they saw as an unfortunate consequence of their industrial society. Reaching back to Jean-Jacques Rousseau, Johan Heinrich Pestalozzi, and Friedrich Froebel, reformers called instead for a pedagogy "that starts with the child" (vom Kinde aus): teaching strategies must be tailored to each student and must embrace the unique qualities of childhood.[17]

While the motivation for creating such an innovative system was manifold, including the influence of building nationalism and political and social control, it was also based on Enlightenment ideas of the child. Enlightenment conceptions of childhood, the child, and education, and the Prussian education system, in particular, greatly influenced educational ideas and practices in the long nineteenth century. The reform education movement, as it played out across Europe, the Americas, and some parts of India, among other places, was intimately tied to a particular conceptual understanding of childhood that evolved, in part, through its relationship to educational ideals and results. While changing concepts of childhood and youth drove education reform, they also provided an aggressive and confining logic of exclusion or restriction.

British education, though mandatory after the 1880 Education Act, was of varying effectiveness and brutality, depending on class, gender, and geographical area. Robert Roberts, who was a boy in Edwardian Salford (England), later described his childhood in the slums in devastating detail. He wrote of a highly stratified existence, where everyone had to cross numerous class-, gender-, and age-based emotional frontiers, which constantly informed life at home, at school, on the streets, and in the workplace. Roberts described "appalling conditions" in his Church of England school (built in 1839), which had 450 students and eight, mostly unqualified, teachers.[18] In this school, he wrote,

> the staff worked earnestly but with no great hope. The building itself stood face on to one of the largest marshalling yards in the North. All day long the roar of a work-a-day world invaded the school hall, where each instructor, shouting in competition, taught up to sixty children massed together.[19]

FIGURE 3.1 Edwardian infants sitting at their desks during a nature lesson, circa 1908. *Source:* this life pictures / Alamy Stock Photo.

As a boy, Roberts recognized that this sort of environment was not conducive to academic success, yet he was one of the "bright boys" who was good at his lessons and wanted to stay in school. Because of a lack of support, he failed the exam to obtain a technical college bursary and needed to find work instead. Class, as with race elsewhere, could be a determining factor in deciding which children were entitled to a childhood.

This description of schools for working-class children is in marked contrast to the experiences of upper-middle- and upper-class children. Schools for elite boys, such as the famous English public schools, have received much attention from historians, in particular for their fashioning of a distinct brand of masculinity pointed at colonial leadership, military prowess, and a conceit of physical superiority as honed by the games ethic. The classical historiographical narrative is of a shift in focus among elite schoolchildren from forms of manliness connected to a Christian piety to a muscular Christianity expressed on the playing field. While this has been challenged in terms of the actual experience of elite children, and its importance reassessed in the light of the rise of middle-class imperial settlement, it remains true that the imperial future was often rhetorically staked on the physical prowess and sporting ethics of elite boys.[20] Public boarding schools, through their sometimes brutal emotional and physical conditioning, were intended to form and educate leaders in every sphere of endeavor and to produce men who felt that they were at the top of gendered, social, racial, and imperial hierarchies.[21] These hierarchical ideas pervaded all levels of societies in the metropoles and the colonies and profoundly impacted children, whether European (settler) or Indigenous.

COLONIZED CHILDREN'S EDUCATION

Educational ideas within European colonial regimes in the first third of the nineteenth century were predicated on the hope of universal potential: that education could transform and "civilize" the colonial subject.[22] This civilization, of course, was borne out of specific European ideas of what an education to produce civilized future adults entailed. As Bowersox explains in the case of Germany, instruction was colonial in orientation and served to encourage children and youth "to think that they, as Germans, belonged among the colonizers and that they could promote the cause of progress at home and abroad when they grew up."[23] British children, and those in settler colonies, were taught much the same, with similar goals in mind. Focusing on the history of colonizing ideas around race and civilization points to a hardening of views in the latter part of the century. It was viewed as increasingly unlikely or even impossible to "elevate" other races to the level of the European and thus what was most required was control through education. These racist beliefs arguably did more to shape education policies in various locations throughout the imperial world than did pedagogical theory.

As the nineteenth century progressed and the concept of childhood narrowed and became more entrenched, children's needs were differentiated from their parents' and adults' in general. This development ran parallel to an entrenchment of racial theory as biological rather than cultural. These two factors had major consequences for Indigenous people and children who were set apart because of their age, and who simultaneously became the focus of ideological chauvinism. These children's "childhood" did not fit the "dominant" mode. Sanjay Seth has argued that colonialism itself was viewed as an "essentially pedagogic enterprise."[24] Rebecca Swartz has recently encouraged scholars to take seriously the larger context of colonial education since this enterprise was a "pedagogic process in which Indigenous people were taught new ways of seeing and being."[25] As Edward Said famously wrote, students in India were not just taught English subjects but rather "the inherent superiority of the English race."[26] Educative ideals and practices were never neutral but rather an integral part of a political agenda of cultural erasure, of European dominance, and of taught inferiority and quiescence. Furthermore, Swartz emphasizes the point made by scholars in many colonial contexts that childhood was viewed as the opportune time to form, through mandatory education, Indigenous peoples into the kind of citizens colonizers wanted to make them.[27]

In European metropolitan centers and among settler colonists, education increasingly became concerned with teaching children about their nation, their empire, and consequently, their own place in the world. Ideas about imperialism, social Darwinism, modernity, religion, and science infused teaching and classroom material and were combined, confused, and popularized into a sometimes heady mix. Education became entangled with discussions about modernity. Both the manipulation of the concept of childhood and the education of children were of paramount importance to colonial powers, who understood that the child embodied potential futures: "nothing less than the future of the nation was at stake."[28]

In India, as Satadru Sen argued, "native childhood" came to be seen as "an oxymoron." The normative nineteenth-century model of childhood did not serve an age group, but a socially and racially idealized group. "Reformatories, boarding schools and authoritative texts," according to Sen, "were energized by the putative plasticity of the child, but they were also paralyzed by an articulation of difference that implied that native children were essentially small, perverse adults."[29] Casting young people as deviant, precocious, dangerous, and not-quite children was a prevalent mechanism for precluding a universal childhood from belonging to all children.[30] According to Sen:

> Childhood was thus an important ingredient in the making of empire, race and nationhood at a time when new meanings were attached to perceived distinctions between white and black children, girl and boy children, aristocratic and middle class children, "westernized" and "authentic" children, and between the offspring of the elite and those of the poor and provincial. One set was central (as future adults) to the colony and the emerging nation, while the other was relegated to the fringes.[31]

In Latin America in the early part of the nineteenth century, independence leaders spent a great deal of time and effort in creating an education system that would reflect their political goals. More specifically, early republican education and school policies in Colombia demonstrated the perceived need to manage the collective emotions of children (and via them, their families) through education. It was a desire to imbue children with a "unity of sentiment" directed at a prescribed political goal.[32] While the British government, via the Colonial Office, did not construct a uniform system of indigenous education, the space was filled by missionaries, local governments, and organizations who saw value in the opportunity to shape children according to imperial ideals of Christian religious observance, cultural bearing, or profit.[33] Sen's understanding of the political clashes over children in the British Raj can be applied much more widely in other colonial and national settings.

Many colonial educators and missionaries believed that boarding schools were far more effective than day schools as the former removed children from the influence of their parents and communities. As Karen Vallgårda demonstrates, Danish missionary Carl Ochs, the founder of one such school, made the link between the modern conception of childhood, children, and education plain:

> One is inclined to return to the circle of people among whom one finds more fruit of one's work, less evil, hypocrisy and deception than among the old,

namely to the children. [With respect to] the generation which has grown up and has become old in heathenism, there is but little to do and in order for the following generations not also to become like it, the youth must be educated and properly raised.[34]

The Danish Missionary Society argued that Indian parents provided problematic education for their children, though they lauded "a universal 'mother's heart'" among Indian people. For the most part, however, Indian parents were viewed as inadequate and harmful, exposing children to "sinful" and risky talk and behavior. They were portrayed as willing to kill or harm their children, motivated by their religion or the need to compel the children to work too hard, or else they were too lenient and indulgent. According to missionaries, as Vallgårda puts it, Indian parents displayed "distorted affective dispositions" and "either loved too much or too little."[35]

Although Danish missionary Sara Ochs, Carl Ochs's wife, seemed to have been aware that the families' material situation often necessitated children's contribution to the household economy, she nonetheless interpreted what she considered children's excessive work as a sign of bad parenting. As Vallgårda argues, the missionaries' views on Indian parents and their children was one "where class prejudice intersects with religious and moral condemnation," and where "the plea was not for the material support of poor Christian families, but rather for interventions in their parenting."[36]

According to Vallgårda, missionaries could not remove children from their families by force. They waited for parents or guardians to sign over their children to the boarding school, mainly because of some emergency situation, not because of an overwhelming desire for their children to be raised in that setting. This finds echoes in the Canadian Indigenous Residential School example which will be discussed below. Once parents had signed over their children to missionary-run boarding schools, however, parents lost their authority over them and the children could not return home.[37] Indigenous parents in Canada also did not have this choice and their children were forced to stay at school, away from their parents and their communities.

CANADIAN RESIDENTIAL SCHOOLS

Canadian residential schools operated in the nineteenth and twentieth centuries. The last one closed in 1996.[38] The stated goal of these schools was to "civilize" Indigenous children, to remove them from the "corrupting" influences of their parents, families, and communities, and to forge new Canadian citizens out of them. The premise was that children were more malleable than their irredeemable parents. These boarding schools were the sites of emotional, physical, and sexual abuse and cultural belittling and denial, giving children a uniform and a number in a concerted effort to strip away the individual. These practices have

FIGURE 3.2 R.C. Indian Residential School Study Time, Fort Resolution, N.W.T.
Source: Library and Archives Canada / PA-042133.

been described as "cultural genocide."[39] The Canadian government concluded a Truth and Reconciliation Commission in 2015 with several highly instructive reports. Many survivors of residential schools gave testimony and have cogently explained how this fusion of ideas of childhood, racism, and nationalism/ imperialism impacted them as individual children through their schooling. The legacy of this school system remains in the physical and emotional health and welfare of Indigenous people. This system is not a blip in the Canadian national story but rather a foundational element in the British imperial project and in the creation of Canada as a nation. It is the fusing of Enlightenment ideas about childhood and education, in their late nineteenth-century guise, with contemporary notions of racial hierarchy, nationalism, and imperialism. Doris Young, who attended the Elkhorn residential school in Manitoba, testified under the auspices of the Truth and Reconciliation Commission:

> Those schools were a war on Aboriginal children, and they took away our identity. First of all, they gave us numbers, we had no names, we were numbers, and they cut our hair. They took away our clothes, and gave us clothes [...] we all looked alike.[40]

Residential schools were not really about education but the tight link established in the nineteenth and twentieth centuries between education and childhood enabled them under that guise. They were more accurately about control and re-forming Indigenous children into Canadian subjects worthy of a "childhood." In so doing, their indigeneity and ties to their cultures, communities, and families were stripped. In justifying the investment in industrial schools to parliament in 1883, Canadian Public Works Minister Hector Langevin argued that,

> if you wish to educate these children you must separate them from their parents during the time that they are being educated. If you leave them in the family they may know how to read and write, but they still remain savages, whereas by separating them in the way proposed, they acquire the habits and tastes—it is to be hoped only the good tastes—of civilized people.[41]

In 1883, Canada's first prime minister, Sir John A. Macdonald, made the goal explicit: "When the school is on the reserve the child lives with its parents, who are savages; he is surrounded by savages. [...] Indian children should be withdrawn as much as possible from the parental influence."[42] By 1920, Canada's infamous deputy minister of Indian Affairs, Duncan Campbell Scott, had a certain confidence in the efficacy of the project in declaring: "Our object is to continue until there is not a single Indian in Canada that has not been absorbed into the body politic."[43] The Bagot Commission Report of 1842 and the 1879 Report on Industrial Schools for Indians and Half-Breeds both concluded that residential and industrial schools, with children separated from their families, were the best ways to "civilize" Indigenous children.[44]

The result through education was to be "the enforced acculturation" of Indigenous students, as Jim Marten has put it.[45] Marten discusses the situation in the United States, which shares a history with the Canadian residential schools system. Similar projects occurred in various colonial settings, where particular kinds of "enforced acculturation" were desired. In the later half of the nineteenth century, the United States provided a model for the Canadian system, complemented by developments in Britain to deal with "juvenile delinquents." The model for residential schools, both in Canada and the United States, was not the English public school of the elite but rather the European and North American reformatories and industrial schools for the urban poor. These institutions were often violent places where students were physically punished with straps and meager food rations.[46]

Residential school children crossed the starkest of emotional frontiers when they first entered the schools, but they repeatedly did so on the infrequent occasions when they saw their families or were allowed to return home for holidays. We are fortunate to have the recollections of residential school survivors who have directly addressed this issue. Children's indigenous emotional formations prior to their entry into school were fundamentally and intentionally re-formed. As Mary Courchene, formerly a student at the residential schools at Fort Alexander in Manitoba and Lebret in Saskatchewan, testified before the Truth and Reconciliation Commission:

> And I looked at my dad, I looked at my mom, I looked at my dad again. You know what? I hated them. I just absolutely hated my own parents. Not because I thought they abandoned me; I hated their brown faces. I hated them because they were Indians [...]. So I, I looked at my dad and I challenged him and I said, "From now on we speak only English in this house," I said to my dad. And you know when we, when, in a traditional home where I was raised, the first thing that we all were always taught was to respect your Elders and never to, you know, to challenge them. And here I was, eleven years old, and I challenged [...] my dad looked at me and I, and I thought he was going to cry. In fact his eyes filled up with tears. He turned to my mom and he says, [...] "Then I guess we'll never speak to this little girl again. I don't know her."[47]

The extremity of this child's negative feelings toward her parents, and by extension toward her community, her culture, and the entirety of her life prior to entering school, is telling of the destructive effectiveness of this system in instilling a new self-understanding in students, predicated on a prescriptive emotional formation. Crossing the emotional frontier between school and home became exceedingly difficult, if not impossible. The schools drilled Indigenous children to police themselves to avoid their own languages and traditional cultural practices. In the above example, the father devastatingly no longer "knew" his daughter; the process of estrangement and alienation was a sinister and effective tool in ripping apart communities, families, and individuals.

Agnes Mills, a former student at All Saints residential school in Saskatchewan, explained: "I wanted to be white so bad, and the worst thing I ever did was I was ashamed of my mother, that honourable woman, because she couldn't speak English."[48] Residential school students frequently express that residential schools made them feel ashamed of their families, their communities, their languages, and their indigeneity. They tried to look, act, and sound "white" to "fit" into European Canadian society at a terrible price. Such brutal practices and attitudes have led to premature death for many former residential school attendees, and lifelong trauma for survivors. As Jim Miller reported after a residential school reunion: many "spoke of wasting years and decades in alcohol, drugs, and violence before they managed to put their lives back together, confront the pain that had been driving them to harm themselves, and get on with the business of living."[49]

Indigenous young people in Canada bore the brunt of imperial and national policies even before the country was officially founded. They supply a clear example of the ways in which a narrowing definition of childhood could be distorted to exclude. These young people were often considered not really to be children but were not adults either. Racist settler understandings of the sensuality and cunningness of Indigenous young people were mixed with ideas about their greater malleability when compared with Indigenous adults. That malleability was to be harnessed through education to produce a more European/Canadian Indigenous population in the next generation. The force of many of these policies is suggestively apparent in education policy. Residential schools are the clearest example, but not the only one. Nationalist agendas (often including the cultural genocide of Indigenous people) permeated social and cultural life in many places globally. Though the rate of Indigenous child removal to residential schools accelerated in the twentieth century, the premise and justification for the creation, continuation, and expansion of these schools had an insidious nineteenth-century logic, fusing ideas about childhood, race, nation, and colonialism. It is a telling paradox that Indigenous children were recognized as children and therefore malleable, but also as not entitled to a childhood, with all the rights and freedoms that entailed for white children elsewhere.

CONCLUSION

After the horrors of the First World War, the twentieth century was styled the "century of the child."[50] Ellen Key's international bestseller was taken up as a rallying cry to make children the central focus of societies in the twentieth century.[51] American activist Florence Kelley echoed others around the world in saying that young people had "a right to childhood."[52] The Declaration of the Rights of the Child, adopted by the League of Nations in 1924, reinforced this "modern" view of a universal childhood. Children, "beyond and above all considerations of race, nationality or creed," possessed rights as *children*.[53] It contained these clauses pertaining to education: "The child must be given the means requisite for its normal development, both materially and spiritually"; and "The child must be brought up in the consciousness that its talents must be devoted to the service of fellow men." The ideas embodied in these clauses represent a refinement of the ideal of childhood and implied further reform in the education of children, irrespective of context. But, as the long nineteenth century bore witness, ideals and promises of reform did not necessarily play out at the level of policy and practice. Many children were either excluded from modern ideals of childhood or else these ideals served to justify and bolster educational regimes of coercion or oppression. Gender, class, race, and location mattered in defining who was a child, who deserved a childhood, and what the conditions of that childhood would be. Education—both at the level of policy and practice—is a crucial indicator of the formative power of ideals of childhood and their global impact on children.

CHAPTER FOUR

Family, Community, and Sociability

CATHERINE SLOAN

In 1875, twelve-year-old pupil Frank Bunting diligently wrote a long essay on "The Albatross" during free time at his school, the Croydon Friends' School, a small Quaker boarding school near London.[1] By doing so, he was most likely surpassing the educational achievements of his widowed mother, Lydia, who at age twelve had already started working in the family business after her own mother was widowed.[2] Frank's experience suggests the impact of the rise of schooling in nineteenth-century Western societies. However, if we take Lydia and Frank's lives together, we can see other influences on education: the priority on maintaining the family unit, and traditions of formal or informal apprenticeship within families.

Family and education were intertwined in the nineteenth and early twentieth centuries in a range of ways. The shifting values and habits of families shaped pedagogies, books, and institutions, while families intervened in schoolchildren's lives and the running of institutions. Families facilitated informal educational practices such as conversation and reading, and attendance at clubs and societies. This chapter examines individual experiences such as Frank's in order to consider the enduring influence of family on the development of education in this period. Family, as a growing body of research suggests, was vital to imperial and global networks and economic strategies.[3] British families, in particular, benefited from their global position, with even small businesses tied to the slave trade, plantations, and the transcontinental flow of goods.[4] In the "family enterprise," education was a key strategy to secure this imperial and global position.[5]

Much of the work in histories of education focuses on the rise of institutions such as schools and colleges. Indeed, the nation played an important role in the rise of institutional education, as campaigners and educators were prominent in political networks, institutions were subject to state policies, and schools and colleges were tasked with selecting books and activities that promoted national identities and histories.[6] Yet these were also transnational phenomena. Networks of educators and organizations, policies and institutional structures, and pedagogies all crossed national boundaries.[7] As a result, emphasis has shifted away from the "trickle down" of educational practices from nation-state and metropole to other parts of the world, instead examining the more complex patterns of interaction and identification between institutions, associations, and communities in different geographical locations.[8] This scholarship largely focuses on institutions in order to develop our understanding of the entangled networks and systems that emerged in a period of colonization and globalization.

However, education also expanded due to the growing number of middle-class families seeking schools and colleges to instil the values of domesticity, public service, and self-improvement, which would ensure the family's financial security and success.[9] British colonization was often justified in terms of its spreading domestic and public virtues through legislation, policies, missionary activities, and education.[10] Therefore, family did not exist merely within national bounds but was an ideal shaping politics, personal life, and education across the world.[11] Family is a promising scholarly lens, as it brings into view the varied familial strategies, educational spaces, and forms of childcare, chores, and work that characterize education across the world, and it complicates a chronological narrative of the rise of institutional provision.[12]

This chapter uses the educational experiences of four learners—Frank Bunting (1862–1910), Anna Legge (1865–1946), William Barron (c. 1865–?), and Sydney Frankenburg (1881–1935)—to reexamine the role of family in shaping experiences of education. While Frank, Anna, Sydney, and William were educated in Britain, the chapter highlights how family practices in Britain were shaped by the imperial and global circulation of ideals, pedagogies, books, and clubs and societies. The chapter also draws attention to their families' global and imperial connections and their encounters with people and places outside Britain. Examining such circulations, connections, and encounters has enabled historians to challenge existing historiographical assumptions about the "trickle down" of influence from the nation-state, or from the West to other regions.[13] This includes a rich body of biographical studies that provide intimate insight into the economic and personal benefits imperialism brought to individual Western families or groups of interconnected families.[14] A biographical approach has also benefited histories of education by providing a more individual perspective on overarching developments, particularly in a period when the gradual emergence of state education meant most learners continued to vary considerably in their experiences.[15] Indeed, these individual variations are a key characteristic of education in this period, as demographers emphasize that the modern life cycle—with a neat trajectory of home, school attendance, work or further education, and marriage—did not emerge until the middle of the twentieth century.[16] The family therefore provides a powerful lens on education in this period by connecting the ideals, institutions, and practices that were circulating globally with the uneven and varying opportunities and expectations at a local level.

FAMILY

In 1884, eighteen-year-old pupil Anna Legge published an essay on "Women in China" in the *Oxford High School Magazine*, at a newly established girls' high school in Oxford, England. Anna was benefiting from the expansion in girls' schooling across Britain. However, her essay also gestured toward her family. Her father was the missionary and scholar of Chinese literature, James Legge, and by displaying her knowledge of his specialism, Anna's essay draws attention to the continued importance of family conversation, home education, and familial intellectual traditions in her education.

From the seventeenth century onwards, European educational philosophy had represented the home as the ideal site of education. The instructive and morally improving conversations of a mother with her young children served as a model of early education for Swiss educational philosopher Johann Pestalozzi (1747–1827) and one of his collaborators, the German Friedrich Fröbel (1782–1852). Their approaches provided a new theoretical underpinning for long-standing traditions of home education.[17] Print production boomed in the early nineteenth century, so that educational treatises and books for home education popularized the idea of family conversation as a powerful pedagogical tool.[18] The give-and-take of family conversation was thought to foster the rational independent selfhood that was the ideal product of an enlightened education. The books recommended content deemed particularly engaging for young readers. First and foremost was natural history, which claimed to appeal to children's affinity for nature, and formed the basis of the familial conversations represented in books by Maria Edgeworth, Maria Hack, and Priscilla Wakefield. Parents were to take cues from these books and draw their children into the habits of rational discussion, independent thinking, and accurate observation of the world exhibited in Anna's essay.[19] Scholars frequently present this pedagogy as child-centered, as freeing the young writer to articulate their own perspectives and observations, in contrast with rote learning adult-authored books or responding to religious indoctrination.[20] It was also a two-way process, as instead of children passively receiving parental dictates, both children and parents honed rational and independent habits of mind through family conversation.[21]

The educational experiences of the four British learners in this chapter suggest the wide reach of these ideas. In 1875, for instance, thirteen-year-old Frank Bunting took on an important role as a librarian at the Croydon Friends' School.[22] The school library was packed with books of rational and improving conversations by authors such as Edgeworth, Hack, and Wakefield or organizations such as the Society for the Diffusion of Useful Knowledge.[23] In this period, the more traditional, overtly religious and didactic texts were superseded by books on factual and improving subjects.[24] While these publications boomed in Britain, the veneration of home education was influenced as much by European educational philosophers such as Pestalozzi, Fröbel, and Rousseau, as it was by British philosopher John Locke.[25] In Britain, however, the pedagogies held a special appeal for dissenting communities such as the Quaker community surrounding the Croydon Friends' School. Observation and rational recreation harmonized with the religious beliefs of dissenting authors such as Edgeworth, Hack, and Wakefield, and organizations campaigning for secular and democratic education.[26]

Studies have emphasized the uneven nature of the books' appeal. Like the dissenting communities in Britain, the books struck a chord with particular communities in Europe, the British Empire, and other areas of the world. A study of Spain suggests that pedagogies of home education were popular due to Catholic beliefs about the susceptibility of children's minds to sensory information and the potentially dangerous influence of strangers or other children.[27] The books also held a particular importance in colonial regions. There was a significant demand for books on home education among white settler families such as those in rural Australia, where access to schools was limited.[28] However, circulation was not constrained to imperial networks. Studies have traced the circulation of popular works beyond Britain and the British Empire to Spanish America and the United States.[29] This form of home education is striking in its wide and enduring appeal in this period, but instead of an even diffusion, it is important to consider how it was configured and understood by different families across vast geographical spaces.

Books on home education by Wakefield, Edgeworth, and Hack remained in the Croydon Friends' School in the 1870s, unaffected by the shift toward institutional education or the new trade in fictional children's books and periodicals from the 1860s onwards. In fact, consumption of such texts increased because the books were reprinted and recirculated in cheaper editions targeting new markets of working-class children and adult learners.[30] Beyond Britain, books from earlier periods were reprinted and repurposed into the twentieth century.[31] Moreover, rational and instructive books did not overtake more catechistic or religious children's books in all areas. Duff shows how the evangelicalism of some Cape Colony communities fueled a flurry of child-rearing books by the Dutch Reformed Church, which sold well across Europe and America, as they addressed a gap in the global market for evangelical literature.[32]

Likewise, home education was not neatly displaced by the rise of institutional education but endured into the twentieth century.[33] For instance, when Anna Legge started at Dollar Academy in Scotland in 1872 at age seven, census records for 1871 show she had previously studied under a governess.[34] For the majority of middle-class British school-goers like Anna, early education—learning to read and write—still happened at home.[35] Noting the gradual introduction of elementary education in England, historians argue that working-class British children too learnt some reading and writing at home throughout the nineteenth century.[36] Across the British Empire, early education remained a family activity where parents, older siblings, and other relatives could be involved in teaching.[37] Studies of white families in Australia and South Africa note that the lack of schools in rural areas meant home education by literate parents was often the only option.[38] While the numbers entering schools increased, home education remained a common feature of many children's lives and a commonplace function of the family.

For British pupils, education could implicitly signify their privileged imperial and global position. In her essay on "Women in China," Anna Legge lamented the "general degradation" of the stereotypical Chinese girl.[39] The sentiment stood in implicit contrast with the family background and education that enabled her to write and publish her essay. Enlightenment notions of educability, rationality, and independence were constructed around the domination and exclusion of those "others" encountered through globalization, enslavement, and colonization.[40] This was not necessarily a subtle or implicit contrast. Enlightenment educational texts and children's textbooks were laden with references to the "primitive" others who lacked the supposedly civilizing influence of the British middle-class home and were therefore depicted as innately ineducable.[41] At school, Frank Bunting had access to a wide range of books by white colonists and missionaries observing the landscape while also promoting the conversion of enslaved, Indigenous, and Native peoples, such as Robert Moffat's *Missionary Labours and Scenes in Southern Africa* (1842), and J.J. Gurney's *A Winter in the West Indies* (1844).

In this context, Anna's remarks on Chinese girls form part of a common feature of factual and instructive books, in situating British readers as agents in colonial spaces. Girls, in particular, benefited through what Alison Twells terms a "missionary domesticity," which carved out a female space in global and colonial politics by emphasizing their abilities to spread family life and education throughout the British Empire.[42] Indeed, Anna had spent her early years in the missionary circles of Hong Kong. For child readers and writers in white settlements, family and home education naturalized and justified their presence in colonial or indigenous landscapes. Australian and Canadian books represented white children as rational and knowledgeable observers and affectionate curators of the land, while insinuating Indigenous communities lacked these qualities.[43]

Globalization and colonization forced some of these communities to negotiate ideals of family and education which pivoted on their exclusion. As Erin Millions has shown, white settler men who married Indigenous women in nineteenth-century Canada strategized to educate their children away from home. This was often motivated by concerns that their children's claim to respectability and status was weakened by a home life with their Indigenous mothers.[44] These decisions suggest the implicit racial taxonomies in Enlightenment notions of independence and rationality. However, concepts such as family and education were fluid enough to be widely adopted and adapted. Banerjee, for example, argues that middle-class families in colonial India adapted the ideal of the European mother who imparted a rational "enlightened" education to her children by combining it with the virtues of the Hindu woman.[45]

In other cases, these ideals were used to push back against and criticize colonization. Roldán Vera shows that children's books and textbooks imported from France and Britain had a special appeal in Spanish American countries recently freed from Spain, as they legitimated the independence, rationality, and modernity of the new nation-states.[46] Children, too, could mobilize ideals of family as a criticism of their treatment by colonial government. Lee's brief study of children's letters in interwar Nyasaland explains that multiracial boys wrote to the colonial government to demand financial support for their education from the white fathers who had abandoned them.[47] While from a British perspective, many families across the British Empire and the world lacked the European family seen as necessary for home education, there was a far from uniform response from readers in different geographical locations, who could adapt or mobilize this concept to their own ends.

While family shaped educational books and pedagogy, education shaped family bonds and relationships. A future schoolmate of Anna Legge, Violet Bonner, had contributed "The Scornful Monkey" to the mainstream periodical *Little Folks* as a small girl, when learning to read and write at home.[48] Of course, writings such as this served an educational purpose as a practical application of children's literacy and an outlet for self-improving discussion between isolated home-educated children. Pooley demonstrates that working-class families also wrote collaboratively, as the cheap availability of print brought contributing to mainstream periodicals within the reach of working-class children.[49] However, studies of British families show that such writing was equally important in consolidating the bonds between family members.[50] Some children took charge of writing round robins or family newspapers, which circulated via post around the extended family.[51] Studies of America and Germany also highlight how the process of learning to read and write was intertwined with tasks such as letter-writing and diary-keeping, thus consolidating the bonds between family members.[52] The affective value of literacy practice increased for families separated by colonial employment. Education sustained the family as a "transnational institution," as children wrote letters to relatives in Britain and the colonies.[53]

Education at home was not limited to literacy practice, however. Frank's mother, Lydia Ann Bunting, began helping her mother with the family drapery business at age twelve, and when her husband died in 1866, it was this early training that helped her maintain herself and her son.[54] In this period, institutions began to prolong the time spent in education by many British children, but examining individual families highlights the uneven nature of this development. Lower-middle-class children continued to leave school for apprenticeships or work at fourteen or fifteen years old, and indeed fourteen was the official leaving age at the Croydon Friends' School. While scholars note the decline of formal traditions of apprenticeship across Europe in the nineteenth century,[55] England in 1868 still had enough schools with a leaving age of fourteen or fifteen that they comprised one of the three classes identified by the Schools Inquiry Commission.[56] For many, the family continued to be a source of informal occupational training. Thus, while Lydia's son Frank left school at fourteen for an other apprenticeship, his education and apprenticeship did not interrupt longer-standing traditions, as he later took over his mother's drapery business.[57]

Education remained a varied collective strategy to maintain a family's prosperity, which might involve schooling, but could also involve the informal transmission of trade or business skills.[58] With the priority on the family unit, children within one family did not necessarily receive the same education. Parents might give one child a longer stint in schooling, apprentice another to the family business, but send others to acquire new skills and techniques through apprenticeships elsewhere, thus ensuring a strong and varied set of skills and training for the family as a whole.[59] Generally, middle-class families in this period were becoming more reliant on institutions to mediate access to the national examinations and formal qualifications increasingly necessary to enter the circles of public and professional life.[60] Sydney Frankenburg, the son of a Manchester rubber manufacturer, attended the Manchester Grammar School with his brother Leonard. While attending the school enabled Sydney's brother Leonard to do national examinations and go on to Cambridge University, this was not the case for Sydney, who joined the family firm.[61] While Frank, Anna, and Sydney all benefited from the expansion of educational institutions, their educational experiences cannot be reduced to school attendance. Instead, their lives are a reminder of the messier and more varied nature of educational experience, as home education and informal training were valued and commonplace parts of education across this period.

INSTITUTIONS

In a textbook in use at Frank Bunting's school, the teacher was advised to "place fifteen or twenty familiar objects on a desk or table before the class, and request the pupils to [...] writ[e] on the spot the names of the articles."[62] This is an example of the object lesson. In this pedagogical approach, the teacher drew pupils into conversation about the appearance and production processes of objects such as glass and india rubber, and pupils then wrote down the descriptions. This conversational format suggests that Frank's schooling, far from diverging from home life, was shaped by the ideals, factual and instructive pedagogies, and educational practices associated with the middle-class family.

Like the two-way conversations of the middle-class family, the object lesson has been presented as child-centered for freeing the young learner to articulate their own perspectives and observations, in contrast with the rote-learning format of many other textbooks.[63] And indeed, a study of a middle-class Pestalozzian school suggests teachers experimented with a varied and engaging syllabus.[64] However, transplanting these conversations into the school frequently operated as a criticism of families from lower social strata. The middle-class veneration for family and home education was not extended to other families across Britain, or to all the families they encountered through their imperial and global connections. In Britain, working-class families were often represented as incapable of providing the environment and conversational stimulus required for home education, as their lives were defined by manual or monotonous labor and pressing material concerns. Learners were to be detached from the home and educated in institutions such as charity schools, elementary schools, and mechanics' institutes.[65]

Frank Bunting's education was typical of lower-middle-class children, focusing on literacy and practical skills, with no Latin or Greek. While children from better-off families were expected to receive a classical and literary education, other children were expected to learn through the more material and sensory processes deemed within the grasp of their limited social and cultural experiences.[66] After all, Johann Pestalozzi and Friedrich Fröbel had initially developed their lessons for impoverished and working-class children. In their schools, the middle-class teacher recreated the rational conversation and practical lessons of the middle-class home, curtailed to fit the children's supposedly limited social and cultural experiences. Middle-class educational campaigners objected that too abstract or literary a syllabus would put working-class children out of step with their "natural" pace of intellectual development.[67] As state elementary schooling expanded in 1870s England, pedagogies based on bestsellers such as Elizabeth Mayo's *Lessons on Objects* (1839) provided reassurance that education for working-class children would be confined to appropriately material and practical concerns. The popularity of the object lesson was connected to global developments in education, as Britain began to fear the economic and technological competition from better-educated nations.[68] Girls' learning was curtailed even more, with subjects such as needlework taking up a large part of the school day, as they reassuringly linked girls' education with the ideal of a thrifty, clean, and orderly working class.[69]

Indigenous and Native family life was seen as an even greater hindrance to children's moral and intellectual development, and so British observers, missionaries, and educators recommended children be detached and educated in institutions.[70] The object lesson was also recommended. Charles and Elizabeth Mayo, for example, had developed the object lesson when involved in the Home and Colonial Infant School Society. As the popularity of European philosophers such as Pestalozzi and Fröbel indicates, this pedagogy was embedded in global and imperial developments in education. German experiments such as kindergartens served as a model of rational secular education in Britain and America from the 1830s onwards.[71] In imperial spaces, the object lesson fit with white missionaries' perceptions of Indigenous and Native intellectual inferiority, and was used to acculturate and modernize communities in Ireland, India, Canada, and New Zealand.[72] As the nineteenth century progressed, white educators, philanthropists, and members of colonial governments were informed by increasingly rigid ideas about the relationship between race and educational ability.[73]

It was the institution rather than the family that was prioritized by many colonial administrators and missionaries. Colonial administrators in India promoted sending elite Indian sons to school, as their homes were thought to lack the social and cultural environment to cultivate masculine independence.[74] However, global studies emphasize that European educational experiments were adapted as they spread. An analysis of the kindergarten and the monitorial system demonstrates how these systems underwent a process of "diffusion and transformation" across the United States, Asia, the Ottoman Empire, South America, and Haiti.[75] While object lessons could be a deliberately rigid and confining form of education, communities and individuals could interpret their education differently. Thirteen-year-old Frank Bunting may have practiced object lessons in the classroom, but he used his literacy skills to write a lecture on the complex topic of "The Human Frame."[76] Children and young people could transcend restrictive pedagogies but also circumvent them. Pupils endured brutal conditions in Indian boarding schools in Canada, where their practical education sought to erase their kinship ties and culture. However, Griffith notes that Indigenous girls sustained their sense of family by using blankets and other everyday items to mimic and remember their grandmothers' language, posture, and gestures.[77]

Scholarship generally represents institutional education, especially school attendance, as a break with the ideals, bonds, and habits of the family. In boarding schools for middle-class boys in England, John Tosh argues that the switch from vacation to term time meant "home and school [were] always experienced in polarized terms."[78] Yet tracing the trajectories of individual learners through their education uncovers that home and school repeatedly overlapped. Frank Bunting was born in London, but he started school at a "Friends' First-day Sch[ool] Cheltenham"—that is, a Quaker Sunday school—where his mother had set up her drapery business. Then he lived away from home by attending "a boys' school in Witney for 3 years—boarders & day scholars."[79] After the Croydon Friends' School, Frank was briefly apprenticed to another business, before returning to work with his mother. His varied experience of Sunday school, private school, boarding school, and apprenticeship was typical of the "mixed economy," which characterized experiences of education into the twentieth century.[80] Using family as a framework rather than an institution brings to light the mixed nature of individual experiences, in which even a school that diminished contact with family may have been simply a brief interlude in the family's educational strategy.

Family remained a key influence on education across Britain in the period. Even elite public schools waned in popularity in the early nineteenth century due to parental frustration about the poor living conditions, low educational standards, and lack of adult supervision.[81] The subsequent restoration of public schools' reputation in the mid-nineteenth century is frequently linked to Thomas Arnold's introduction of a more morally serious Christian manliness to Rugby School in the 1830s, which appealed to middle-class ideals of domesticity.[82] Learners, too, carried these values to school and college, and recreated the comfort and intimacy of family life by using furniture, mementoes, and domestic occasions such as tea parties.[83]

Scholars suggest that girls' education was hampered by the supposed break of schools from domesticity. Whereas boys' schools were valued for instilling independence from the home, girls' schools promoted themselves as home-like and capable of preserving their ties to domesticity.[84] The rise of girls' education is thus associated with the advancement of women into public life in the second half of the nineteenth century.[85] Yet individual educational trajectories reveal how girls' and boys' education continued to be entangled with family life in complex ways. For instance, Frank Bunting lived apart from his mother while attending school at Witney, but census records show he lived with his aunt.[86] Schooling was not necessarily a break from home life. Women educators used motherhood to associate their schools with the benefits of family, creating a female form of authority and expertise that justified women's entry to the teaching profession.[87] At the same time, educational reforms sought to domesticate the public school in the nineteenth century, with Thomas Arnold introducing "houses" overseen by married teachers at Rugby School, with pupils living alongside the teacher's wife and children.[88] Small private schools for boys, too, catered for such families by marketing themselves as "home-like."[89] Even for schools with few women, studies note the watchfulness and care parents exerted via letters to ensure their values and habits were sustained by children away at school.[90]

For many middle-class British parents, day schools were a practical strategy to educate their children while maintaining family life. The parents who chose the Manchester Grammar School often thought "home rather than school ought to be the centre of a boy's life," a teacher complained in an 1874 issue of the school magazine *Ulula*.[91] Indeed, one of Sydney Frankenburg's schoolmates at the Manchester Grammar School, Alfred Frederick Hertz, recalled asking his parents to be sent to Rugby School as a boarder instead of his local grammar school, but his parents "would not consider the possibility of allowing me to be away from 'home influence'."[92]

The rise of the institution provided new educational opportunities for families across Britain, but despite commonalities, schools in different parts of Britain were not homogenous. Day schools were particularly subject to family influence. Although the Oxford High School was governed by a committee, many of the schoolgirls came from a group of university families, including the Legges, who were involved in setting up the school and acted as its governors or shareholders.[93] Manchester Grammar School was a day school located in the north of England, where parents persistently demanded grammar schools be repurposed to provide the modern education of benefit to local commercial and industrial families.[94] Pupils like Sydney and Leonard Frankenburg attended the school for its science stream, established in the 1870s in response to these demands for a modern German-style science education.[95] Manchester public figures were particularly proud of the school for creating a local educational trajectory, which meant boys could move from higher grade schools into further education through scholarships to the Mechanics' Institute and Owens College, or to Oxford and Cambridge universities via the grammar school.[96] We need to know more about how the broader institutional developments of the period played out in different communities, possibly creating, as in Manchester, a new educational life cycle uniquely benefiting local families. For instance, Tamson Pietsch has demonstrated colonial institutions such as universities and schools drew learners from the community nearby rather than relying on boarders, and thus like Manchester Grammar School prioritized the ideals of local colonial elites.[97] Even elementary schools, which had initially sought to create a "little artificial world" detaching working-class children from the home environment, gradually ceded to their families' worldview, with teachers and government inspectors accepting that using learners' dialect and expressions would make lessons more meaningful.[98]

Transnational families were integral in shaping education in Britain. William Barron was a Catholic pupil at the Jesuit Stonyhurst College in Lancashire, and published a school magazine *El Curioso* in Spanish and English with a friend from Gibraltar, John Recano. William was likely one of the generations of the Barron family whose children were sent from Mexico or California to receive a gentleman's education in England.[99] Elite families such as the Barrons did not have to confine their educational strategies within national bounds but could use their transnational social networks to seek an education in line with their values and culture. The strategies of these imperial families could shape institutions in Britain, with Stonyhurst College largely relying on a transnational Catholic elite drawn from the Americas, Europe, and Ireland, as well as Britain. Other British schools catered for international students, such as white children sent from colonial India. Their parents were striking a balance, determined to lessen the effects of their children being brought up in domestic intimacy with Indian servants, but at the same time relying on occasional letters to remind their children of family bonds, Indian words and phrases, and the patterns of colonial domestic life.[100] Some British schools received Indigenous children sent from Canada. While their white fathers were often concerned to separate them from Indigenous kin, their Indigenous mothers sustained family bonds through letters of advice and censure, at times mobilizing other family members to write on their behalf if their own literacy was limited.[101] As these cases suggest, there were complex geographies of imperial education even within Britain, created by the imperial and global networks in which many families were embedded.

Studies of global and transnational education have demonstrated that European-influenced pedagogies and educational institutions varied at a local level, suggesting the impact of family on patterns of global education.[102] Children followed what O'Neill terms a "horseshoe pattern" as they moved along educational and family networks for an education overseas, then returned home with a prestigious education, which shored up their family's status. Daughters with a French education could signal a family's status, with the added benefit of gaining Catholic girls a place in a transnational Catholic elite.[103] An Irish elite was formed as families selected schools and universities, such as Stonyhurst College, which were located in England, on the Continent, or in the Americas.[104] The white families in Cape Colony studied by Duff relied on family and educational connections in Scotland and the Netherlands when sending their children away to school.[105] As a lens on education, family sheds light on complex educational trajectories that passed through a range of locations, crossed national boundaries, and generated a global demand for new institutions.

Beyond these transnational elites, families across the British Empire and other areas of the world intervened and reconfigured the education on offer in institutions. The popularity of housewifery as a subject in elementary schools was not wholly down to middle-class interventions but at least partly influenced by the strategies of working-class parents to secure the family's well-being.[106] In imperial spaces, parents varied considerably in their response to colonial schools. Some responded positively, such as the parents in Gaitskill's study of girls' missionary schools in colonial South Africa, which suggests some parents saw the domestic ethos as beneficial for family life.[107] In other cases, such as the schools set up in Natal, African parents distrusted the motives of missionary schools and had more trust in those organized by the government.[108] In cases where Indigenous families were systematically broken up by institutions, such as the Indian boarding schools in Canada studied by Griffith, Indigenous parents actively strategized to ameliorate their children's living conditions, in some instances by reporting abuses to the local press.[109] Children, too, could alter the educational practices of their families. In one such study, Duff examines the piteous appeals written by white middle-class children from school in Scotland and the Netherlands to their parents in the Cape Colony. The letters speeded up plans to construct a school nearer home and the development of a system of Dutch Reformed Church schools in the Cape.[110] It is important to consider the extent to which the rise of institutions was not solely shaped by emulating elite or European models of education but was also embedded in the expectations and educational trajectories of individual families.

COMMUNITY

The encouragement of rational conversation between parents and children was a part of wider ideals of self-culture and mutual improvement in middle-class and working-class communities in Britain.[111] Frank Bunting's lecture of "The Human Frame" was given before a mutual improvement society at his school, and in 1874 he had also won a prize for his careful fretwork as a member of a second society at the school.[112] Alongside the pedagogies of the home and classroom were a range of improving leisure activities that were equally valued for nurturing intellectual independence and a sense of public duty.

A key characteristic of nineteenth- and twentieth-century institutions in Britain was the growth in clubs and societies. Like Frank, Anna Legge was a member of the Oxford High School Guild of Charity, Sydney Frankenburg and his brother Leonard were active in the debating societies of the Manchester Grammar School, while William Barron participated in making a school magazine. The rise of a cohesive British middle class in this period is often connected to the rise of institutions with a strong associational and corporate life, capable of inculcating ideals of public duty and independence.[113] Associational life enabled participants to fashion themselves as rational and independent members of a wider community, particularly important when the social makeup of the student body began to include lower-middle-class young people, girls and women, and colonial students.[114] School rebuilding in rural areas is argued to have consolidated this sense of belonging to a cohesive community by adding shared spaces such as chapels, quadrangles, play spaces, gyms, and dining halls.[115] The isolated location meant children were separated from their religiously and politically divided middle-class communities, and united through collective events and group activities on school grounds.[116] The focus on elite institutions means that this community ethos has been assumed to have trickled down from the authority figures of elite institutions, with increasingly pale and less powerful imitations created in schools further down the social hierarchy.[117]

Yet moving beyond the small circle of elite public schools, the division of school from town and family was not always so stark. It is only more recently that historians have begun to explore societies and clubs as part of families' collective strategies of education. Frank's active involvement in school societies was a continuation of his home life. His mother Lydia was active in the local Quaker Meeting, the temperance movement, and the Missionary Helpers' Union, a Quaker organization that supported missionary work in Africa, Asia, and the Middle East and published material to engage younger members.[118] Associational life at the school received strong support from parents, and Frank Bunting's classmate and fellow society member Frank Farrington's father donated money and supplies to the school's mutual improvement societies.[119] Habits of collective activity at school or college would seldom have been learners' first experience of working as a cohesive community, with many arriving well versed in processes of meetings, minute-taking, and voting.

Scholarship on family life shows that, from the early nineteenth century, children and youths were drawn into the orbit of the associational activities of their families by attending societies, public meetings, and lectures together.[120] The clubs and societies for mutual improvement, which enriched family life in the nineteenth century, gained new life in the twentieth century as they created a route to evening classes and training courses with more formal qualifications.[121] Moreover, family meant that individuals attending the same school or college had varied experiences of clubs and societies. While Frank was immersed in the temperance and missionary activities of the Quaker community in Britain, Manchester Grammar School pupil Sydney Frankenburg came from a family active in the associational life of Manchester's Jewish community. His father Isidor was involved in the Jewish Board of Guardians, the Great Synagogue, and the establishment of lads' clubs for Jewish boys, activities that Sydney himself was to support as an adult.[122] Learners had access to the same clubs and societies at their institution, but they carried with them the varied attitudes and knowledge of associational life gained from their family background.

Late nineteenth- and early twentieth-century associational life was characterized by its spread across national borders, from the temperance movement, philanthropic societies, and youth groups, to educational organizations.[123] Yet the communities and values created by these societies were often contingent on the networks of interconnected families who supported them in particular locations. While Cohen examines how clubs in colonial India purported to emulate the independence and masculine sociability of

British associational life, in practice they reproduced the complex and shifting dynamics of Indian society. Cohen notes that white men were sometimes the only members permitted, but regulations were fluid and contested, and as associational life took hold, new clubs emerged for men and women, different religions, and different races, with admissions ages sometimes set as low as twelve years old.[124] Beyond the British Empire, kinship also drew individuals into clubs and societies. Mary P. Ryan's study of nineteenth-century New York points to the same surnames repeating in lists of temperance and missionary societies.[125] School and college associational life was not a separate development, but suggests the ways in which for learners of all ages attending lectures and talks was already an everyday part of their social and cultural worlds.

Discussing school and college societies solely in the context of isolated rural boarding schools obscures the equally important connections between institutions and the broader educational practices of towns and cities. While most schools had a debating society, the one attended by the Frankenburg brothers at the Manchester Grammar School was called the Philosophical Society, echoing the name of Manchester's famous Lit & Phil. The name presented pupils as participants in Manchester's vibrant associational life. Early nineteenth-century clubs and societies are regarded as instrumental in creating a sense of values and interests in middle-class communities in Britain.[126] There is a rich historiography on civic associational life, but historians have only begun to explore the important role played by juvenile associations, for instance in the missionary and temperance movements.[127] Even a brief examination of society names shows a rich two-way influence between schools and towns, with "Dorcas" societies sewing for the poor, debating societies, natural history societies, and team sports commonly featuring in towns and schools in Britain and across the empire. Participation in institutional clubs and societies was not necessarily just an expression of corporate pride but could articulate a more local identity, expressing a sense of civic pride and duty.

Historians note the impact of family and community has been obscured by the "great man" approach to understanding reforms in British education.[128] At Sydney Frankenburg's school, the Manchester Grammar School, pupils wrote to the school magazine to demand a school cap and colors.[129] The letter captures the contemporary concept of self-government, where learners themselves organized and supervised leisure activities, clubs, and societies, as well as maintaining discipline and creating and sustaining new values and habits.[130] Across this period, a sense of community was engendered by simple and cheap stratagems such as caps and team colors, badges, and pins; songs and sports chants; school magazines; and communal events such as prayers, team games, and society meetings, all of which became part of the everyday life of most institutions, particularly those that could not afford expensive rebuilding projects.[131] Indeed, historians note this associational life did not originate in elite institutions such as the English public schools or Oxford and Cambridge universities but newly established institutions seeking to establish a sense of community.[132] Associational life enabled populations new to institutional education such as women and middle-class men to redraw this notion of an educational community in ways that included and empowered themselves.[133]

This sense of community did not evolve in isolation in Britain but was underwritten by Europe-wide fears of white degeneration and the perceived need to build a healthier, fitter white community.[134] In 1898, Manchester Grammar School held an event where pupil Arnold Meyer ("Max") Aronovich won praise for his performance of Shylock.[135] Arnold was Romanian-born and his family were among the Jewish refugees seen as a threat to Britain when they arrived in the 1880s and 1890s, fleeing persecution in Eastern Europe.[136] His participation in a Shakespeare play could be read as the successful assimilation of a migrant youth into British culture.

The presence of migrant and colonial learners is a key yet under-theorized aspect of the impact of globalization and colonization on education in Britain.[137] The Oxford and Cambridge student community frequently emphasized itself as a white, male, and elite enclave, which was in part a response to the social and imperial shifts, which brought in a growing number of non-Anglican Christian, non-Christian, foreign, and women students.[138] Other responses to Britain's increasingly imperial and global population included planning "efficient" infant schools and elementary school buildings with ventilation, light, and space to nurture a healthy future population.[139] In Manchester, new associations were set up to acculturate and assimilate colonial and migrant families. Established Jewish families like the Frankenburgs sought to deflect rising anti-Semitism through assimilative associations such as the Jewish Lads' Brigade.[140]

Historians are only beginning to explore the betrayal and confusion experienced by learners as they navigated organizations and institutions designed to tackle their supposed racial inferiority.[141] We cannot know what Arnold felt, for instance, when reading praise in the school magazine for his performance of Shylock, and "the power and Irving-like style with which he 'craved the law and due penalties of his bond'."[142] Some pupils like Arnold were active in school life, but as the gestures toward his Jewishness suggest, they were negotiating a community that was seeking to assimilate, marginalize, or exclude them. As more students came to Britain from its colonies for education, these young people managed their trying circumstances by setting up associations of their own. These associations were looked upon favorably by colonial government as a way to create a sense of loyalty and duty toward Britain. However, scholars note that students' associational life contributed toward the creation of nationalist communities with coherent ideals and identities of their own.[143] West African student groups in Britain deployed the language and motifs of a self-governing educational community to demand independence from the scrutiny and oversight of colonial government.[144] The rise of associational life did not only reflect the rise of a homogeneous conformity in British education but was entangled in the complex national identities and collective strategies of its increasingly diverse institutional communities.

From the perspective of those born in Britain, associational life was inaccessible to children born elsewhere in the British Empire and the world. In her essay in the *Oxford High School Magazine*, Anna lamented the typical Chinese girl's supposed lack of institutional education and outside friendships which meant she "does not hold her proper place in society [...] owing to the fact that she has never been taught its duties nor has exercised its privileges."[145] Children across the British Empire were assumed to lack the values and duties instilled by the associational life of British families, communities, and institutions. Thus, buildings and activities attempted to enforce adherence to European work and leisure rhythms by housing children in a regimented space that severed them from their families, as noted in studies of institutions in New Zealand and America.[146] In a study of Canadian schools, Mona Gleason notes the significance of school photographs in presenting the community as ordered and cohesive.[147] Indeed, a perceived lack of community caused anxiety about white settler populations of the British Empire such as Ireland and South Africa, where modern school buildings were seen as a way to develop citizenship.[148]

At the end of the nineteenth century, associational life became increasingly prominent in a transnational educational culture. In 1915, a former pupil of Dollar Academy in Scotland in 1915 wrote to the school magazine about his recent visit to Hong Kong. He had met an old schoolmate Wei Yuk who "has dozens of old photos, boys and girls, that woke up very pleasant memories of those days."[149] Wei Yuk was a Chinese boy brought to Britain by James Legge as part of his missionary work and educated alongside Anna and her siblings at Dollar Academy.[150] The letter suggests that, in adulthood, the school photograph was an object that continued to evoke a meaningful sense of belonging to a privileged global educational community.

The adoption of caps, colors, photographs, and other emblems in schools across Britain and the British Empire represented their membership of a transnational educational community. Institutions remained important in their development, as clubs such as the Girl Guides often took places in community focal points such as churches, libraries, and schools, which had space and resources.[151] Far from capitulating to British or European ideals, associational life created a sense of community that enabled people in a range of locations to articulate and pursue their own agendas. Kristine Alexander emphasizes that transnational organizations such as the Girl Guides were far from homogenous but instead characterized by conflicting ideals and practices. In India, the establishment of all-white Girl Guide companies led to Indian girls turning to missionary organizations to help them set up their own groups. Indian girls' autonomous groups unsettled British authorities enough for the British Scouting and Guide headquarters to change the rules and admit Indian girls and boys.[152] Indigenous learners in colonial spaces also used associations to claim a place for themselves in a wider transnational community.[153] The implicit racial ideologies in imperial and global networks could be simply sidestepped or ignored. While Empire Day connoted British racial superiority to white learners, educators, and officials in Britain, for black African and Caribbean learners it was sometimes celebrated as a marker of their belonging and status in a British community.[154]

Associational life was both multiethnic and transnational, but gives insight into how clubs and societies were adapted to the shifting values and strategies of families in different geographical locations. As an adult, Wei Yuk and other parents petitioned the colonial government in Hong Kong to support new schools for their children. The families demanded schools with the "public spirit" that would enable their children to position themselves as the new Chinese elite.[155] Anna's description of "Women in China" may have reinforced the superiority of English over Chinese girls, but her former schoolmate Wei Yuk deployed these ideals to the advancement and advantage of his own community in Hong Kong. Learners across the world used membership of transnational organizations to gain a sense of privilege and status. The Girl Guides may have proclaimed equality, but Wu's detailed study of Malayan girls explains that some joined not as an assertion of equality but for the social mobility offered by interacting with European girls.[156] Through membership of transnational associations, young people could display the modern ideals and elite status of their families.

CONCLUSION

The purpose of this chapter has been to explore the multiple links between family and education in the nineteenth and early twentieth centuries. The family—as an influence on ideals, pedagogies, books, institutions, and associational life—has rarely been considered a framework for understanding the development of education at local, national, imperial, and global levels. However, by introducing four learners—Frank, Anna, Sydney, and William— this chapter has shown educational experiences in this period to be impacted as much by family strategies and educational practices as by institutional reforms and state policies. Moreover, home education, books in the familiar format, object lessons, and associational life were not shaped within national bounds but gained currency through conversations and borrowings within Europe, the British Empire, and on a global scale.

Education in nineteenth-century Britain is often seen in terms of cohesive, isolated, and racially and culturally homogenous institutions. However, we should be attentive to the complex and messy educational trajectories of individuals across the life cycle, as much as to the values of particular institutions. For Frank, Anna, Sydney, and William, their educational trajectories brought them into contract with learners, society members, or family in California, Mexico, Hong Kong, Gibraltar, and Romania. This biographical approach enables us to connect the messier and more contingent strategies and aspirations of individual families to the broader narratives of imperial and global education.

CHAPTER FIVE

Learners and Learning

TOM WOODIN

A formidable legacy of educational ideas and practices was bequeathed to learners in the nineteenth century. At a time of great social, economic, cultural, political, and educational upheaval this inheritance represented a force for change but was contested, transformed, and blended into existing patterns. The Reformation and Enlightenment took different forms in different countries, but one salient theme challenged mysticism and religious dogma in favor of apprehending reality through the senses. Potentially everyone might gain access to knowledge and salvation. The profound implications of this message were blown open by the French and American revolutions, which were crucial historical turning points in the history of learning. They were the most visible symbols of the overthrow of an old aristocratic order even if many ideas and practices from the old regime would endure. They made it impossible to ignore the demands of the people, not just as subjects but increasingly as citizens, and education was one place where this struggle for equality was played out. In addition, new technologies, tied into rapidly emerging capitalist relations of production, made communication faster and promised greater control over nature through the discovery and application of knowledge. The technology of education, so familiar to us today, predated the nineteenth century but certainly became more extensive through the proliferation of schooling and the classroom. Progress was in the air—industrialization, democratization, and urbanization appeared to be unstoppable forces that were improving societies and their populations, symbolized by the image of the factory across Western nations. The accumulation of wealth, partly from colonial adventures, as well as the accumulating numbers of wealthier people, created an insatiable demand for education and learning.[1]

Yet, revolutionary ideas were to be stymied by forces of reaction and tradition. Nascent class-based industrial nations evolved new forms of inequality to replace the old. During the nineteenth century, waves of industrialization and migration, while spatially diverse, were becoming pervasive across Europe, the Americas, and Australia. Although the American Revolution threw off British shackles, the story of imperialism was far from over and the nineteenth century would witness an intensification of colonialism, with significant implications for education and learning. Imperialist expansion provided raw materials but also traded hierarchies and assumptions about civilization and learning. Important distinctions in terms of age, class, gender, sexuality, and disability hardened. Moreover, not all societies developed in the same way and colonial nations had different trajectories of learning. Accessing actual processes of learning helps to reveal some of these multiple and complex social relations.[2]

The Enlightenment notion of individual autonomy championed by Immanuel Kant in his 1784 essay "What is Enlightenment?" was not available to everyone but implied the need for resources and a sense of entitlement. The issue of who could be educated, who was capable of civilization, was embedded into most educational encounters of the nineteenth century. Whether elites considered "natives," the working class, disabled people, women, and other groups capable of civilization, of being improved and able to learn, was a crucial matter. If the answer was no, then only basic forms of learning were considered possible or realistic, and there was tenacious opposition to the spread of learning that might upset social relations. If the answer was yes, then a different set of assumptions resulted, for example, marginalized groups might ultimately be integrated into the nation and granted the franchise or independence.[3]

THE EXPANSION OF LEARNING

The early nineteenth century, up until the European revolutions and uprisings in 1848, was marked by contrasting reactions to the French and American revolutions, highlighting secularism, equality, and modernity on the one hand, and church authority, hierarchy, and tradition on the other. The influence of Jean-Jacques Rousseau on learning was to be profound. Key thinkers such as Johann Heinrich Pestalozzi, Friedrich Fröbel, and Johann Friedrich Herbart all highlighted the need to start from the needs and activity of the child rather than impose a pre-given structure of knowledge upon the developing mind. Pestalozzi was unsuccessful in founding an orphanage but went on to establish an inspirational boarding school at Yverdon, which was feted by educators internationally and would help to ensure the dissemination of his ideas. The head, heart, and body were to be utilized in drawing out human potential in both intellectual and physical senses, as part of a pioneering science of human nature. Cultivating skills and recognizing daily experience was to contribute to moral growth among all sections of society. Pestalozzi's ideas, in *Investigations in the Course of Nature in the Development of the Human Race* (1797) and *How Gertrude Teaches her Children* (1801), would be grafted onto a range of practices and meanings.[4]

Similarly, Fröbel's "kindergarten" was founded in the early nineteenth century and helped to generate new ideas about learning. He formulated play as a vital aspect of social development, alongside song, games, and caring for animals and plants. His "gifts" or playthings were to stimulate controlled and regulated learning in order that children would come to appreciate the connections between the inner unity of the child and that of the universe, encompassing God, humanity, and nature. Kindergartens, crèches, and infant schools would become part of the national landscape in many countries. In a further contribution, Herbart infused learning with an understanding of psychological processes and moral philosophy in works such as *Aesthetic Revelation of the World as the Chief Work of Education* (1806) and *General Pedagogy Deduced from the Purpose of Education* (1806). He offered an early version of educational evolution, which was linked to the stages of individual growth.[5]

The revolutionary upheaval in France built upon the ideas of the "radical enlightenment."[6] In 1791, revolutionaries in France proclaimed the universal right to education, which would resonate across the Western world and beyond. If everyone had a right to education, then everyone was in theory educable. Jean-Joseph Jactot, in *Enseignement universel*, argued that intelligence was evenly spread and that all were able to teach themselves. One fascinating instance arose from Jean-Marc Gaspard Itard, who worked with the so-called "wild boy of Averyron," who had been discovered naked in a forest in 1799. Against the claims that the boy was "incurable," Itard preferred an environmental explanation of his apparent deficiencies, which he argued resulted from a lack of human interaction and, borrowing from John Locke and Etienne Condillac, he asserted that understanding could be gained by training the senses. While the progress of the boy was partial, Itard nevertheless represented an early example of developmental ideas and a rejection that even "difficult" children were uneducable.[7] These ideas would find traction later in the nineteenth century when Itard's student, Édouard Séguin, popularized sensory-training and devised a nonverbal intelligence test, which would influence Maria Montessori.

The early nineteenth century was a time of great conflict, in particular over the uses of literacy. Social and economic changes were fueling a demand for learning, and many people were eager to gain literacy, but the terms on which this was to be achieved and the values that were to permeate learning were far from settled.[8] Learning implied control, power, and the autonomy of individuals and groups, so could not easily be contained. There was an unmistakable "thirst for knowledge" as early radicals adopted the adage, commonly attributed to Francis Bacon, that "knowledge is power." E.P. Thompson opened his groundbreaking study of the working class with the recognition that the membership of the London Corresponding Society was to be "unlimited," open to all, as one of the "hinges upon which history turns." Learning was becoming a necessary corollary of popular participation and demands for reform.[9] One of Thompson's preoccupations was the engraver, critic, and poet, William Blake, whose work helped to embed a romantic notion of the child as innocent and resisted the rationalism of the Enlightenment. His now celebrated poem "London" highlighted the harmful role of the institutions of the church, monarchy, and army, which resulted in "Marks of weakness, marks of woe":

> How the Chimney-sweepers cry
> Every blackning Church appalls,
> And the hapless Soldiers sigh
> Runs in blood down Palace walls.[10]

He also identified the "mind forged manacles" that imprisoned people, adding complexity to learning that was not simply a matter of putting in or taking out but required the active engagement of learners themselves. Breaking out of these manacles could be a lifelong process; self and collective expression had to be constructed over time.

Working-class autobiographers built upon puritan traditions in which the individual had charted their life before God; now the working-class writer examined her/his path to learning and progress through a range of social movements. While their early experiences of education might be sketchy, they were buoyed up by a family member or close relative and friend, and often devoted long hours to study and learning. This tendency is explicitly illustrated in Thomas Cooper's autobiography where he outlines his ambitious program of learning:

> I thought it possible that by the time I reached the age of twenty four I might be able to master the elements of Latin, Greek, Hebrew, and French; might get well through Euclid, and through a course of Algebra; might commit the entire "Paradise Lost" and seven of the best plays of Shakespeare to memory; and might read a large and solid course of history, and religious evidences; and be well acquainted also with the current literature of the day.[11]

Cooper reflects a key point about such "autodidacts" who delved into eclectic knowledge that appeared important. This was to be done through private reading and study, memorization of key texts but, crucially, discussions in a network of domestic, public, and political forms. The learning of another "autodidact," William Lovett, was articulated as part of social and political movements that embraced libraries, reading rooms, discussion groups, and individual study. Lovett's sense of adventure and free exploration is encapsulated in his title, *Life and struggles of William Lovett: in his pursuit of bread, knowledge & freedom with some short account of the different associations he belonged to & of the opinions he entertained.* His experience formed the basis for imagining a complete reform of learning. Spending a year in Warwick jail for sedition, Lovett and John Connor wrote *Chartism: A New Organisation of the People*, which argued for educational change to accompany political reform. "Schools for the people" were to include lectures, readings, dancing, music, and entertainments as well as libraries.[12] The political reformer Francis Place recalled that his library "was a sort of gossiping shop for such persons as were in any way engaged in public matters having the benefit of the people for their object," it was a "common coffee house room."[13] Jürgen Habermas has argued that the eighteenth-century coffeehouse, as an engine of civil society and business, represented a bourgeois public sphere; it would be complemented by a proletarian public sphere.[14]

A further aspect of early nineteenth-century radicalism was the flowering of utopian thought and practice, particularly in France with the Saint Simonians, communitarians in the United States and community builders in Britain. Utopians aimed to prepare for and prefigure a future state of society that required educated participants.[15] For example, Robert Owen and the Owenites would be influenced by the work of the Swiss educator Philipp Emanuel von Fellenberg, who worked with poor children by building shared learning between pupils and teachers as well as by fostering mutual support and self-help. Owen established model infant schools and formed communities on the land where there were attempts to live out utopian ideas and more equal relationships, but such communities found it difficult to sustain themselves in the long run. A more enduring case influenced by Owenism was the Rochdale Society of Equitable Pioneers; started in 1844 and, as the first successful consumer cooperative society, it stimulated a movement that was as much educational as it was economic. Its Law First stated that it intended to "arrange the powers of production, distribution, education and government, or in other words, to establish a self-supporting home colony of united interests."[16] Education was to form the basis for a new state of society in which members exercised power. Co-operators were practical people who responded to the emerging industrial system and related struggles over "useful knowledge." In 1826, fearful of revolutionary tendencies, Lord Brougham's Society for the Promotion of Useful Knowledge provided information to the people by publishing cheap tracts and pamphlets. However, the application of these ideas to the working classes was fiercely contested and many radicals argued for "really useful knowledge" that would bring emancipation and put workers on a par with the middle and upper classes.[17]

Reactions to industrialism were varied. The "monitorial" system, developed by Andrew Bell and Joseph Lancaster, helped to address the potentially expensive cost of education, and lack of teachers to meet demand, through educating large groups of children by using monitors who were taught in stages by a single teacher. The emphasis tended to be on drill and memory and monitors also kept order, organized examinations, and carried out other administrative tasks. It was an economic model that could easily be adopted by other countries, for instance, it proved to be long-lived in South America. A comparison with the Lunar Society, which from the late eighteenth century met in the British Midlands on the nights on or near the full moon, is instructive in shining light on divergent responses to industrialism. The monitorial system tended to systematization and order in mimicking industrial processes. By contrast, the "lunaticks" such as Erasmus Darwin, James Watt, Matthew Boulton, and Richard Lovell Edgeworth came together at each other's houses to share and test out their heterogeneous ideas and learning in an informal and free atmosphere, unhindered by hierarchy, which stimulated innovation and change in science, thought, and industrial application.[18]

Domestic spaces provided an important arena of education well into the nineteenth century, although gender and class were to refract experiences in distinct ways. Protestantism gave weight to Bible reading in the home and the long tradition of girls producing samplers frequently carried religious and moral messages. *Practical Education*, written by Maria Edgeworth and her father, argued for enriching the early experience of childhood based upon practical experimentation. In order to produce well-rounded individuals steeped in moral values, they weighed up the relative merits of school and home as sites of learning. While the home was a place where it was possible to devote "hourly attention to each of their pupils,"[19] wealthy parents were also censured for neglecting the education of their children and leaving them to the servants, which led to "vice and falsehood."[20]

Clearly, "proper" education was being targeted at a higher social group. By contrast, William Cobbett eulogized the self-sufficient rural household and independent sprit that it nurtured; it provided a necessary corrective to the "system," in dire need of political reform, which was in danger of producing mere "word-mongers."[21] Rather the purpose of education should be highly practical "breeding up, bringing up, or rearing up; and nothing more." Fearing the schoolmaster as a spy, he thought the school system would educate children into servility and an acceptance of poverty.[22] Initiatives such as the Ten Hours Movement, which aimed to restrict the hours of labor, relied on similar conservative assumptions about the family.

A different example of home education is provided by the celebrated case of John Stuart Mill whose *Autobiography* revealed the intensive education pursued by his father James Mill, who subjected his child to Greek at age three and Latin at eight as well as a program including Greek and Roman classics, political economy, philosophy, science, metaphysics, maths, and languages. His father, in his "frequent talks about the books I read, he used [...] to give me explanations and ideas respecting civilization, government, morality, mental cultivation, which he required me afterwards to restate to him in my own words."[23] Such domestic tutorials would sharpen Mill's academic abilities, although he also suffered from a mental breakdown in his twenties.

REACTION AND COMPROMISE

Others foreshadowed dire unintended consequences of learning. Older practices and ideas were not wiped out by the new educational movements and thinking. Even in France, traditional ideas about divine right, rank, and hierarchy were to be translated into the new language of learning. For instance, under Napoleon the education of the bourgeoisie and upper classes were prioritized, and nationhood and citizenship were differentiated according to class, gender, and race. With the Restoration of the monarchy in 1814, education once again fell under the church. The remarkable longevity of Jesuit schools and teaching orders illustrates the ways that older practices were reinvented in changing times. They had been created during the Renaissance but continued to exert considerable influence having grafted humanism onto the doctrines of the Catholic Church. Their restoration coincided with the defeat of Napoleon after which their educational influence would expand across Europe, the Americas, and Asia, particularly China, in a context where the nation-state was exerting control over education. The *Ratio Studiorum*, or "Plan of Studies," produced in the sixteenth century, laid out ambitious programs of study that aimed to venerate God, save souls, and support the Society of Jesus. This would be adapted to diverse local settings where languages, sciences, and humanities were taught alongside a familiar mastery of classical studies as a basis for the development of character and to train pupils in reasoned argument.[24]

Despite the difficulty of implementing ideas of equality in France, the revolution nevertheless reverberated across Europe. One of the most notable, anxious, and lengthy rejoinders was Edmund Burke's *Reflections on the Revolution in France*. For Burke, the Revolution was a destroyer of all that was valuable in life. He identified an educated elite who were necessary to defend civilization and learning. They were to provide guidance and instruction for the poor through the state, the church, and education. The most quoted phrase of Burke's *Reflections* appears in a passage that lauds a tradition of learning in terms of a hierarchical social structure:

> Nothing is more certain, than that our manners, our civilization, and all the good things which are connected with manners and with civilization, have, in this European world of ours, depended for ages upon two principles [...] the spirit of a gentleman, and the spirit of religion. The nobility and the clergy, the one by profession, the other by patronage, kept learning in existence, even in the midst of arms and confusions [...]. Learning paid back what it received to nobility and to priesthood, and paid it with usury, by

enlarging their ideas, and by furnishing their minds. Happy if they had all continued to know their indissoluble union, and their proper place! Happy if learning, not debauched by ambition, had been satisfied to continue the instructor, and not aspired to be the master! Along with its natural protectors and guardians, learning will be cast into the mire, and trodden down under the hoofs of a swinish multitude.[25]

In Britain, the MP, Davies Giddy, opposed the Parochial Schools bill of 1807 in terms that reflected the fear that hierarchy would be challenged as the people embraced learning. Giving education to the laboring classes would

be prejudicial to their morals and happiness; it would teach them to despise their lot in life, instead of making them good servants in agriculture, and other laborious employments to which their rank in society had destined them; instead of teaching them subordination, it would render them factious and refractory [...] it would enable them to read seditious pamphlets, vicious books, and publications against Christianity; it would render them insolent to their superiors and, in a few years, the result would be, that the legislature would find it necessary to direct the strong arm of power towards them, and to furnish the executive magistrates with much more vigorous laws than were now in force [...] he never could admit it to be just or reasonable that the labour of the industrious man should be taxed to support the idle vagrant.[26]

These impulses were also built into learning that targeted the poor. Ragged schools, industrial schools, and foundling hospitals, which had spread across Europe, could feel like the new workhouses, draconian forms of welfare created after the Poor Law Act of 1834, in which control was a primary concern as was the placing of the poor in appropriate employment. A mean and narrow fact-based learning would be parodied in Charles Dickens's *Hard Times* and was echoed in Mr Buckle's prize in London in 1873 which was awarded to the "headmaster who could produce the best results at the lowest cost" alongside the chilling award to the superintendent who managed to achieve the lowest death rate on his patch.[27]

In Russia, repeated half-hearted reforms proved no match for the stern forces of reaction. As in France and Britain, educational opportunities for peasants gave rise to corresponding fears of rebellion and the need to reassert hierarchy and tradition, a pattern that was to be repeated throughout the nineteenth century. Alexander I introduced statutes in 1803 and 1804 for scientific and secular education. Some state schools were established and peasants were to be taught reading, writing, arithmetic, and agriculture in parochial schools alongside provincial schools that prepared wealthier pupils for white-collar jobs. In 1825, Tsar Nicholas I realized that the educational tide could not be completely turned back but sought to ensure that students might be funneled in such a way as to retain social divisions when he decreed that parochial schools were for peasants, district schools for merchants, and *gimnazii* for gentry and civil servants.

> It is necessary that in every school the subjects of instruction and the very methods of teaching should be in accordance with the future destination of pupils, that nobody should aim to rise above that position in which it is his lot to remain.[28]

Widespread illiteracy remained as educational reform only scratched the surface. But out of unpropitious circumstances, suggestive experiments could blossom, albeit short-lived ones. The acclaimed writer Leo Tolstoy set up a peasant school on his Russian estate, Yasnaya Polyana. He was deeply moved and impressed by the storytelling capacities of the children, which showed the value in their writing and its relevance for literary culture.[29] Locating knowledge and understanding within the peasantry carried revolutionary potential that would feed into discussion among the intelligentsia, some of whom were countenancing fundamental change in a semi-feudal system that was collapsing by the early twentieth century.[30] Tolstoy's paradigm of mutual learning between teacher and taught would impact upon educators in the twentieth century.

The struggles and compromises between revolution and reaction were also very apparent in the transition of Spanish and Portuguese South American colonies to independence, which represented a problematic journey involving a variety of educational experiences for the diverse populations of the continent. The bulk of South American countries gained independence in the 1810s and 1820s and learning was directly integrated into these struggles. Leaders would establish and lend their names to educational institutions as a continuation of independence struggles. The military liberator, José de San Martín, inaugurated the National Library and the Normal Lancasteriana, a teacher training school, in Lima; Simón Bolívar created many schools; and Bernardino Rivadavia, the first president of Argentina, also stimulated the growth of learning through the establishment of the University of Buenos Aires; in Mexico, Benito Juárez would champion educational reform. The University of Mexico, because of its links with colonialism, was suppressed for a time but other universities in Latin America were formed on the wave of independence including the University of Buenos Aires in 1821. Battles over the curriculum of learning would ensue, especially between the still-powerful Catholic Church and the newly empowered liberals who favored secular, state-supported education. While in Colombia religious education became the norm, elsewhere secular education prevailed for a time. Ties to the Catholic Church would be retained or renewed in some instances such as the Catholic University in Chile in 1888 and the Pontifical Catholic University of Peru in 1917.

The spread of positivism in Latin America stimulated scientific and educational change, embracing science and pedagogy. Juan Bautista Alberdi, the Argentine political theorist and diplomat, gained a scholarship to the College of Moral Sciences but subsequently reflected that "my classmates and I were so ignorant in natural and physical sciences." He believed this had mixed blessings and reveals a shift from independence fighter to practical politician concerned to stimulate industrial development via polytechnical education. He argued that, by encouraging moral sciences, Rivadavia had believed "he was encouraging his country to be free. Tyrants are afraid of moral sciences [...] neglecting the natural sciences revealed his ignorance of the real needs of our countries, which cannot ignore technology and must prepare themselves by learning practical subjects, with utilitarian application."[31]

Yet, limited public funds made the expansion of schooling problematic. It was in this context that the Lancaster model became popular, particularly in Argentina, Chile, Colombia, Peru, Brazil, and Mexico. Gradually teachers' colleges would be created and pedagogical ideas from Pestalozzi, Fröbel, and Herbart would be introduced, but the lack of teachers, effective administrative arrangements, and inequalities between classes, Spanish-speaking and Indigenous non-Spanish-speaking groups, and between urban and rural areas all acted as a break upon learning. A missionary near Buenos Aires, Father Álvarez, wrote in the 1880s, in patronizing terms that "the little Indians progress perfectly but [...] lack books, paper [...] I am going to Buenos Aires just to beg for books."[32]

These obstacles could not be overcome immediately, especially in economic and social systems that were not conducive to building an educational system. Moreover, elsewhere, social divisions took on diverse forms. For instance, the Ottoman Empire divided learners according to religion and ethnicity. Mahmud II, Sultan from 1808 to 1839, created the *rüşdiye* schools, which taught mainly Muslim boys in Turkish, reading, writing, arithmetic as well as geography and history. However, an educational system remained only a vision until the dismantling of the empire after the First World War when Mustafa Kemal Atatürk would embark on a program of educational reform.[33]

SCHOOLING, NATIONAL IDENTITY, EVOLUTION

Increasingly, the need to educate more people to a higher standard was accepted. From the mid-nineteenth century, the school incrementally became a dominant means of organizing learning through the creation of systems of universal, mass compulsory schooling across most Western nations. In turn, this had the effect of marginalizing other practices and places of learning.[34] A powerful grammar of schooling would prove to be deeply persistent, embracing classrooms, blackboards, and subject divisions that became central to educational experience. Subsequent reform would work within this basic structure.[35] The coming of compulsory education was overdetermined by multiple factors, including the influence of industrialization, urbanization, secularization, technology, and nationalism. There were contested arguments on childhood and child labor, the economy, health, politics, and international competition.[36]

The expansion of the state in the nineteenth century was a major shift predicated upon cultural change. The school contributed to a cultural revolution that slowly changed the habits of whole populations in making them pliable to rational thought and action and fitting them for varied employments. Gradually, religious impulses would be partly replaced by and partly overlaid with secular ideas of progress, a process that also squeezed out facets of eighteenth-century popular culture.[37] In many countries the school became coterminous with the spread of literacy, especially in Southern Europe, but in countries such as the United States, France, and Britain universal compulsory schooling had to contend with existing literacy practices. Schooling was also closely tied into the building of national identity and citizenship.[38]

In fact, state education had roots in the absolutist state formations of the seventeenth and eighteenth centuries, which required an educated but compliant populace who would help to ensure the continuance of authority and the systematic and rational control over nature. For example, Frederick II introduced compulsory schooling in Prussia in 1763. State authority over education was exerted in many ways, including via entrance to the civil service. With the expansion of government, these posts were opened up to a larger number of people with the requisite skills and training. Degrees would be introduced for entry to key professions such as medicine, law, and teaching.

In the United States, despite popular wariness of state and federal government, the common school developed early in the century. The extension of democracy, the "manifest destiny" of westward expansion, and industrial growth challenged privilege and elitism. Fears about the potentially deleterious influence of waves of immigrants were to be countered by the Americanizing role of the school, symbolized by the national flag in the classroom. Each of these forces facilitated ideas about the common school, which received a boost in 1837 when Massachusetts established a state board of education that was to be led by Horace Mann who championed the extension of schooling, as did Henry Bernard in Connecticut and Rhode Island. Mann argued that "Two divine ideas filled their [Pilgrim Fathers] great hearts—their duty to God and society. For the one they built the church, for the other they opened the school." Schools were to represent a continuation of puritan traditions and, although church and state were kept separate, they would help people to read the Bible and achieve social mobility in a dynamic society.[39]

However, a great variety of educational experiences can be identified in the United States where race and ethnic divisions were prominent. The contrast between the common school in New England and the lacklustre provision in many Southern states was stark. In the antebellum South, slaves were obviously denied an education but maintained cultural, religious, and educational traditions from "sundown to sunup," which fed into the creation of African American schools and colleges in the post-Civil War period, institutions that would in turn provide vital sustenance to communities that suffered exclusion and segregation for most of the twentieth century.[40] For Native Americans the so-called policy of "assimilation," which denied cultural traditions, led to both symbolic and physical violence against tribal groups that did nevertheless manage to assert some control over their learning.[41]

Thus, at the same time that schooling was developing as a common experience, the diversity of schools reflected social divisions. The application of ideas of citizenship, culture, and character to the working class, peasantry, freed slaves, the colonised, women, and the disabled remained problematic. Generally, elementary education was a completely separate track to secondary education, whether that be at the private schools, lycées, grammar schools, or gymnasium, which often enjoyed better resources and a more academic curriculum. However, once elementary education had become a part of an accepted framework, it gave rise to tendencies toward more advanced learning, for instance, the French *écoles primaires supérieures,* the higher-grade schools in England, or the US common schools, which ultimately paved the way for the high school. In Britain, a few "bright" children were able to win scholarships. A related perennial debate concerned whether schools were experienced as controlling or liberating places—willingly or unwillingly to school? Public support for education has been outlined by various scholars but so has the widespread reluctance of many pupils as well as the harsh punishments. Equally, for much of the nineteenth and early twentieth centuries, the experience of schooling could be fleeting, and later adult reflections and autobiographies did not always dwell upon it.[42]

The complementary forces of war and nationalism also led to the enforcement of learning in state schools. Education provides some supporting evidence for Eric Hobsbawm's argument that the nation was a product of state action. Schools acted as a conduit for Benedict Anderson's print culture of nationalism.[43] In Germany, the rector of Berlin University, Johann Gottlieb Fichte, feeling the effects of defeat by Napoleon, in his Addresses to the German Nation (1807–8), had emphasized the potential for the nation to be rebuilt though a system of schools that was to educate all children in intellectual ideas and manual training. After the Franco-Prussian War, the Third Republic in France supported compulsory, free, and secular education.[44] In Britain, national identity became entwined with citizenship through Empire Day, which commenced in 1902, although the empire could appear as a diffuse and intangible entity.[45]

With the unification of Italy, Massimo D'Azeglio is popularly associated with the phrase that "we have made Italy, now we must make Italians." The 1859 Casati Law introduced elementary schooling. Texts such as Carlo Collodi's *Pinocchio* and Edmondo de Amicis's *Cuore* emphasized the interconnections between loyalty, schooling, and the nation. Written as the school diary of eleven-year-old Enrico Bottini, *Cuore* features the arrival of a boy from Calabria in the south. The text explains that it was "a glorious land which gave Italy illustrious men [*sic*], and which gives her strong workers and brave soldiers, in one of the most beautiful parts of our country [...] inhabited by people of ability and courage. Cherish him [...]. Make him see that an Italian boy, no matter which Italian school he sets foot in, finds brothers there."[46] As a nationalist text influenced by socialism, it gained traction in twentieth-century fascist Italy, communist eastern Europe, as well as Latin America.

Nationalist impulses did not efface social divisions. Most German schools adhered to Prussia's lead, which stressed devoutness, obedience, and efficiency on class lines. While the *volksschule* became universal and compulsory, there were to be multiple types of school. The prestigious nine-year gymnasium with Latin, Greek, and modern languages became the route to universities and the civil service. The *realgymnasium* offered Latin, modern languages, natural science, and mathematics, and the *realschule* or *oberralschule* accentuated natural sciences and maths.[47] In the 1870s, the composer Richard Strauss attended the *Ludwigsgymnasium* in Munich, which still felt the impact of Alexander von Humboldt's school reforms early in the century that had promoted literature, art, philosophy, and classical languages as a way to cultivate the individual. Georg Wilhelm Friedrich Hegel, Gotthold Ephraim Lessing, and Friedrich Schiller had advocated a new humanism around the turn of the nineteenth century in order to create a middle ground between science and theology. It was to have a profound influence upon Strauss, who came to see himself as part of a cultural elite, a Goethean figure, tasked with maintaining a tradition of learning and European culture stretching back to the Greeks and Romans. He recalled that the gymnasium was "the benevolent guardian of European culture." Strauss blended academic study with his prodigious musical talents. It inculcated a notion of *bildung*, so that intellectual improvement remained central to the rest of his life. Following two world wars, at the end of his life, Strauss would lament the subsequent turn to mathematics, science, and vocational education. Indeed, from 1890, Wilhelm II had opposed what he saw as a harmful hierarchy of schools and argued that, "It is our duty to educate young men to become young Germans and not young Greeks or Romans." From 1900, greater equality between schools was introduced.[48] The learning needs of a larger segment of the population was tied into military and national histories to justify the unification of Germany under Bismarck.

Traditions of learning were not to be replaced completely, and modernity was birthed with instruments and ideas from an older world. As in Latin America, religion was complemented by a belief in science and progress, and the salvation of the soul was accompanied by the secular education of the individual. Religious influences on learners continued to be felt with the onset of state authority. Even in Prussia, where the cultural struggle or *kulturkampf* over the role of religion in schools led to the assertion of the right of the state rather than the Catholic Church to supervise schools, they remained denominational and teachers were appointed according to religious faith. The coming of state education could ironically lead to an intensification of battles over religious control of education with various denominations vying for preeminence. For instance, in Australia a dual system of national and denominational schools was instituted in the 1840s. The British North America Act of 1867, while conferring educational authority on Canadian provinces, guaranteed denominational rights if they already had legal recognition. These measures created diverse educational systems and meant that religion at least remained part of the assumed backdrop for many learners.

From the late nineteenth century, impulses and movements for change coalesced within educational systems. The school became embedded in national cultures and there was a gradual professionalization of teachers. Systematic learning theory responded to social changes in technology, urbanization, industry, organized labor, and demography. There was a greater focus on a more defined sense of childhood, exemplified by the Swedish reformer Ellen Key's *Century of the Child* and G. Stanley Hall's popularization of "adolescence." Learning came to be viewed as a natural process of individual and social growth related to personal expression and citizenship within an expanding notion of welfare. Pestalozzi and Fröbel were taken more seriously. In terms of the curriculum, learners were presented with a wider range of content in elementary education, broadening out from literacy, arithmetic, and moral character, to other subjects including geography, history, science and practical subjects which all invoked citizenship, nationalism and individual development.

Greater emphasis was placed upon the learner's experience and understanding. The language of psychology and psychoanalysis would be adopted into everyday language with great rapidity and would inform twentieth-century education as a whole. Psychology had an accumulative impact upon the classroom and teacher training. In the United States, William James established a psychophysiological laboratory at Harvard in 1891 and wrote *Principles of Psychology*, which advocated behaviorist ideas and viewed education as a means to organize children and fit them for their future social and physical environment. His student Edward L. Thorndike went on to publish *Educational Psychology* in 1903. John Dewey would play a key role in shifting educational assumptions about human development. The University of Chicago Laboratory School, founded in 1896 and directed by Dewey, complemented a plethora of other experimental schools. Dewey saw schools as societies where life happens, not just as a preparation for life; as such, they should be organized more democratically. Other examples included the Play School and Walden School in New York and William Wirt's 1908 Gary Plan in Indiana, which embraced work, study, and play. In 1919, the Progressive Education Association was formed and Helen Parkhurst's Dalton Plan was launched in 1920 at Dalton, Massachusetts.

Child-centered learning also featured in Europe. Herbart's psychological ideas were applied more systematically. Wilhelm Wundt, who wrote *Principles of Physiological Psychology* in 1874, established a psychological laboratory at the University of Leipzig in 1879 to examine consciousness and experience. Ovide Decroly's École de l'Ermitage (the Hermitage School), set up in Brussels in 1907, aimed to transform the classroom into a workshop where pupils would extend their individual interests through a framework addressing food, shelter, defence, and work. Montessori's Casa dei Bambini (Children's House) highlighted experiential and tactile learning by deploying a range of didactic materials to train the senses of the child through stages of mental growth. In Poland, the children's author and director of the Dom Sierot orphanage, Janus Korczak, produced influential ideas on pedagogy, working with "difficult" children and encouraging pupil participation. In Britain, Henry Caldwell Cook's *The Play Way* stressed the importance of play, experience, and the wholeness of the child. Open-air schools, which spread from Germany across Europe and beyond, attempted to reintroduce a sense of nature into learning, working outdoors to improve the health of children. The headmistress of Birley House open-air school in Britain observed that the results of the school were "marvellous" in transforming "neglected and ill-nourished children, who had improved by leaps and bounds, while those suffering from organic weakness made slower but steady progress."[49]

Progressive education also related to a process of systematization and socialization, involving measurement, study, and control of children and learners. The progressive concern with the young child, which linked learning to health and social efficiency, was to have far-reaching effects. Care and control overlapped in contexts of learning.[50] Progressive educators were attracted not only by democracy and creative pedagogies but also by scientific study and intelligence testing.[51] Herbert Spencer had argued in favor of evolutionary thought, apparent in much educational thinking at the time, from eugenicist views to recapitulation theories, which argued that children grew through the "stages of mankind," from "savagery to civilisation," that could be found even in anti-militarist youth organizations such as the Woodcraft Folk.[52] Ironically, Russian anarchists such as Peter Kropotkin challenged evolutionary thought derived from Charles Darwin and Thomas Malthus in arguing the case for the kind of cooperative organization that would be championed by the Folk after its formation in 1925.[53]

New pedagogical ideas had a symbiotic relationship with universities where many theories of learning were refined. Higher education was indeed an important aspect of embryonic education systems. German universities exerted an international influence on learning. Under the guidance of Humboldt, the University of Berlin was founded in 1809 and was to become associated with the notion of academic freedom and the education of the individual along classical lines. It dedicated itself to scientific knowledge, a complementary mix of research and teaching, and a range of academic activities. By the end of the nineteenth century there had been a widespread adoption of *Lernfreiheit*, the freedom of the student to choose their program, and *Lehrfreiheit*, the freedom of the professor to research any topic. This had the effect of advancing the division of knowledge into various disciplines, which were supported by the organizational politics of higher education and ultimately impacted upon programs of learning, especially in the United States, for instance, with the foundation of Johns Hopkins University in 1876. These functions only emerged gradually. Until the end of the century, research was generally done outside universities. In Britain it was the Royal Society and other institutions that encouraged research. It was the function of a university, J.H. Newman stressed, to prepare young men for leadership, "to fill any post with credit, and to master any subject with facility."[54]

Throughout the century, higher education was extending to the middle classes and offering training in commercial skills. In 1877, the University of Tokyo was founded and included departments in law, physical sciences, literature, and medicine, with teaching in English and German. In Britain new universities formed away from Oxbridge, partly to replace the dissenting academies, and centers of higher learning flourished in London, Durham, Manchester, Sheffield, Birmingham, Liverpool, and elsewhere. Very gradually, women were allowed into universities although progress was sporadic. In the United States, girls' and women's education was influenced by the utopian socialist wave of enthusiasm and included the coeducational Oberlin College in 1833, and Antioch College in the 1850s with Horace Mann serving as the first president.

As universities engaged with constituencies beyond the upper classes and on a range of social issues, the curriculum would begin to move away from the classics toward science, modern languages, literature, and economics. Adult education, people's universities, and university settlements all provided opportunities where university academics connected with working-class people and the poor in order to build "fellowship," but the process also generated self-reflections on how universities could construct curricula more suited to the modern world.[55] Tutors such as R.H. Tawney learnt from working-class people in tutorial classes as much as he did from soldiers in the First World War trenches. Universities were being integrated into social movements—Korczak would study at the Polish "Flying University," which developed a nationalist agenda hidden from Russian eyes.

WESTERN LEARNING FROM THE OUTSIDE

Rapidly multiplying ideas and practices of learning within education systems were also being extended beyond Europe and the West. "Modernization" and "westernization" were complex processes in post-1868 Meiji Japan. Prior to this, schools were organized hierarchically with the ruling samurai studying literature and Confucianism at *hankō* (domain schools) and others attending *terakoya* (temple schools), where they learned reading, writing, and arithmetic from both monks and lay teachers. They were complemented with a network of private schools. The Meiji Restoration did lead to important educational reforms based upon Western ideas, notably the 1872 Gakusei (Education System Order) that was initiated to create a national education system. However, Western ideas encountered a conservative reaction and could not be implemented overnight in a non-Western context. In 1890, Motoda Nagazane drafted the Imperial Rescript on Education, which reemphasized Confucian and Shinto values, moral education, national identity, and imperial authority. Traditional Chinese learning (*kangaku*), perhaps comparable to a Western classical education, would retain considerable hold and influence in Japan until the 1890s when it was replaced by history, literature, and philosophy that would, in fact, adopt many features of the older practice. In addition, the inability of the state to devote adequate resources to education meant that many small private schools cropped up offering traditional learning. Miwada Masako opened a school in Matsuyama in 1880, which aimed to study texts (*dokusho gakuka*) over three years including important works of the Chinese classical canon and histories of Japan written in Sino-Japanese. The teaching involved traditional methods of lecture, group readings, and group discussions, and exams were held each month. Over time, temple schools would be converted into primary schools and domain schools into secondary schools and universities.[56]

In China the Manchu dynasty came under pressure, especially after the humiliation of the Opium Wars and defeat by the Japanese in 1894–5. In 1898, the Hundred Days of Reform proposed to reorganize the military, broaden civil service exams, and introduce modern schools but it generated considerable opposition, epitomised by the Boxer Rebellion in 1900. Despite the limited structural changes, learning was developing as part of a "New Culture Movement," which introduced many Western ideas, including Marxism, and the spread of vernacular language. Mao Zedong himself read extensively, much in the style of an autodidact, within the walls of the Hunan Provincial Library, where he studied books by Adam Smith, Charles Darwin, J.S. Mill, Rousseau, Spencer, and Montesquieu: "During this period of self-education I read many books, studied world geography and world history. There for the first time I saw, and studied with great interest, a map of the world [...] I mixed poetry and romances, and tales of ancient Greece, with serious study of history and geography of Russia, Armenia, England, France and other countries." Geography in particular created a tangible sense of national identity as it enabled students to see the country whole. As a library worker at Peking University, Mao would be treated with contempt and indifference by arrogant professors, and this helped him to reflect upon the need for cultural change to end feudalism, convinced that education and learning should not be the sole preserve of elites.[57]

In colonialized countries, the relationship to Western learning took on a different set of meanings. The two-way transfer of resources, people, inequalities, and ideas was to have a profound impact upon both the metropole and the colony.[58] Colonial issues did occasionally flare up in public debates, as in Britain in the wake of the 1865 uprising in Morant Bay, Jamaica, and in the lead up to the 1867 Reform Act, when tensions were exposed that directly affected the way that education and learning were apprehended.[59] Commonly, the colonial story was integrated into a Whig version of improvement, as in Thomas Babington Macauley's argument in 1848 that the "history of our country during the last hundred and sixty years is eminently the history of physical, of moral, and of intellectual improvement":

> in America, the British colonies rapidly became far mightier and wealthier than the realms which Cortes and Pizarro had added to the dominions of Charles the Fifth [...] in Asia, British adventurers founded an empire not less splendid and more durable than that of Alexander.[60]

These assumptions were to come under considerable scrutiny and challenge, not least from the diverse range of colonized peoples. It is possible to discern a number of overall themes that pervade colonial education: the tensions between traditional learning, religion, and Western models; debates over the language of instruction; the desire to educate a cadre of local people necessary for colonial leadership and administration but not to create an idle educated class who might turn against colonial authority; the considerable conflict between and within key groups—missionaries, the state, and various local religious and ethnic groups and independence movements; the partial nature of learning opportunities that tended to be half-hearted imitations of the country of origin; and the exportation of hierarchies based on class and gender, which became intertwined with racial hierarchies. Crucially, colonial nations confronted a dilemma: the nationalism that suffused the expansion of organized learning at home posed a danger of generating independence abroad.

From the advent of the East India Company, India would play a central role in British culture and was a place where debates on learning took on great significance. Although the company was initially a trading concern, it moved into government and administration. Educational grants were made from 1813, and in 1823 a General Committee on Public Instruction was formed in Calcutta (Kolkata).[61] Many of the members were Orientalists who promoted teaching Sanskrit and Arabic and translating English works. Missionaries also supported some vernacular education but were disturbed about aspects of Indian culture that they considered unchristian. Reformers considered oriental learning to be condescending and unhelpful to reform and progress. Macauley's famous *Minute on Education* in 1835 stipulated that instruction should be in English, which marked a shift toward prioritizing Western knowledge.

Some Indians supported the move. The reformer Ram Mohun Roy argued for English education and founded the Hindu College in Calcutta, which helped to stimulate the setting up of schools and the expansion of Western learning in Bengal. However, surveys carried out by Baron Curzon of Kedleston after 1898 revealed the parlous state of education and continuing lack of schools. The colonial power had neither resources nor commitment to education, so much was left to private provision where rote learning, memorization, and passing examinations became standard.

There was a growing opposition to British control and some resentment of the priority accorded to Western learning as opposed to Indian languages. This movement would also receive support from the founding of the universities of Calcutta, Bombay (Mumbai), and Madras in 1857, the same year as the Indian Rebellion. They would become engines of nationalist thought that energized the Swadeshi movement, which boycotted foreign goods. The promise of white-collar jobs in the colonial administration had created unrealistic expectations, among a "babu" class, that could not be fulfilled. Following a government crackdown and a boycott of the University of Calcutta, accused of producing "slaves," the National Council of Education organized literary, scientific, and technical education. The movement was to influence Rabindranath Tagore, who founded a school in West Bengal in 1901, which started with open-air education and eventually transformed into a university. In 1921, the Indian constitution transferred education to Indian control. It did not quell the urge for independence and Mahatma Gandhi would launch the non-cooperation movement, which intensified protest and built further national schools and "national universities," where some Hindi and mother-tongue teaching took place.[62]

In Africa, great diversity of learning existed according to historical and religious context. This included Christian-influenced education in Ethiopia; Qur'anic schools in East Africa; and English and Afrikaans schools for settler communities in South Africa.[63] But for the bulk of sub-Saharan Africa, traditional education prepared children for the roles they were to play in their homes and villages as well as tribal duties. It involved what we might call socialization, vocational learning, and initiation into religious customs. By the end of puberty young people would have been taught the myths, stories, and religious beliefs of their tribes as well as fishing, hunting, or farming in addition to community responsibilities, learning that was often differentiated according to gender. It might vary from basic instruction to more complex educational systems. The dispersed Poro society of West Africa maintained a quasi-community government, fortified by religious belief. Its primary responsibility was to train mainly men for participation in community life for which families would pay a fee. A few women were also accepted into membership or formed their own society. Full initiation might last several years and involve remaining in the bush for weeks where not just practical skills of hunting and crafts but secrets and passwords were imbibed, symbolized by rites of passage and the paying of homage to ancestral spirits.[64]

Missionaries in Africa came with the aim of converting the population to Christianity and, by 1900, there were an estimated 100,000 European missionaries on the continent. The array of missions in Uganda, Kenya, and the Gold Coast (Ghana) included those of the Society for the Propagation of the Gospel in Foreign Parts, the Wesleyan Methodists, Roman Catholics, the White Fathers, the Church Missionary Society, the Universities Mission to Central Africa, and the London Missionary Society. Initially, the Christian faith would confirm rather than dispel traditional modes of life although the long-term impact would work in the latter direction.[65] To win converts they studied African languages, translated texts, and gave Christian lessons in Indigenous languages. Attempts to convert people could backfire and meet with resistance, as when the Basel Mission in the Gold Coast took a strong stand against "pagan" participation in rites of passage.[66] Assumptions about class, gender, and race inequalities were also carried across to the new setting. For example, missionaries in Sierra Leone imposed a gendered curriculum with the creation of an Anglophile elite as opposed to other girls who were socialized into a Christian vision of obedience, fidelity, modesty, and piousness. A disproportionate amount of time was devoted to needlework in comparison to boys who were able to concentrate on arithmetic, reading, and writing. At the Female Captured Negroes School in Freetown in 1816, girls spent two hours forty-five minutes a day sewing and one hour forty-five minutes reading and writing.[67]

Indeed, educational provision was frequently limited and policy ideas half-baked, governments being content to leave the field to missions and private schools. It would not be until the 1920s when indifferent attitudes to education changed with the circulation of the League of Nations' concept of trusteeship. In 1922, the Phelps-Stokes Commission noted the passing of the tribal system although many traditions would persist. Indeed, the British remained attracted to the idea of "adaptation" to the specific cultural needs of Africa, which was often resisted by Africans who demanded British education.[68]

In the very different setting of Southeast Asia, colonial expansion also led to debates over the role of Western education. Prior to conquest, education in Southeast Asia had been based around family, community, and religious traditions including Confucianism, Islam, Buddhism, Daoism, and Hinduism. Learning centered upon the transmission of cultural values and memorization, which acted as a buttress to religious and cultural hierarchies. Western colonization introduced technologies of schooling including a secular curriculum, age grading, examinations, and qualifications that might provide the opportunity of employment in colonial administrations. However, the impact of Western schooling would again be inchoate. In Burma (Myanmar), traditional Buddhist

schools were complemented with Western schools after the British occupation
of 1886, which also led to some recognition of women's education and the
development of higher education that resulted in the University of Rangoon
in 1920.[69] Vietnam, Cambodia, and Laos became integrated into the French
Indochina Union where some primary education along French lines was
provided. Even in the Dutch East Indies (Indonesia), where the Dutch
government committed itself to the provision of schooling, actual outcomes
were curtailed. Rather, schools tended to cater to the children of colonial classes.

In Thailand, which was not colonized, Western influences were still felt.
Traditional education drew upon Buddhism, support for the king and loyalty
to the family. From 1897 the King Chulalongkorn set up a department for
education with mainly English advisers who initially addressed themselves to
the learning needs of a leadership class. Temple schools were established, a
medical school, a law school, and a royal pages' school for sons of nobility,
which became the Civil Service College in 1910.[70]

CONCLUSION

The history of learning in the nineteenth and early twentieth centuries reveals
important oscillations between modernity and religion, equality and hierarchy,
social change and social reproduction. Places of learning came to proliferate with
the school and university becoming dominant institutions that helped to embed
social practices that remain familiar today. New ideas of the learner emerged
based upon educability, personal exploration, and social engagement. But the
basic equality implied by learning was not to be achieved as institutionalization
entrenched social divisions. Long-established forms of learning, ranging from
traditions of scholarship to cultural practices imbued with religious meaning,
did not disappear and have recently been rediscovered as a means of coming
to terms with changes in current times. This was not immediately apparent in
the early twentieth century when ideas of progress and modernity still held
sway. By 1920, there was considerable hope that education was to be extended
considerably. Proponents of new education believed that their ideas and plans,
although blunted by the First World War, augured well for the future. Sites
of learning multiplied as a result of changes in technology and the means
of communication. Colonized countries experienced the strengthening of
independence movements in which learning featured prominently. In Russia,
wide-ranging educational reform would generate equal measures of hope
and fear as the Bolsheviks attempted to counteract historically low levels of
education. Learning was to remain a site of struggle throughout the century.

CHAPTER SIX

Teachers and Teaching

MARIANNE A. LARSEN

Histories of teachers and teaching are generally told through the lens of the nation-state with a focus on Europe. In contrast, this chapter paints a picture of teachers and teaching in the age of empire (1800–1920) beyond and across national boundaries and a wider range of formal and informal educational settings. The chapter is organized into five sections. First, the theoretical framework—transnational new cultural history—is outlined. This is followed by four salient topics, which together illustrate the transnational, entangled, and embedded nature of teaching in the age of empire. These topics comprise: a discussion of teaching early in the nineteenth century characterized by close community relations in Indigenous and non-Indigenous communities; missionary-teachers in the Americas and Africa as cultural-brokers; teachers and their formal training within the context of the spread of state-controlled schooling; and finally, the spread of two different pedagogical approaches, the Pestalozzian and the monitorial methods, across numerous colonies and countries. Together, these examples provide excellent illustrations of the interconnected, intercultural, and transnational nature of teachers and teaching in the nineteenth and early twentieth centuries.

THEORETICAL FRAMEWORK: A TRANSNATIONAL NEW CULTURAL HISTORY

The theoretical framework guiding this account is a transnational new cultural history. The terms "new cultural history" (NCH) and "transnational history" (TNH) highlight important topics previously marginalized and inadequately conceptualized by historians, and provide nuanced understandings of existing topics by focusing on intercultural relations and transfers, entanglements and flows, especially those that are transnational.[1] Transnational historians and cultural studies theorists critique approaches to the study of history that position Europe at the center of analyses and measure non-Western societies against some kind of ideal, universal image of the West. NCH and TNH urge us to shift our attention away from this privileged role of the West in historical research to examine histories of the "Other."[2]

Following Randeria, who has critiqued the privileged view of the West in historical research, this chapter illustrates the more complex ways in which nineteenth-century teachers and teaching were constructed through interconnections both within and beyond nation-state and colonial boundaries.[3] In particular, this chapter is positioned against all-too-common English-language Eurocentric accounts that trace how a dominant set of reforms about teachers and teaching traveled from Europe outwards to the rest of the world. Thus, the narrative presented shows the multidirectional flows between teachers and teaching across a wide variety of educational settings within and outside of Europe, and, in doing so, demonstrates how there is not one single idea of what teaching and teachers were like during the age of empire.

Specifically, attention is paid to the concepts of connections and mobilities to demonstrate how teachers were embedded within relations with one another and the communities where they lived and taught. Many teachers, as we will see, operated as mobile subjects connecting different worlds, Indigenous and non-Indigenous, North and South, East and West. Transnational and cultural mobilities scholars have shown how mobility has always been a key constituent element of human life across time and place.[4] As Greenblatt explains, "even in places that at first glance are characterized by homogeneity and stasis rather than by pluralism and change, cultural circuits facilitating motion are at work."[5]

A broad conception of culture is central to this analysis in all its complex and changing forms across different social, economic, and political contexts.[6] This analysis necessitates focusing on interconnections, flows, and links between and among cultures, connecting various parts of the world to one another and creating the conditions for cultural change to take place within and across borders.[7] This account moves beyond focusing on elite culture, to embrace aspects of collective culture, and especially the role of the social and thus educational in everyday life. Drawing upon the notion of entanglement, we see the mutual influences between the "West" and the "rest" of the world, which resulted in nineteenth-century societies being bound to one another through cultural transfers of pedagogical knowledge and practices.[8] Therefore, this chapter engages with notions of cultural transfers such as cross-border flows of pedagogical approaches and the role of teachers as cultural brokers, shaping local teaching cultures and translating foreign educational ideas and processes through their everyday practices.[9]

Finally, commonly accepted binaries such as East–West and colonized–colonizer operate to classify and normalize the teaching subject in narrow ways. As a result, many teachers have been excluded from historical narratives about teachers and teaching, especially Western-based histories focusing on the professionalization of teaching over the nineteenth and early twentieth centuries. In contrast, this chapter reaches beyond traditional histories that focus on trained teachers within state-funded schools to include stories of educators such as Indigenous Elders, missionary teachers, dame-school teachers, and teachers in Christian church-run schools as well as infant and elementary schools to illustrate the complexity of teacher and teaching experiences across varied settings within the age of empire.

TEACHING AND THE COMMUNITY: INDIGENOUS AND DAME-SCHOOL TEACHERS

Teaching in the early part of the nineteenth century was embedded within close community relations, which were particularly evident within Indigenous communities, working-class communities in Britain and continental Europe, and in pioneer colonial settings. Within North American Indigenous nations, teaching was embodied and grounded within the whole local community. The community was at the center of all educational endeavors. As Weaver explains, "community is the highest value for Native peoples, and fidelity to it is a primary responsibility."[10] We see this concept of the community as teacher in other Indigenous communities. In New Guinea "in the sphere of social relationships, the individual learns what the community requires of him, simply by participating in its regular life."[11] And in West Africa, the entire community was responsible for educating the young: "parents and the wider circle of kinsmen consider it a sacred trust to discharge their obligations regarding the child's 'socialization'."[12]

Indigenous children learned knowledge, skills, and values such as respect, sharing, and self-reliance through observing exemplary adult role models in their communities. The community taught children through methods drawn upon since time immemorial to prepare these "students" for life. Most teaching emphasized experimental, informal, and holistic forms of learning, including oral and tag-along teachings, stories, ceremonies, apprenticeship learning, and games. Teaching and learning were intertwined and integrated with all aspects of family and community life, which were highly valued.[13]

Elders played a central role in instructing the younger generation about the teachings and stories of their ancestors. Daily teaching was defined by close personal and kinship relationships between Elders and students, in a context of family support, with the community as a classroom. Elders taught children how to manage and prosper in harmony with the environment for economic survival.

Specific skills related to food production such as hunting, fishing, trapping, and cultivating crops for survival were taught, as well as manufacturing skills including homebuilding, tool making, and weaving. Elders also taught younger generations moral principles by which they should live and urged the sharing of inter-nation or inter-tribal goods. As teachers, they were an example of how to live without conflict, and if conflict did occur, how to settle differences according to Indigenous customs and laws.[14]

Outside of Indigenous communities, teaching was similarly entangled within close community relations across Britain, North America, and Australasia. Prior to the development and spread of state-schooling, a variety of small, private schools emerged during the early part of the nineteenth century to serve the needs of local communities. Such schools were called common day, private pay or private enterprise, venture, gaffer, or dame schools. Dame schools were early forms of private elementary schools usually taught by single women in their homes. Pupils were generally between the ages of three and eight and came from poorer and/or working-class families. Dame-school teachers taught basic reading, writing, and arithmetic skills as well as catechism and simple prayers. Girls were taught sewing, embroidery, and other household skills (see Figure 6.1).[15]

The phenomenon of the dame school is an excellent example of transnational cultural transfer traveling from Britain to British colonies in Australia, New Zealand, and North America through immigrants who desired education for their children.[16] In response to these demands, female immigrants set up dame schools in their homes to provide education for the children in their rural settlements, villages, and towns. In colonial America, these schools were

FIGURE 6.1 Thomas Webster, *A Dame's School*, 1845. Tate Modern, London. From *Social England*, volume 6, edited by H.D. Traill, D.C.L. and J. S. Mann, M.A. (London: Cassell and Company, Limited, 1904). © Getty Images.

established by New England women, providing them with a source of income, at a time of limited opportunities for female employment.[17] In Australia, the first two teachers from abroad were ex-convicts, Isabella Rosson and Mary Johnson, who opened dame schools in the late eighteenth century. By the middle of the nineteenth century, Adelaide was full of dame schools, which accepted children of all ages and taught them basic reading, writing, and arithmetic skills.[18]

Working-class and pioneer parents (in the North American colonies) supported dame schools because they provided an inexpensive basic education, accepted children of all ages, and were sufficiently flexible in not requiring regular attendance. The dame had much in common with local mothers, as both engaged in additional work within the home to supplement their income. Moreover, many dames, empathizing with demands placed upon families, would receive children at various hours during the day, especially if the parent was engaged in other household work, and take care of children until later in the evening. In the case of colonial pioneer communities, dames were flexible in allowing children to be pulled out of school for the economic needs of the family, which in rural areas were based on the seasonal agricultural cycle.[19]

Dames and local parents worked out the terms of teaching, including what was to be taught and school fees. For example, in Massachusetts, Goodwife Mirick was contracted by local parents in the late nineteenth century for "training up the children, and teaching the children to read, and that she should have three pence a week for every child that she takes to perform this good work for."[20] In this way, parents and teachers were interconnected in a relationship of mutual obligation; parents needed to have their children educated and teachers needed to make a living. If teachers did not ensure that parents' needs were met, children would be withdrawn from school and shifted to another. If parents did not pay the school fee, the teacher would close down the school and move to another more viable locale.[21]

MISSIONARY TEACHERS AS CULTURAL BROKERS

Another example of close relations between teachers and the communities where they worked were transnational missionary teachers and Indigenous students trained to teach in mission schools. However, before proceeding, it is vital to acknowledge the devastating impacts on Indigenous communities where many missionary teachers taught, including forms of cultural genocide through, for example, residential and other missionary schools run by both the state and the church. The narrative that follows is not intended to downplay this history of religious imperialism but rather to show how some missionary teachers challenged the colonizing "Othering" paradigm through the development of empathetic relations with those they served.

Nineteenth-century missionary work in Africa was first carried out by English-speaking Protestants and then by Protestants from continental Europe. US American Baptists and Roman Catholics joined in the missionary movement in Africa after mid-century.[22] US missionaries established churches and mission schools to convert Indigenous nations to Christianity early in the century, and in the British North American colonies (present-day Canada) religious orders and societies continued their proselytizing work begun many hundreds of years ago. Mission schools were considered indispensable to missionary aims to win converts. Thus, the relationship between the school and church was often close, and missionaries served within the church and as teachers at mission schools.

Within the context of Africa, Carpenter refers to such individuals as village preacher-teachers: "The village school teacher and the 'catechist' or lay-leader of the Christian fellowship were often the same individual. At dawn and perhaps again in the evening he would lead the group of Christians gathered for prayer. On Sundays he conducted more extended services of worship. For several hours a day he would conduct a primary school for the children."[23] Indeed, as this letter from 1828 to the London Missionary Society illustrates, missionaries held many different roles: "The missionary, especially when initially establishing a station, was preacher, pastor, catechist, (secular) teacher, nurse, medical doctor, gardener, instructor in practical subjects and trades like building, carpentry, gardening, wagon-making and so forth—all at the same time."[24]

These teachers worked in small mission schools, which provided an elementary education for children and interested local adults. Given that the primary goal of mission societies was to convert locals to Christianity, there was a heavy emphasis on Christian moral principles in these schools. Female students received instruction in hygiene, cooking, sewing, spinning, gardening, clothes-making, childcare, housework, Christian family life, storytelling, and the Bible. Depending on the skills of the teacher, building, furniture-making, and other trades (for example, carpentry, blacksmithing, wagon-making) were also taught.[25]

Above all, missionary teachers provided a basic education in reading, writing, and arithmetic. The primary aim of teaching reading was to enable pupils to read the Bible and other religious texts. The White Fathers mission in Northern Africa, for example, was deeply interested in teaching literacy in the mission schools and did so by "producing alphabet sheets, word lists and grammars, later full-scale dictionaries, textbooks and manuals, translations of portions of the Gospels and later of the whole New Testament" in local, native languages.[26] Indeed, nearly all of the teaching in the mission schools was done in African languages. Missionary teachers recognized the need to learn local languages so as to better understand the cultural contexts within which they taught. The work that these teachers did in translating African languages (and Indigenous languages in North America) was pioneering and laid some of the foundations for the development of written literature in Indigenous languages. Learning the local language, customs, values, and beliefs enabled the teacher-missionary to develop empathetic and interconnected relationships with those they served.[27]

Hundreds of African American missionaries also journeyed to Africa during the nineteenth century. They established schools for children, set up homes and orphanages, and translated grammar books, dictionaries, hymns, proverbs, etc. into the local Indigenous languages. Lulu Cecillia Fleming, Clara Ann Howard, and Nora A. Gordon, who worked in central sub-Saharan Africa as mission teachers, stand out for their unique understanding of the Africans they worked with given that they were born in the southern United States to former slaves. They focused on getting children and especially girls from surrounding villages to attend the mission schools with the aim to improve their lives through education. As African Americans, they were in a unique position to identify to some degree with the local culture and empathize with the lives and plight of the Congolese women and children with whom they worked.[28]

Within the Americas, missionary teachers also established schools alongside churches. US missionaries engaged in educational work in Hawaii in the 1820s, teaching basic literacy skills to local Hawaiians through the development of a written form of the Indigenous language.[29] In northeastern North America, mission schools were established among the Haudenosaunee Confederacy in the early 1800s, including the Seneca (see Figure 6.2). The American Board of Commissioners for Foreign Missions (ABCFM) established many mission

FIGURE 6.2 Dennis Cusick, *Seneca School House*, 1821. Object ID A7841. © Rock Foundation collection, New York.

schools throughout the continental USA among the Cherokee, Creek, Choctaw, Chicksaw, and Seminole. Cherokee leaders encouraged the American Board missionaries to open schools, to provide their children with opportunities to become literate and learn skills associated with the colonizer settlers.[30] By the late 1820s, the ABCFM Cherokee schools had become "an international showcase" with eight schools and an enrollment of approximately 200 students, overseen by thirty-five missionary teachers and other staff.[31]

Similar to African mission-schools, ABCFM schools taught basic skills in reading, writing, and arithmetic as well as religion. However, missionary teachers quickly learned that they did not always have the full support of Indigenous communities when it came to conversion to Christianity. For instance, while some Cherokees converted to Christianity for pragmatic reasons, many removed their children from school when it was time for conversion.[32] Another example illustrates how missionary teachers had to navigate within a zone of intercultural contact and conflict with the Indigenous communities they served. An 1811 agreement between a Haudenosaunee community and the first missionary teacher, Jabez Hyde, acknowledged that the teacher would not teach religion or enforce attendance.[33]

Good missionary teachers, like dame-school teachers, understood and respected the communities within which they worked. Among the Cherokees, Evan Jones and John B. Jones were successful and well-respected missionary teachers who sought the views and cooperation of the people they served and accepted the adaption of the Christian faith with Indigenous spiritual beliefs. Like missionary teachers in Africa, they supported bilingual education and learned the local language, translating the Bible and other educational materials into Cherokee. Moreover, they both supported the education of Cherokee children. Jones recommended state funding of Cherokee secondary schools where "farming, gardening, and the mechanic arts should be taught."[34]

Over time, missionary societies recognized the importance of training local Indigenous students as teachers for the mission schools. There are numerous examples of Africans trained to become teachers in mission schools. Some were trained as assistant teachers and others took over the complete running of their local mission school. For example, Tamrat Emmanuel, a Beta Esra'el pupil from Ethiopia, trained as a teacher and ran a school in Addis Ababa for members of his community.[35] Similarly, in North America, Indigenous students were trained to become teachers in mission schools. By the middle of the century, in Hawaii the vast majority of the teachers in mission schools were native Hawaiians.[36]

In Alaska, some Indigenous students were sent to northeastern US institutions for teacher training. Frances Willard, a Tlingit woman, spent five years training in a New Jersey seminary, graduating in 1890 and returned to her community in Alaska to become a teacher at the Sitka Industrial Training School. As the first Alaskan to take charge of a local school, she was highly regarded in her community. Upon her return, the local newspaper wrote: "We are highly pleased with the education and the culture which she has acquired in the short space of five years [...]. Miss Willard shows a commendable spirit and a sincere desire to elevate her people."[37] Of note is the fact that Willard, although integrated within the white settler world, did not sever her ties with her own heritage. She wrote about Tlingit mythology for the *North Star* and regular reports about her school, her high expectations for her students, their eagerness to learn, and her joy in teaching them.

Another example of an Indigenous woman trained to teach in a mission school was Catharine Brown, Brainerd ABCFM Mission School's first female Cherokee schoolteacher. In 1820, she became a teacher and left her family to teach a school of girls 100 miles from her home.[38] When the local Cherokee leaders learned that she was moving to their community to take up a position teaching, they quickly erected a school building at their own expense and with their own labor before she arrived.[39] Brown's 1822 letter to her missionary sponsors provides a picture of her work at the school: "The school here is very small; only about 15 scholars attend constantly and 10 of these beside myself, board in Brother Pother's family. The pupils in general make good improvement."[40] Indeed, her letters and her diary illustrate the transnational nature of her teaching: "a Cherokee woman working on behalf of her Nation by writing into existence a cross-racial and transnational network of supporters."[41]

The examples of missionary teachers outlined above are what Gaul calls cultural intermediaries and Szasz calls cultural brokers.[42] As cultural brokers, non-Indigenous missionary teachers who worked in North American and African communities, learned the local language, reached out and sought the views and opinions of local citizens, and in so doing demonstrated their respect for Indigenous/native cultures. They bridged diverse worlds through their preaching and teaching work. Indigenous women missionary teachers such as Frances Willard and Catharine Brown also became cultural brokers, creatively negotiating the complex and conflict-ridden cross-cultural worlds they straddled. Their education at mission schools, proficiency in their Indigenous languages as well as in English, enabled them to act as cultural brokers between their own people and white settlers—as students, interpreters, and teachers, contributing to "the relatively successful and mutually beneficial relationship that existed between the groups."[43]

Missionaries from abroad who learned Indigenous languages opened up to understanding the local cultures within which they were working. And Indigenous people trained within mission schools to become teachers, learning the language of the colonizer, also became educational intermediaries, bridging two disparate worlds through their connections with each. Tragically, this was not the case for the majority of Indigenous communities where bigoted colonial and religious attitudes contributed to abuses of power over Indigenous children, the loss of culture, and in some cases, lives. However, the examples provided above do provide a brief snapshot of the work of more empathetic missionary teachers and instances of transnational, cross-cultural encounters. Mission schools could be sites for both intercultural contact and missionary teachers were at the heart of such encounters. Nonetheless, while missionary teaching work continued though the century, much began to change with the development of state-controlled schooling.

NINETEENTH-CENTURY EDUCATIONAL REFORM: THE SPREAD OF FORMAL TEACHER TRAINING

During the nineteenth century, public education systems were constructed across a wide range of settings as a part of broader processes related to state formation. Former colonial societies undergoing modernization processes associated with new nationhood also turned their attention to constructing state-funded, compulsory school systems. Many of these processes were associated with breaking the close connections between teachers and local communities, characteristic of the informal schooling practices discussed above, as well as the role of other actors such as religious, voluntary societies and missionary teachers. Above all, education reforms were about tightening state control over students and their teachers.[44]

While the timing and processes associated with key educational reforms differed across settings, the central importance ascribed to mass education and the role of teachers and teacher training did not. Before examining the role of the state in developing formal teacher training, a brief overview of broad state modernizing processes, which involved broadening control over education through the development of state-funded, compulsory, secular, and standardized school systems, is provided. In Europe, in the early nineteenth century, state-funded and controlled education came to be associated with the economic and political development of the nation-state. By mid-century, state control of education was established in France, Holland, Switzerland, and across Germany. In the second half of the century, national education reform played out in other European countries such as Italy, Denmark, Sweden, and Finland.[45]

State modernizing processes similarly took place in East Asian countries. The development of a state school system began during the early Meiji period in Japan as a strategy for social order and consolidation of state power. In 1872, the Meiji government passed the Fundamental Code (FC) of Education "to place the task of schooling Japanese children firmly in the hands of the new educational system."[46] China's Self-Strengthening movement, which began in the 1860s, involved broadening state control over schools and the curriculum. The movement was also referred to as the Westernization movement given the influences from the West on the development of the Chinese state education system.[47]

State-controlled schooling was also established during the final stages of the Ottoman Empire aimed at building citizenship and loyalty among diverse populations. The 1869 Education Act, adopted from the French model, introduced a centralized and compulsory education system. Again, we see the intensification of state control over all aspects of schooling, including students, curricula, books, and teachers. The Ottoman Empire, according to Evered, "sought to become known as an educator state, a development on par with worldwide innovations in the realms of both educational and citizenship-building projects."[48]

The development of mass education in England over the course of the nineteenth century was slower and haphazard compared to other European countries. However, by the 1840s, dissatisfaction with the state of educational provision offered through the voluntary societies, the British and Foreign School Society (BFSS) and the National Society, led to a realization that the state ought to adopt greater responsibility for public education. Processes associated with constructing a state-controlled education system began in 1846 and continued hesitantly from the 1850s until the 1870s with the passage of the Elementary Education Act in 1870.[49]

Although the British state was reluctant in the first half of the century to extend its control over schools, it was more active in the construction of public education systems in its colonies. In India, Macaulay's 1835 "Minute Upon Indian Education" called for the East India Company to provide funding for the provision of public education. Through the 1830s to 1850s, the British colonial state in North America gained further control of the education system by funding schooling, making it compulsory and under the control of Departments of Education. Constructing Australian state systems of public education began in 1851, and legislation in New Zealand in 1877 established state-funded, compulsory elementary education.[50]

Constructing a public education system across the United States developed rapidly after the 1830s in the period known as the "Age of the Common School." Public education systems were first established in New York, followed by Pennsylvania, Ohio, Massachusetts, and Michigan, which laid the foundations for expansion of state-funded elementary education. The movement to provide mass schooling expanded westward during mid-century and southward after the Civil War. By 1865, state systems of common schooling had been established throughout the northern, Midwestern, and western states.[51]

While initiatives to extend state control over education systems occurred at different times throughout the nineteenth century and involved different actors (the government, voluntary/religious societies, colonial trading companies, elites, reformers), there were some remarkably similar aspects to these reforms. Education reform involved creating an educational state bureaucracy; a standardized systems of schooling (with nomenclature to designate particular schools for particular ages of students); state-funding for schools; and state control over curricula and examinations. However, it is the role of the state in enhancing its control over teachers through teacher training that is of interest to us here.

Political and educational reformers claimed that the greatest problem facing prospects for the spread of compulsory education was the need for properly trained and certified teachers. In response, they promoted the establishment of state-funded, formal teacher training institutions to properly prepare individuals to teach the masses. This idea spread outwards from Europe to many other regions of the world. Normal schools (based on the idea of teaching the norms, rules, and principles of education) were first established in France in the seventeenth century. By the nineteenth century, a two-tier system developed with primary school teachers educated at *départemental écoles normales*, and secondary school teachers at the *Écoles normales supérieures*. By the early 1840s, there were seventy-five normal schools in France.[52]

In Prussia, normal schools (seminars), specialized schools for the training of teachers, were founded in the early nineteenth century. By 1834, there were thirty such seminars offering two- to three-year courses in teacher education as well as eleven smaller seminars. Public and private teaching seminars also opened up outside of Prussia. The first seminar for women teachers opened in Berlin in 1830 and soon after others were established across other German states. By 1904, Germany (which had become a united country under Prussian leadership in 1871) had 133 state-run teacher training colleges for men and ten for women.[53]

Leaders in the Ottoman Empire, in their quest to build a strong and unified state, looked to France for inspiration for educational reform. Significant efforts were made to train more teachers as educators "and as agents of the state and of modernization."[54] As in Germany, separate men and women's teachers' training colleges were established in Istanbul, focusing on training teachers for Muslim and non-Muslim primary/middle schools as well as secondary schools. All teachers, both Muslim and non-Muslim, became subject to mandatory retraining and certification in these colleges.[55] And within Africa, in colonies such as Madagascar, missionary societies established normal schools based on the French model (see Figure 6.3).

In England, from 1839 onwards, under the stimulus of government grants, the number of training colleges run by the BFSS and the National Society multiplied. By 1845, the National Society operated twenty-two training colleges, while the BFSS continued to run the Borough Road. In 1846, legislation was passed to provide state assistance to these training colleges, as well as to initiate a system of teacher certification following successful completion of standardized merit examinations, which included state-funded salary augmentations.[56]

In the United States, the first normal school was opened in Vermont in 1823 by Samuel Hall. Due to the efforts of educational reformers, Horace Mann and James C. Carter, a normal school was opened in Massachusetts in 1839. These men

FIGURE 6.3 Interior of a normal school, established by the London Missionary Society, Antananarivo, Madagascar, illustration from the magazine *The Graphic*, vol. 19, no. 498, June 14, 1879. © Getty Images.

were all influenced by the normal schools in Prussia they learned about through their educational study tours in Europe and through reading about Pestalozzian pedagogies used in the Prussian normal schools (see below). The spread of the normal school to other states can in part be credited to the twenty-six graduates of the Massachusetts normal school who went on to become normal school head teachers as far away as Illinois and Michigan. By 1865 there were twenty-two normal schools throughout the northern, Midwestern, and western states.[57]

Teacher training institutions were established later in the nineteenth century in Japan and China. The first teacher education institution in China, the Normal School of Nanyang Gongxue, was founded in Shanghai in 1897. The Qing government first issued regulations on teacher training programs in 1904, and further normal schools were established throughout the country. By 1909 nearly 50 percent of primary and secondary school teachers had graduated from one of these institutions. The establishment and spread of normal schools in China was influenced by similar trends in Europe and the United States, and after 1904 by similar trends in Japan.[58] The Fundamental Code in Japan ushered in a formalized system of teacher training as well as mandatory licensing procedures for teachers.[59] The Tokyo Normal School as well as other similar training institutions were set up, and existing classroom teachers were expected to attend a two- to three-month training program to be licensed to teach.[60]

Formal teacher training spread through many other regions of the world as well, following in large part the examples of earlier reforming nations such as France and Prussia. There were remarkable similarities in the pedagogies taught in these institutions. Scottish educationists and philosophers throughout the century wrote many books on the science and art of teaching that spread throughout teacher training institutions across the British Empire. For example, headmasters of the High School of Edinburgh wrote pedagogical texts that were republished in London, referred to in English and other North American educational journals, and in the writings and speeches of reformers across Britain, Europe, and North America. In addition, David Stow's 1853 book *The Training System*, which went through ten editions, was of considerable influence in the establishment of teacher training in England and North America.[61]

Similar pedagogical ideas and practices circulated between and within Europe, Britain, and North America through these texts and their writers. Both Forrestor and Reid, educationists who immigrated to Canada from England and became school principals, published pedagogical textbooks read by many North American schoolteachers. Other pedagogical texts such as Thomas Tate's *Philosophy of Education; or the Principles and Practice of Teaching* (1857) and Henry Dunn's *Principles of Teaching; or the Normal School Manual* (1837) were widely used in normal schools across North America.[62] Two popular pedagogical approaches, the monitorial and Pestalozzian methods, were also taught across a wide variety of normal schools. These constitute the next topic of this chapter.

The transnational spread of pedagogy: The monitorial method and Pestalozzian pedagogy

Although quite different from one another, both the monitorial and Pestalozzian pedagogical approaches circulated widely through parts of Britain, continental Europe, the Americas, and in the case of the monitorial method, in Africa and Australasia. The global spread of these pedagogies is an excellent example of the transnational nature of teaching in the age of empire.

The monitorial method was established in the late eighteenth century to educate large numbers of pupils cheaply and efficiently, meeting the needs of growing public education systems described above. Two teachers stand out for developing and promoting the method. The first was Andrew Bell who practiced this approach in his school for soldiers' orphans in Madras, India. His method became known as the Madras system. Bell returned to England in 1796 and urged the adoption of his system as the most effective way to spread popular education. He published *An Experiment in Education, Made at the Male Asylum of Madras*, providing an account of his use of monitors in his school.[63] Two years later, Joseph Lancaster opened a day school in London, England, and also needed a system that was cheap and easily applied to educate large numbers of children from the poor classes. The Lancastrian method, similar to Bell's, required the teacher to first teach a group of older children who would then teach a smaller group of younger children.[64]

The Madras, Lancasterian, Bell-Lancaster systems, and monitorial method (different names for the same approach) necessitated the active role of the teacher in the classroom. The teacher was responsible for training a group of ten- and eleven-year-old pupils (monitors) outside of school hours. The teacher would supervise all of the pupils in a single large classroom, while the monitors taught groups of younger students, drilling the pupils in ways he had been previously drilled by the teacher. The teacher remained in charge of the school and, while hundreds of pupils were receiving instruction, he would organize, reward, and punish the monitors. Lessons were tightly and efficiently organized and planned by the teacher, in terms of the time spent in each part of the lesson and content covered.[65]

The monitorial method spread throughout five continents (Africa, Australasia, Europe, North and South America) in the first half of the nineteenth century. The diffusion of the method occurred through diverse processes, including the work of UK-based voluntary societies as well as political and educational reformers. However, above all, the system was spread through the work of teachers, initially Bell and Lancaster, and thereafter hundreds of missionary teachers and teachers trained in the method either as monitors themselves or at various monitorial training institutions.[66]

The Lancasterian method was initially associated with the BFSS and the Madras (Bell's) method with the National Society. Both societies developed model schools in London to train monitorial teachers: the BFSS Borough Road (BR), and the National Society Central School. These institutions, especially the BR, became sites where teachers trained in this method and then traveled abroad and established monitorial schools, creating the conditions for the transnational circulation of this approach. As Kaestle explains, "the system passed from teacher to monitor and from school to school. This training process illustrates the recursive nature of the system; it could recreate itself, expanding to occupy all the vacuum of ignorance in the world."[67]

Lancaster was not only a successful teacher but also an excellent promoter of the system he claimed to have invented. In 1810, he made seven separate tours and gave seventy-six lectures in England. In 1811, he visited Ireland and helped to establish the Kildare Place Society, which ran a model school training institution based on the monitorial method, directed by a BR graduate. That same year, the *Edinburgh Review* announced that Lancaster's lectures had resulted in the establishment of over 150 schools in the previous five years. By 1825, there were over 1,100 monitorial schools in Ireland alone.[68]

After 1815, teachers across continental Europe took up this pedagogical approach, addressing the demands for growing state-funded education systems. A model school was first established in Paris in 1816, under Reverend Francis

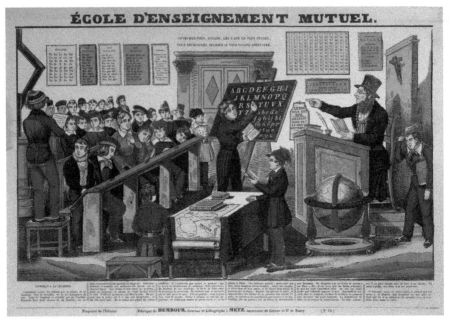

FIGURE 6.4 Teaching with the Monitorial System (School of Mutual Instruction), nineteenth century, engraving, Paris. Carnavalet Museum. © Getty Images.

Martin, who was trained at the BR. The method spread throughout France with 1,200 schools running by 1820 (see Figure 6.4). Teachers were sent from Russia to train at the BR and returned to spread the method within their country. Monitorial schools were also established in Bulgaria, Denmark, Sweden, Italy, and the Ionian Islands in Greece.[69]

Reformers in Spain engaged in the quest to build a modern educational system also took interest in the monitorial method and soon it was considered "the only plausible alternative for spreading schooling in a short time and at a low cost."[70] The system became the centerpiece in the Spanish government's modernization plans and spread throughout the country following the establishment of the first schools in Càdiz in 1818. The first monitorial model school in Madrid became the main institution for training teachers in the system.[71] The system also spread throughout Spanish America, meeting the demands of those engaged in building mass education systems. The teacher-missionary, James Thomson, implemented the method in Buenos Aires in 1818. Five years later, Lancaster arrived in Caracas to promote the benefits of his method. Eventually, teachers in Argentina, Brazil, Chile, Colombia, Cuba, Ecuador, Guatemala, Mexico, Panama, Puerto Rico, and Uruguay established monitorial schools. By the end of the 1820s, approximately one-eighth to one-third of all primary schools in South America were using the method; and by the 1830s it was also spreading through Central America.[72]

The monitorial method similarly spread across the northeastern and parts of the southern United States in the early nineteenth century. The Free School Society in New York City, organized by teacher Thomas Eddy, was running eleven monitorial schools by 1825. In Philadelphia, Thomas Scattergood opened a monitorial school in 1808. By 1819, when Lancaster arrived in the United States, there were more than 150 monitorial schools there.[73]

The monitorial method also spread to British and French colonies, mainly through the work of the voluntary societies and missionary teachers. Students from Madagascar and Ghana traveled to London to train in the monitorial methods, returning to their countries and establishing monitorial schools there.[74] Monitorial schools were also established in Sierra Leone and South Africa as it was "considered advantageous for use in colonial settings due to the reduced need for multiple teachers."[75] Other colonies where the monitorial method took root included Australia, Ceylon, and India; and Jamaica, the Bahamas, and Dominica in the Caribbean.[76] And finally, the method was taken up within the Ottoman Empire in the later nineteenth century. An English writer described a typical monitorial school in Istanbul with 100 to 200 pupils, under the supervision of the monitors and direction of the teacher, learning and reciting verses written in Arabic from the Quran.[77]

The impact of the spread of this pedagogical method was immense. As Kaestle writes, "in an international context, the monitorial school movement was the most important single development in education in the first three decades of the nineteenth century."[78] Key to the spread of this method were the training institutions/model schools themselves, which became sites of cultural encounter between teachers and monitors (in training). Monitorial model schools were established in London, Bogota, Dublin, Madrid, Paris, and Philadelphia. Teachers were trained in monitorial methods at these institutions and once they returned to their home settings they either taught in existing schools using the new method they had learned or established their own monitorial schools. Monitorial teachers then trained further monitors who would then, over time, establish their own schools, demonstrating the recursive nature of the system.[79]

Others were involved in the spread of the monitorial method, including missionary teachers, educational and political reformers, and proponents of the method associated with the two voluntary societies. The diffusion of the method resulted in many interconnections between such individuals, all committed to spreading the system. Teaching was thus constructed within the global interconnections and flows of the monitorial method. The movements of teachers, missionaries, and educational reformers made possible the spread of the method as a form of cultural transfer. This is not a story of a one-way transfer of a pedagogical approach from the West (England) to the "rest" of the world. The origins of the method were multiple (England, France, India) and the spread of the method occurred in crisscrossing directions across England,

Wales, Ireland, many continental European countries; through parts of Western and Southern Africa; and across the Atlantic Ocean to the Americas. In their social network analysis of the spread of the monitorial system throughout Spanish America, Roldán and Schupp describe the mobility actions of the early adopters of the system: "geographic mobility occurred in several directions: among the first introducers of the method in Spanish America we find both 'foreigners'—British, French or Spaniards who travelled to Spanish America where they implemented the method—and the 'locals'—Spanish Americans who travelled to Europe, learned the method there, and then put it into practice when they returned to their countries."[80]

By the 1830s the monitorial method had begun to be discredited as educational reformers and teachers developed interest in more progressive pedagogies such as those espoused by the Swiss educator Johann Heinrich Pestalozzi. Pestalozzi was concerned about the condition of the poor and his schools in Switzerland primarily served poor populations. In 1800, he opened a school in Burgdorf and, while teaching there, systemized and codified many of his methods and ideas about education. Five years later, he established a new institute in Yverdon. Pestalozzi emphasized that every aspect of a child's life contributed to the formation of her/his personality, character, and capacity to reason. Pestalozzi believed in the ability of every individual to learn and in the right of every individual to education. The pupil was viewed as an active learner, learning from experiences and observation. Through such an education, the well-being of each individual could be improved and each could become a responsible citizen.[81]

According to Pestalozzi, the teacher played a significant role in the classroom. Pestalozzian methods of teaching placed a premium upon movement and activity in the classroom. Teachers were instructed to be kind and gentle, and to keep children in constant activity, not to lecture to them or require that they merely listen. Lessons were to be in the form of a continual conversation, using the method of simultaneous repetition. Teachers were instructed to stimulate pupils' interests and create in them a desire to learn by talking with them, telling them curious anecdotes, giving them something interesting to expect from one lesson to the next, and using illustrations and physical objects from the natural world.[82]

Pestalozzi's methods were based on individual differences, sense perception, and the student's self-activity. Each child's faculties were to be developed in harmony with one another. The principle of harmonious development of all the faculties necessitated that instruction be progressive, proceed from the known to the unknown, with facts taught before causes, the concrete before the abstract, and simple principles before rule. From amongst the various methods of instruction available, the teacher was to select the best approach(es) for teaching each pupil.[83]

Pestalozzi's schools drew pupils from many countries, becoming sites of cultural transfer in the diffusion of Pestalozzian methods. In the early 1800s, individuals from Switzerland and Germany visited Pestalozzi's institute at Burgdorf. Later, the Yverdon Institute became famous, drawing in visitors from across Europe, Britain, and North America. Initially, Pestalozzian methods spread through Switzerland, and then more widely outside of Switzerland, largely due to the geographic mobility of teachers who studied at Pestalozzi's institutes and then went on to implement Pestalozzian pedagogies within their own teaching contexts. For instance, German educators Friedrich Fröbel and J.F. Herbart went on educational study tours to Yverdon to observe the teaching methods deployed there. Fröbel spent two years at Yverdon and in 1805 was hired as a teacher at the Pestalozzian Frankfurt Model School. Inspired by Pestalozzi's ideas about children and learning, Fröbel established the foundations for the Kindergarten system in Germany.

From Germany, the system spread outwards. As Pinoche explained, "Pestalozzi's ideas had the most rapid and most widespread influence, and the best application, one may even say that it was through Germany that it penetrated into other countries."[84] The Pestalozzian school in Berlin and model school in Königsberg, which opened in 1805 and 1809 respectively, became so popular that "the first course of lectures was attended by 104 superintendents and pastors, and the second by 70 clergymen and teachers."[85] Infant schools were established in France based on Pestalozzian pedagogy due to the influence of Marie Pape-Carpentier (1815–78), a Pestalozzian-inspired inspector general of infant schools.

Individuals from England and Ireland also visited Pestalozzi's Swiss Institutes. John H. Synge spent three months at Yverdon in 1814 and then returned to Ireland to establish a school based on the Pestalozzian system in Abbeyleix, Ireland. Charles Orpen, an Irish teacher of students with disabilities, spent three months in 1817 visiting Pestalozzi in Yverdon. Upon his return, he began to promote the Pestalozzian method within Ireland, leading to the spread of Pestalozzian methods into the Society for Promoting the Education of the Poor in Ireland. From England, James Greaves visited Yverdon in 1818, teaching there until 1822.[86]

Pestalozzian ideas also enjoyed widespread popularity outside of Britain and Europe. Anne Langton, from England, was tutored at Pestalozzi's Yverdon Institute. She immigrated to Upper Canada (at that time a British colony) in the 1830s and established a school based upon Pestalozzian pedagogy.[87] In 1803, William Mure, impressed with Pestalozzi's schools, which he studied during a trip to Europe, convinced a Frenchman to establish a Pestalozzian school in the United States. The Pestalozzi movement gained momentum in the United States in the 1860s, primarily through the efforts of E.A. Sheldon who imported Pestalozzian teaching materials to Oswego, New York, where he was the school superintendent. This led to the establishment of the Normal School of Oswego, which became the center of US Pestalozzian education.[88]

Pestalozzian methods were taken up in other teacher training institutions. During the 1850s, the Normal School of Upper Canada began to provide lectures on Pestalozzian methods of teaching; the headmaster from 1847 to 1866 introduced Pestalozzian object teaching into the model schools. And, as noted above, Pestalozzian pedagogy was also taken up in US normal schools. Similarly, the Pestalozzi-Fröbel Haus was founded in 1882 in Germany to train early childhood teachers. Pestalozzian pedagogy was also implemented within elementary education teacher training institutions across Britain where students were taught by lectures with illustrations and demonstrations based on the Pestalozzian model.[89]

Pestalozzian methods, such as object teaching, were considered particularly well suited for young children. Object teaching became very popular in Britain following the 1830 publication of Elizabeth Mayo's book, *Lessons on Objects*.[90] Elizabeth Mayo, teacher and educational reformer, and her brother Charles, lived with Pestalozzi from 1819 to 1822 at Yverdon. Inspired by Pestalozzi's ideas, Charles returned to England to work with his sister, and together they established the beginnings of formal education of early childhood teachers in Britain drawing upon Pestalozzian principles in their work.[91] Indeed, many viewed Pestalozzian pedagogies as more appropriate for infant and early years schooling, in comparison to the monitorial school method, which aimed to meet the needs of mass elementary school systems, primarily for the poor.

Both methods gained popularity within England, Wales, Ireland, and many Central, Western, and Northern European countries. The monitorial method spread to a number of French and British colonies in West and Southern Africa, Australia, Ceylon, India, Jamaica, and the Bahamas. To meet the needs of emerging public education systems, the monitorial method was implemented through the work of educators and educational reformers in many parts of the United States as well as emerging nation-states in Latin America. The spread of these methods was not linear but rather teachers, reformers, schools, and training institutions from different nations became interconnected with one another through processes associated with the spread of both approaches. This is why a nation-state focused history is unsatisfactory in teasing out the complexities of what teachers and teaching were like in the age of empire. A transnational lens helps us to see the ways in which teachers using and being trained in monitorial and Pestalozzian methods across a range of settings, both nation-state and colonial, were entangled with one another through these cultural transfers.

CONCLUSION

Using a theoretical framework of new cultural transnational history, this chapter has provided a broad overview of teachers and teaching by shifting our attention from the nation-state to other actors such as individuals, communities, institutions, and societies that shaped and influenced teaching during the age of empire. Attempting to write such a chapter on the history of teachers and teaching from

1800 to 1920 inevitably means having to neglect some topics. These include the feminization and professionalization of teaching as well as histories of teachers in South Asia, the Middle East, and many other parts of the world. Nonetheless, this chapter has decentered Europe by addressing teaching and teaching across a variety of non-Western settings, and included the experiences of Indigenous educators, dame-school teachers and missionary teachers with the aim to illustrate the multiplicity of narratives about teachers and teaching. In this way, our notion of whose story counts within histories of teachers and teaching has been broadened, reaching beyond accounts of teachers in formal, state schools to teachers in a variety of nonformal settings outside of public education systems. By focusing on the connections of teachers within their local communities, especially early in the nineteenth century, and then global connections among teachers who traveled for work and training in various pedagogical methods, this chapter has shown the ways in which teachers and teaching, in the age of empire, were constructed in interconnections enabled through movements and entangled flows between different people, places, sites, and regions.

CHAPTER SEVEN

Literacies

MAXINE BURTON, HEATHER ELLIS, AND GARY MCCULLOCH

INTRODUCTION

Historical accounts make an unequivocal link between literacy and culture. To take two examples, David Vincent's book title, *Literacy and Popular Culture*, and Jeffrey Brooks's statement that "A popular culture based on common literacy arose in Russia from 1861 to 1917" acknowledge that literacy is not viewed now as an autonomous skill or commodity, but can only be fully evaluated within its social and historical contexts.[1] The immense changes during the nineteenth century in society, education, scientific knowledge, and working patterns were to affect opportunities for acquiring literacy, the requirement to be literate, and attitudes to literacy.

The seminal event in the history of literacy in many different countries is often taken to be the introduction of compulsory elementary schooling. It would be misleading to assume that this in itself created universal literacy, although writers such as David Barton do acknowledge that it created the expectation of universal literacy.[2] As will be discussed below, the relationship between schooling and literacy levels is not a simple matter of cause and effect. And as Vincent notes with respect to England, the consequences of the coming of mass literacy must be sought in the diverse areas of activity in which the skills of reading and writing were practiced.[3] Above all, the history of literacy can only be fully understood in terms of its social and cultural contexts, a position that has been advocated by literacy writers such as Brian Street, Harvey Graff, and David Barton. Likewise, there is no "single monolithic literacy," hence the term "literacies" appears more appropriate than a straightforward reference to literacy.[4]

Over the course of the period covered by this volume, the general trend involved a change from literacy skills being acquired in the home or workplace, to more formal systems of acquisition in the classroom. As Jenny Cook-Gumpertz has argued, we should not think of a "shift from [...] total illiteracy to literacy, but rather from a hard-to-estimate multiplicity of literacies, a *pluralistic* idea about literacy as a composite of different skills related to reading and writing for many different purposes and sections of a society's population to a twentieth-century notion of a single, standardised schooled literacy."[5] By 1920, we can truly speak of "mass" literacy with schooling becoming generally universal and compulsory, and literacy acquisition being firmly linked with childhood and the classroom. However, as Patricia Crain has pointed out, despite this dominance of the concept of "schooled literacy," "new histories of literacy find reading and writing in unintended places."[6]

According to dictionary definitions, the meanings of literacy in the nineteenth century hinged on a question of (formal) education. The term "literacy," to cover the processes and implications of reading and writing, did not exist until at least the late nineteenth century, when it was, as Raymond Williams suggests, "a new word invented to express the achievement and possession of what were increasingly seen as general and necessary skills."[7] Definitions of literacy must avoid reference to a fixed standard; for example, Gordon and Gordon argue that it is "the degree of interaction with written text that enables a person to be a functioning, contributing member of society in which that person lives and works."[8]

The nineteenth-century word "literate" seems to be derived from the earlier term "illiterate," stemming ultimately from the Latin, *illiteratus*, unlettered, making the latter the normal or linguistically "unmarked" label.[9] Nowadays, as Sam Duncan notes, the label of illiteracy comes with a literate society.[10] That label carries a definite stigma, created in part through the construction in the nineteenth century of the stereotype of the illiterate as stupid and oftentimes criminal.[11]

MEASURING LITERACY

Any description of literacies in this period must not neglect to mention the "Literacy Myth" and its corollary, the "Great Divide." The Literacy Myth as a conceptualization of the value of literacy was first expounded by Harvey Graff. It refers to "the belief, articulated in educational, civic, religious, and other settings, contemporary and historical, that the acquisition of literacy is a necessary precursor to and invariably results in economic development, democratic practice, cognitive enhancement, and upward social mobility."[12] The other side of this equation is the Great Divide theory, which is characterized in the following terms:

There is a "great divide" between "illiterates" and "literates." For individuals this is taken to mean that ways of thinking, cognitive abilities, facility in logic, abstraction and higher order mental operations are all integrally related to the achievement of literacy: the corollary is that "illiterates" are presumed to lack all of these qualities.[13]

Graff criticizes the tendency to contrast literacy "in its mythic form with a series of opposing values that have resulted in reductive dichotomies such as 'oral-literate,' 'literate-pre-literate,' 'literate-illiterate,' and other binaries that caricature major social changes."[14] It seems much more likely to have been the case that nineteenth-century literacy existed on a continuum whereby more people could read than write, and where, in practice, a clear line between literate and illiterate individuals must have been difficult to draw.[15]

At a general level, Vincent identifies three phases of literacy growth connected with three groups of countries within Europe. Before 1800, mass literacy in terms of reading skill had been virtually achieved in Sweden, Denmark, Finland, Iceland, Scotland, and Geneva, while parts of France, Germany, and England were not far behind. "Beyond them, in the further reaches of eastern and southern Europe, literacy could not be taken for granted at any level."[16] Over the following century, literacy rates increased in most if not all countries. Yet there were different measures of literacy, and these are often difficult to gauge with certainty. Reliance on quantitative evidence can be misleading, although the development of qualitative methods in this area helps to provide a more rounded picture of the uses no less than the incidence of literacy.

In England, the main quantitative sources of evidence since the mid-eighteenth century (after Hardwick's Marriage Act of 1754) have been signatures on marriage registers, with all spouses being required on marriage to sign the marriage register or to make a mark if they were unable to sign. After 1839, the statistics from marriage registers were collected and published annually by the Registrar General of Births, Deaths and Marriages. Since Lawrence Stone's highly influential article on literacy, published in 1969, historical attention to this source of data has grown greatly, and this has raised significant issues in historical method. Relying on these registers can only give a partial account, as signatures—a very restricted definition of literacy—offer no evidence of reading ability or the ability to write anything else.[17]

W.B. Stephens in his major survey argues that, although it provides only a crude and imperfect yardstick, such evidence constitutes "a valuable measure of the maximum numbers able to write."[18] Elsewhere, he acknowledges that signature statistics are not valuable as an absolute measure, but he contends that they are useful as a means of comparison.[19] Evidence is fragmentary and often misleading before the 1830s, but still allows tentative estimates both of general levels of literacy and of differences between localities and genders and ages.[20] With regard to the period 1830–70, Stephens argues that the reservoir of evidence based on census material and on the annual reports of the Registrar General of Births, Deaths and Marriages is "enormous."[21]

Like Stephens, Vincent makes extensive use of marriage registers as his principal source of quantitative evidence. According to Vincent, marriage registers do offer a "standardised body of evidence" and with the requirement to give information on age, occupation, and residence, "permit analysis of some of the more important determinants of literacy."[22] Vincent suggests that literate and illiterate England were almost exactly balanced at the end of the 1830s. By the middle of the nineteenth century, almost all the ceremonies involving middle-class grooms were literate, but only a quarter involving grooms from the skilled working classes were, and the proportion of fully literate ceremonies did not reach 50 percent until 1879.[23] David Mitch's detailed study of the rise of literacy in Victorian England again uses marriage registers as the prime source of quantitative evidence.[24]

In other countries, different quantitative measures have been used. In Sweden, church registers recorded results of examinations in reading and bible knowledge. Only after passing this exam was a person entitled to take Holy Communion and get married, an incentivized literacy.[25] It has often been claimed that Sweden had nearly universal literacy rates from early in the nineteenth century, but more recent research shows widely differing estimates arising from various sources, suggesting that different kinds of literacy are being measured.[26]

Spain is a rather different case, with persistently high levels of illiteracy throughout the nineteenth century. Census data can be used following the first census, in 1860, to provide relevant information. In that year, about 70 percent of the population aged ten or over could not write and/or read, according to this official census. Further analysis indicates that 20 percent could both read and write, while 45 percent could read only. The male illiteracy rate ran at 64.8 percent, while that for females was 86 percent.[27] Military records provide supplementary data from the end of the nineteenth century, suggesting continuing high levels of illiteracy.[28]

Service in the armed forces can often highlight literacies, in terms of records detailing both measurement of literacy levels as well as the desirability or necessity of literacy. As warfare modernized and became more technically complex throughout the nineteenth and twentieth centuries, literacy skills came to be viewed as a prerequisite for effective soldiering. In the British Army throughout the nineteenth century functional literacy became a requirement for all soldiers above the lowest ranks. As early as the Peninsular War (1807–14) soldiers of the Experimental Corps of Riflemen were offered basic education (reading, writing, arithmetic) to enable promotion to the rank of sergeant.

As Barbara Hately-Broad has written, "By the First World War army education in Britain had come to be widely regarded by the authorities as a means of developing motivation and ensuring an effective fighting force, whilst for soldiers themselves it was often a necessary prerequisite for securing promotion."[29] This situation was formalized in 1918 with the creation of the Educational Training Scheme, which included classes in English and arithmetic. There always seems to have been a significant proportion of recruits with literacy (and numeracy) difficulties, statistics that came to the forefront especially at times of mass conscription such as the First World War. This was happening despite the existence of universal compulsory elementary education, first established in England with the Elementary Education Act of 1870. The year 1918 also saw the Fisher Act, which raised the school-leaving age to fourteen.

Elsewhere, in Prussia, by the 1860s literacy was a requirement for obtaining commissions. In Russia, despite literacy levels lagging behind much of Europe, in 1867 reading was made compulsory for all the lower ranks of the army; a reduced term of active service was presented as the incentive.[30] In the USA, the analysis of Northern Army soldiers' educational attainments between 1862 and 1864, during the Civil War, reveals an intake of recruits from predominantly Northern states plus Canada, England, Scotland, Ireland, Germany, and "other countries."[31] Up to 20 percent of those born in Kentucky, Tennessee, Canada, and Ireland had never received any schooling; Scottish-born soldiers had received the most education. With America's entry into the First World War in 1917, all recruits had to undergo literacy tests. According to Gordon and Gordon, "twenty-five percent of all draftees were found to be illiterate. Ten million men registered for the draft. Approximately 700,000 were totally illiterate. It was not uncommon for federal officers to arrest illiterate 'draft dodgers' who did not know of the draft or that the country was even at war."[32]

The case of Japan presents further challenges for historians seeking quantitative evidence for literacy, as signatures were not used as marks of personal identification and there was no national census until 1920. On the other hand, the Army Ministry of Japan has extensive records of examinations given to new recruits from the final years of the nineteenth century, showing that in 1899 about 25 percent of Japan's twenty-year-old males were totally illiterate and a further 30 percent had only "little learning." Moreover, a literacy test given in 1881 to all 882 adult males in the remote village of Tokiwa in central Japan revealed that the overwhelming majority were illiterate, those scoring highest in the test being those from families who performed local administrative tasks.[33]

In Russia, estimates of literacy rates for this period are based mainly on census records. In 1860, the ability to read among male peasants in six out of sixty-nine provinces was only 6 percent (5 percent for serfs, and 9 percent for state and court peasants). This percentage began to increase with the emancipation of the serfs and other reforms of the 1860s, and by the 1897 census, 35 percent of all men and 13 percent of all women could read. Literacy levels varied greatly based on region, estate, and location, urban and rural, but by the time of the 1917 Revolution, 42 percent of the population were literate.[34]

At the same time, qualitative sources highlight the uses made of literacy and the formation of a reading public in many countries during the nineteenth and early twentieth centuries. Jonathan Rose's work has demonstrated the development of a broad reading public inclusive of substantial parts of the new industrial working classes in the context of nineteenth-century England.[35] Vincent has also contributed extensively to this kind of study, by attempting to relate "the often discrete categories of education, family, work, popular beliefs, the imagination and politics," and also by integrating statistical evidence with many different forms of literary evidence.[36] In particular, Vincent utilizes evidence from working-class autobiographies as a complementary means of exploring the application of reading and writing in the distinct areas of the family, the classroom, the workplace, responses to the natural world, the imaginative life of the community, and the political ideology and movements of the nineteenth century.[37] Vincent also highlights the role of the Universal Postal Union in 1874, which linked all European countries in a common system of flat-rate postage (a development from Rowland Hill's penny post in Britain in 1840). It is then possible to look at increasing postal flows as a measure of rising literacy levels.[38]

In the United States, we also see an increasing diversity of reading material toward the end of the nineteenth century, which suggests the growth of a reading public, including the spread of popular magazines from the 1890s.[39] In Spain, too, there were increasing numbers of readers in the second half of the nineteenth century, a new readership for the periodical press, petty literature, and serialized novels, which belied the outward appearance of persistent illiteracy.[40]

Work carried out by historians looking at soldiers' correspondence in the First World War confirms the existence of a broad reading public, stretching across all classes, by the end of the period covered by this volume. As Paul Fussell claims in his seminal work, *The Great War and Modern Memory*,

> By 1914, it was possible for soldiers to be not merely literate but vigorously literary, for the Great War occurred at a special historical moment when two "liberal" forces were powerfully coinciding in England. On the one hand, the belief in the educative powers of classical and English literature was still extremely strong. On the other, the appeal of popular education and "self-improvement" was at its peak and such education was still conceived largely in humanistic terms.[41]

Fussell refers to the "consciousness of a national literary canon" in England, which he claims America lacked.[42] Literary language thus became the medium through which the events of the war were described—"less a problem of linguistics than of rhetoric" because of the presumed inadequacy of language to describe the indescribable.[43] This leads him to make the claim that "only a complete illiterate who very seldom heard narrative of any kind could give an 'accurate' account of a personal experience."[44] Censorship was rigorous, and jargon, cliché, and euphemism conspired with a helping of "British phlegm" to ensure that the reality of the conflict was never revealed to civilians. The essence of this was crystalized in the Field Service Post Card (Form A.2042), the progenitor of modern forms, in which items could be crossed out and blanks filled in by the soldier. It was resolutely upbeat and allowed for no bad news to be transmitted. It required no further censorship and may well have been a boon to the semi-literate soldier (see Figure 7.1).

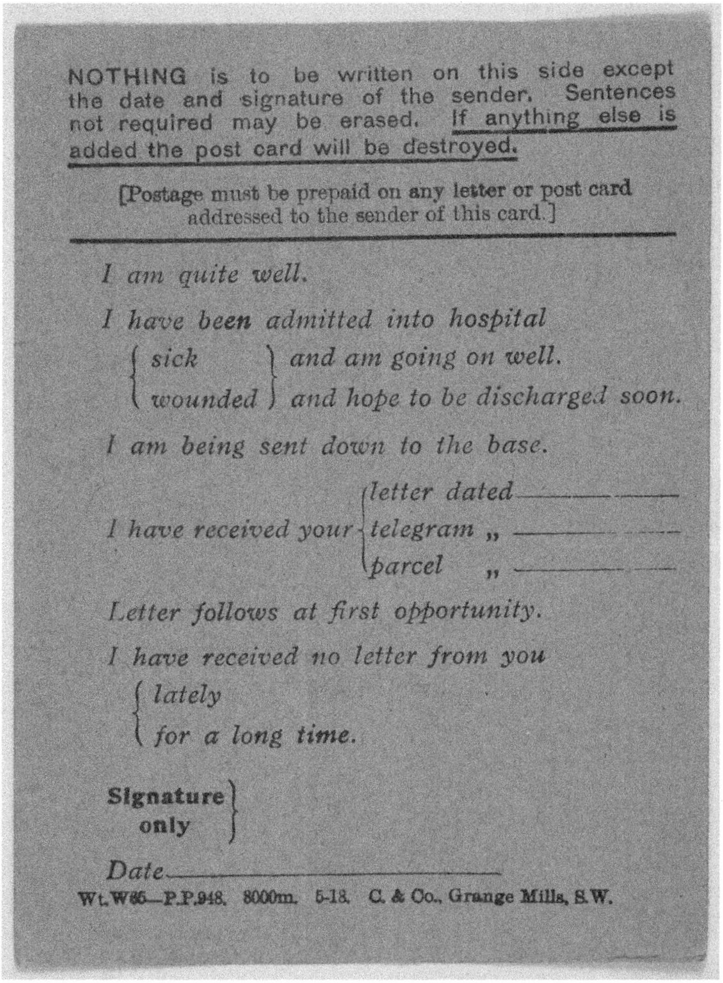

NOTHING is to be written on this side except the date and signature of the sender. Sentences not required may be erased. If anything else is added the post card will be destroyed.

[Postage must be prepaid on any letter or post card addressed to the sender of this card.]

I am quite well.

I have been admitted into hospital
{ *sick* } *and am going on well.*
{ *wounded* } *and hope to be discharged soon.*

I am being sent down to the base.

I have received your { *letter dated* ________
{ *telegram* „ ________
{ *parcel* „ ________

Letter follows at first opportunity.

I have received no letter from you
{ *lately*
{ *for a long time.*

Signature only

Date ________

Wt.W85—P.P.948. 8000m. 5-18. C. & Co., Grange Mills, S.W.

FIGURE 7.1 British Field Service postcard, First World War. © Imperial War Museum.

Further evidence of high literacy levels among soldiers were so-called "war libraries," first set up in Britain between 1914 and 1919 as a sophisticated machinery of book supply for common soldiers. By the end of 1919, Britain had sent to the trenches, to war hospitals, and to prisoners of war no fewer than 16 million books. The Workers' Educational Association, founded in 1903, also took a lead in providing books for its members on the front. Soldiers from many other countries including Australia also took advantage of such schemes for reading books, reflecting the development of literate tastes across society and nations in the early twentieth century.[45]

Nineteenth-century fiction is also a rich source of information about literacy levels and practices,[46] and strikingly illustrates the fact of continuing illiteracy, for example, in Charles Dickens's description of the illiterate crossing sweeper, Jo, in his 1864 novel *Our Mutual Friend*:

It must be a strange state to be like Jo! To shuffle through the streets, unfamiliar with the shapes and in utter darkness as to the meaning of those mysterious symbols, so abundant over the shops, and at the corners of streets, and on the doors, and in the windows! To see people read, and to see people write, and to see the postmen deliver letters, and not to have the least idea of all that language—to be, to every scrap of it, stone blind and dumb![47]

In practice, however, the literate and illiterate were everywhere in each other's company and possessed varying degrees of literacy, and this diversity also emerges from the characters Dickens describes in his novels. Indeed, contemporary fiction of the time—produced, for example, by Victorian novelists in England, especially Dickens and Hardy, Balzac in France, and writers such as Tolstoy, Gogol, and Chekhov in Russia—can give us real insights into literacy practices and attitudes.[48]

SCHOOLING AND LITERACY

The history of literacy in the period 1800–1920 is closely linked to schooling because of the important educational legislation introduced in many parts of the world especially in the final decades of the nineteenth century and the emphasis of elementary schooling on reading, writing and arithmetic. This is not, however, to imply a straightforward causal relationship. Indeed, literacy levels were rising throughout the nineteenth century before universal schooling could have taken effect and it has been argued that this trend might well have continued without state interference.[49] Too often the acquisition of literacy has been treated as an obligation imposed on a population without taking into account the people's desire to acquire it. Working-class acceptance of universal elementary education can also be interpreted as a response to economic developments such as an increase in the number of service jobs and the rise in wages, which helped to compensate for the loss of child labor.[50]

By 1918, most of Europe, all forty-eight states in the USA and many other parts of the world including Japan and some countries in South America had enacted compulsory school attendance legislation. Before the advent of universal elementary schooling, reading and writing could be acquired in a number of different locations, for example, in the home, workplace, or church. Shifting the main responsibility for literacy onto school classrooms was a relatively new concept.[51] In Sweden, responsibility for teaching children had lain entirely with their parents, enforced through the Church Law of 1686. Elementary schools, which taught writing as well as reading, were a later development in 1842, supported by the state rather than the church.

In Russia, it was the peasants themselves who set up their own rural schools long before schooling became compulsory. Primary schooling did not become widely available until the late nineteenth and early twentieth century; before the First World War the majority of peasant children probably attended school but attendance was never made compulsory, and the effect of schooling was limited. Estimates put literacy at 40 percent by 1914.[52] The teaching profession in Russia was not brought under state control until the 1930s; before then priests often functioned as teachers.

The modernization of schooling into mass systems such as the elementary schools in England and the common schools in United States rested in part on the denial and suppression of previously common courses or paths.[53] Before the introduction of universal schemes of elementary education, no form of schooling, or formal schooling itself, had a monopoly.[54] With schooling came the decontextualization of literacy, "increasingly divorced from the child's encounters with language in the home."[55] Ursula Howard expresses this in terms of a real sense of loss experienced by working-class writers in the nineteenth century; while popular schooling may have provided greater numbers of people with more opportunities for skills acquisition this was only at the cost of creativity and self-expression.[56]

With the increasing provision of schooling came the setting up of teacher training colleges for the instruction of schoolteachers and a new focus on the pedagogy of reading instruction. Traditional ABC methods such as those employed in the early modern horn book (see Figure 7.2) came to be challenged by "whole word" methods favored by Pestalozzi, among other educational reformers. These debates continue to the present day. Pestalozzian (child-centered) principles were adopted by, for example, educators Joseph Neef and John M. Keegy in the United States.[57] Schooling also involved a shift from individual to collective teaching.

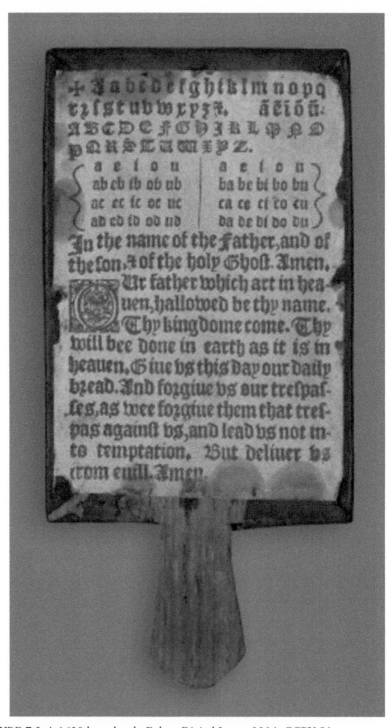

FIGURE 7.2 A 1630 horn book. Folger Digital Image 3304, CCBY-SA.

CLASS, GENDER, AND ETHNICITY

The nineteenth century saw undoubted changes in the extent of literacy amongst the working classes. By then the middle classes and above were for the most part literate; Graff notes exceptions to this generalization, claiming that "illiterate gentlemen and wealthy individuals, some with high-status occupations, are located regularly in historical research."[58] However, this only applied to a small minority and by the nineteenth century the middle class virtually came to wear education and literacy as a badge of status and identification.[59] This is amusingly depicted in Elizabeth Gaskell's 1866 novel, *Wives and Daughters*, in her description of the Hollingsford Book Society, membership of which was considered a "test of gentility":

> No shopkeeper would have thought of offering himself as a member, however great his general intelligence and love of reading; while it boasted on its list of subscribers most of the county families in the neighbourhood, some of whom subscribed to it as a sort of duty belonging to their station, without often using their privilege of reading the books.[60]

To account for the extension of literacy skills—both reading and writing—among the working classes in the period under review requires multiple and interconnected explanations. It is certainly the case that, following the French Revolution of 1789 and the unleashing of revolutionary thought, increased state involvement in elementary education for the masses came to appear more attractive as a way of maintaining control by instilling values, such as piety or patriotism or satisfaction with one's lot in life. But the working and peasant classes in Europe, Russia, and beyond also actively desired and sought out education, especially basic literacy.

According to the "Literacy Myth" explored by Harvey Graff, a close relationship is claimed between literacy and economic development. If literacy did confer social status, to what extent did this affect the working classes? Various writers have attempted to unpack the relationship between increasing levels of working-class literacy and the presence or absence of stigma attached to those who lacked literacy skills. Altick presumes a new status accruing to literacy because of the increasing importance of being able to read under the conditions of industrial life, but both Vincent and Stephens find no evidence for a particular stigma attached to illiteracy.[61] Burton finds a complex picture of the social construction of literacy in nineteenth-century England, with the social mix of literate and illiterate giving way to the increasing portrayal of illiterate stereotypes of deficiency in some respect, notably lack of intelligence.[62] The most straightforward interpretation may hinge on the simple fact of increasing levels of literacy conferring status on literacy; "as the ability to read spread so did its value in social prestige."[63] Conversely, "as literacy became increasingly widespread it is possible that those lacking literacy became increasingly isolated and marginalised both economically and socially."[64] Once universal elementary schooling had been introduced and made compulsory in many parts of the world, literacy came increasingly to be regarded as an individual achievement—or failing.

Geographical considerations played an undoubted role in determining the spread of literacy in Europe, Russia, and North America. A variety of dimensions needs to be considered here including significant differences between predominantly rural, agricultural, and sparsely populated areas on the one hand, and urban, industrial, and densely populated regions on the other. Differences between established regions and newly settled "frontier" areas are also relevant.

Geographical variations played an important role within individual countries too. In England, for example, the key contrast was between urban and rural areas, with the latter lagging behind in terms of literacy levels. This is probably because literacy was perceived to be of less use in agricultural occupations, and attendance at school was likely to be poorer as a result. By the end of the nineteenth century, "the portrayal of the illiterate has marginalised him or her as a rural simpleton."[65] Vincent notes, however, that the increasing mobility of labor, with the movement from agricultural work to industrial employment in towns and cities, expanded the growth of letter writing in order to help maintain family relationships.[66]

For the early New England colonists, there was a close relationship between their Protestant religion and the achievement of literacy; the priority for each household was for their children to be able to read the Scriptures. The War of Independence and the Civil War both had a disruptive effect on educational provision. Soltow and Stevens observe that population density affected the transmission of literacy in the United States, with relatively low levels of literacy in the sparsely populated frontier states to the West.[67] There was also a pattern of decreasing literacy as you moved from north to south.

The difference between levels of male and female literacy in England, which had long seen women lagging behind men, started to change by 1864, when female literacy rates began to overtake male ones, especially in the south of England. Trollope refers to this in his 1875 novel, *The Way We Live Now*, when he describes—for the benefit of his middle-class readers—a Suffolk rural laboring couple in the following terms: the young woman,

> is better educated, has higher aspirations and a brighter imagination, and is infinitely more cunning than the man [...]. She can read, whereas he can only spell words from a book. She can write a letter after her fashion, whereas he can barely spell words out on a paper.[68]

Elsewhere, female literacy tended to lag behind male literacy. Although formal schooling made no distinction between boys and girls in the reading and writing skills being taught, this equality was undermined by the reality of school attendance. Girls were more likely to be kept at home throughout the year to help with domestic duties than boys (who might be required only for seasonal labor), a pattern observed throughout large parts of Europe, Russia, and North America. In her study of literacy and writing practices in nineteenth-century England, Ursula Howard stresses that there were greater constraints on girls' education, which still remained subordinate to family duties.[69] Because of this, nonattendance by girls tended to be viewed as legitimate, whereas boys' nonattendance was considered "truancy."[70]

Nevertheless, female literacy rates did rise, partly in response to the increased middle-class demand for domestic servants, preferably for girls who had attended school; and also due to the very fact of increased opportunities for schooling.[71] Increasing literacy rates among women during the second half of the nineteenth century tend not, however, to be reflected in popular images of women and girls at the time. Howard describes the "gender bias" underlying "popular images" in historical and fictional writing, one assumption being that women learners and writers were the exception rather than the rule.[72] It has been suggested that the working classes in England may even have valued literacy for women more highly than the middle classes did, a finding based on evidence from parliamentary papers and Victorian fiction.[73] This may be related to the dominant (bourgeois) ideology about women which maintained that "the ideal location for women was in the private sphere of the home as full-time wives and mothers" rather than the school or workplace.[74]

In Russia, on the eve of the First World War, the participation of girls in secondary education had increased dramatically, with more girls than boys enrolled. It has been claimed that this fact accounted for the "increasing feminization" of the teaching profession over the years from 1880 to 1914.[75] In America, females also predominated in the teaching profession, to an even greater extent.

In the United States and in many other parts of the world, ethnic considerations also came into play, with the influx of settlers from Europe, to add to the First Nations people, and also African Americans. Literacy was regarded as an important means of acculturation for Native Americans as well as a symbol of freedom and dignity, a significance it also held for African Americans.[76] In the early nineteenth century, slaves were often eager to attend schools to gain instruction, with literacy highly prized as a way of securing privileges, prestige, and acquiring practical skills. In the United States, in particular, literacy was associated with radicalism and freedom, while it also reduced isolation and threatened to overturn the traditional relationship between slaves and their owners long before slavery was banned by constitutional amendment in 1865.[77]

SCIENTIFIC AND TECHNICAL LITERACY

While "scientific literacy" as a term only appeared in the early 1960s, campaigns to increase the "public understanding of science" have much older roots going back to the late eighteenth and early nineteenth centuries.[78] Writing in 1789, on the eve of the French Revolution, the chemist and prominent member of the Lunar Society of Birmingham, James Keir, declared that "the diffusion of general knowledge and of a taste for science, over all classes of men, in every nation of Europe or of European origin, seems to be the characteristic feature of the modern age."[79] The benefits of science were extolled vigorously by a range of institutions, most prominently mechanics' institutes, lyceums, and apprentices' libraries, which began to be established in considerable numbers from the 1820s onwards. Jin-Woong Song has described the Mechanics' Institute movement as "the first major case in which science met the needs of people particularly through education."[80] As the preamble to the Manchester Mechanics' Institute, founded in 1824, stated, its aim was to enable working men "to become acquainted with such branches of science as are of practical application in the exercise of [their] trade, that they may possess a more thorough knowledge of their business."[81]

In his 1995 study, *The Grammar of the Machine*, Edward W. Stevens argued that the changes taking place in the US economy as the country moved toward a manufacturing base and mass production in the first half of the nineteenth century required nothing less than a "new" type of literacy from working men. He described what he termed "technical literacy" as "qualitatively different from (though it included) alphabetic literacy." Indeed, it required familiarity with multiple notational systems including not only the traditional alphabet but also scientific notation, mathematical notation, and spatial-graphic representation. It fell largely to the mechanics' institutes and similar institutions to teach this new literacy, a task rendered particularly difficult, Stevens argued, by the fact that, unlike alphabetic literacy, it required the merger of "a culture of print with a non-verbal culture of experience."[82]

The first mechanics' institute was founded in Edinburgh in October 1821 and was designed to provide technical education for working men in the local area. A second institute in Scotland was established in Glasgow in 1823. This had developed out of an earlier group set up at the start of the century by George Birkbeck who had earlier introduced free lectures on arts, science, and technical subjects in 1800. The first mechanics' institute in England was opened at Liverpool in 1823 followed by the London Mechanics' Institute (which would later become Birkbeck College). By 1850, there were over 700 institutes in towns and cities across Britain and overseas with over 120,000 members.

The movement grew globally, spreading across the Atlantic to the USA and Canada as well as to the rest of Britain's settler colonies in particular Australia and New Zealand. India also had several mechanics' institutes including in Calcutta and Bombay, which offered courses in physical science, manufacturing, commerce, lithography, printing, pottery, metallurgy, and agriculture.[83] Yet it was not only in the English-speaking world that mechanics' institutes proved influential. Writing in 1851, J.W. Hudson noted that an institute had been established in Hamburg in 1848. Yet, as Martyn Walker has shown, mechanics' institutes were not as numerous in Germany as in Britain because of the already well-established system of technical education. Walker also cites the example of the French mathematician and engineer, Charles Dupin, who, having visited the mechanics' institutes in Glasgow and London on several occasions, "undertook the challenge of convincing the French government of the importance of offering working-class adult education through providing state financial support." Institutes were subsequently founded in Lyon, La Rochelle, Nevers, Metz, and Versailles.[84]

Patrick Keane has argued that the expansion of mechanics' institutes across the world should be viewed as an important part of what he terms the "international useful knowledge movement."[85] However, while taking account of its global reach, it is important to recognize mechanics' institutes and technical literacy, more broadly, as particular products of the Industrial Revolution, which began in Britain before spreading to other parts of Europe and the United States in the first half of the nineteenth century.[86]

In addition to mechanics' institutes, we need to gain a fuller picture of the cultural lives, organizations, and mobilities of working men and artisans who were critical in the dissemination of scientific and technical literacy in this period. In seeking the intellectual origins of the Industrial Revolution, Margaret Jacob has investigated artisanal mathematical knowledge, in particular, the widespread diffusion of Newtonian mechanics in England, France, the Netherlands, and Germany.[87] In a French context, Liliane Hilaire-Pérez has researched the personal itineraries of artisans, their collective communities and the ways in which particular techniques spread as artisans traveled within Europe and moved from one trade to another.[88]

By the middle of the nineteenth century, mechanics' institutes and similar institutions offering scientific and technical education had lost much of their original raison d'etre. In Britain, the establishment of the government Education Department in 1856 and the foundation of the civic universities in many provincial cities later in the century saw the provision of technical education move elsewhere. In the United States, colleges increasingly took over the function of scientific and technical instruction, while evening lectures were increasingly attended by members of the middle classes, who demanded talks on a much wider variety of topics.

CONCLUSION

The nineteenth and early twentieth century was a period that saw huge changes not only in levels but also in understandings of literacy. In 1800, reading and writing were practices that took place in a variety of locations including in the home, places of worship, and in the workplace; levels of literacy varied widely with, for example, many more people able to read than write; literacy skills were also used to varying degrees and for many different purposes. By 1920, schools (and mostly schools run by the state) had become the main instructor in literacy skills and the sole custodian of literacy standards; and across large parts of the world, the vast majority of children from all classes and backgrounds would be subject to compulsory instruction in reading and writing with literacy viewed as a necessary personal attribute.

The relationship between the rise of mass elementary education and literacy is complex; but it certainly helped to raise expectations of literacy across large parts of the globe. While literacy levels rose significantly in almost all parts of the world during the nineteenth century, there remained significant differences between men and women, urban and rural communities, working and middle classes, and between different ethnic groups within societies. In this way, while the acquisition of literacy skills could be empowering and emancipatory for some, for others it merely underscored existing power differentials and inequalities.

The period 1800–1920 was one that witnessed unprecedented, large-scale interventions in the literary practices of working-class people and not only through the provision of universal, compulsory mass elementary education. The first half of the nineteenth century, in particular, also saw the widespread provision of scientific and technical education for adults through a range of institutions and organizations, most prominently mechanics' institutes. Here, working men, in particular, received training in what Edward Stevens has termed a new form of "technical literacy," combining alphabetic literacy with the ability to understand and apply mathematical and scientific notation.

CHAPTER EIGHT

Life Histories

ALYS BLAKEWAY, SUE ANDERSON-FAITHFUL,

JOYCE GOODMAN, AND STEPHANIE SPENCER

INTRODUCTION

This chapter explores educational life history through Lawrence Cremin's view of educational biography as a "life history prepared with educational matters uppermost in mind."[1] Cremin maintains that individuals bring their histories to their interactions with "configurations" of educational institutions, which he describes as "the multiplicity of individuals and institutions that educate," which include parents, peers, siblings, friends, families, churches, synagogues, libraries, museums, settlement houses, etc. "Each configuration," writes Cremin, "interacts with the others and within the larger society that sustains it and that is in turn affected by it."[2] As a result, he argues, life histories demonstrate commonalities but also "variegations" as they play out in different ways with different outcomes.

Cremin's approach to life histories and configurations forms part of his cultural definition of education as "the deliberate, systematic and sustained effort to transmit, evoke or acquire knowledge, attitudes, values, skills or sensibilities, as well as any outcomes of that effort."[3] Cohen critiques Cremin's approach to education as overly expansive and unfocused, and for generating a history of "culture," or of "civilisation," rather than a history of education.[4] Critiques of Cremin also situate his scholarship within a "consensus" view of educational history that assumes the development of American educational practices was the result of philosophical choices rather than social and political dynamics.[5] Other educational historians deploy Cremin's cultural approach to open educational history to previously neglected subjects and hitherto overlooked spaces and places of education. Franklin builds on Cremin's distinction between schooling and configurations to contrast the often inadequate substandard segregated schooling made available to black Philadelphians at public expense and the rich and varied, formal and informal educational programs and activities sponsored by African American social, cultural, and political organizations that he argues were underpinned by a distinctive "African-American *paideia*" emanating from the experiences and cultural values of the African American population.[6] Lagemann draws on Cremin's understanding of configurations to open a space for analysis of women's educational activities and writing.[7] Focusing on familial education prior to the establishment of formal educational opportunities for girls, and on women's use of voluntary associations to further their education, Lagemann illustrates both the commonalities and variegations in life histories that Cremin highlights.

This chapter deploys Cremin's notion of life histories to examine aspects of the educational lives of three women whose educational activism during the nineteenth and early twentieth centuries spanned homes, schools, and voluntary organizations: Charlotte Yonge (1823–1901), Mary Sumner (1828–1921), and Charlotte Mason (1842–1923). Yonge, a famous and successful author in her day, whose annual sales were worth over £1,000 in 1854, worked in Otterbourne School as a volunteer teacher, fundraiser, administrator, and manager. As a successful local Anglican author she was in later years invited to be on the founding committee of what is now St. Swithun's, an independent girls' school in Winchester. She also promoted informal education through her novels, where the characters make a point of reading serious books. To fill gaps in girls' education she used essay societies and her periodical, *The Monthly Packet of Evening Readings for Members of the English Church* (1851–99), which contained a high proportion of informative factual articles.[8] Coming from an Anglican family with Unitarian roots, Sumner's 1848 marriage provided her with access to familial and ecclesiastical networks that spanned the hierarchy of the Anglican Church and facilitated her foundation in 1885 of the Mothers' Union (MU). The MU was adopted as an official Anglican diocesan organization after Sumner's address to an audience of women at the 1885 Portsmouth Church Congress.[9] The MU motto "train up a child in the way he should go" encapsulated the MU's aim to educate mothers in morals, parenting, and pedagogy so that through religious witness they might influence future citizens, husbands, and wider society toward behavior thought to alleviate the social evils of drunkenness, ill health, poverty, and crime.[10] The MU grew rapidly as branches initiated by middle- or upper-class women, drawing on traditions of patronage and philanthropy, attracted support from less socially advantaged women. Mason's educational philosophy was grounded in the view that education was "an atmosphere, a discipline and a life."[11] A trained teacher and teacher educator, she began the Parents' National Education Union (PNEU) in 1890 in Bradford with a view to providing a holistic liberal education that could be applied to all social classes, in schools and homes, and across national borders.[12] Her curriculum included art, music, literature, and science, with an emphasis on nature and a recognition of the importance of a Christian God.

The three women's educational lives suggest connections and commonalities that were not just fostered through a relation to Christianity, important though religion was to their educational activism. Yonge in Otterbourne and Sumner in Winchester were well known to each other, especially through *Mothers in Council (MIC)*, the journal that Yonge edited for the MU during the 1880s and 1890s. Both Yonge and Sumner were also involved in the Girls' Friendly Society (GFS), established in 1875. Sumner and Mason both stressed the significance of the educational role of the mother and there are clear resonances between Sumner's *Home Life,* published in 1895, and Charlotte Mason's *Home Education: A Course of Lectures to Ladies, Etc.*, published in 1886.[13] For her part, Mason briefly considered an amalgamation between the MU and the PNEU in 1900.[14] The three women's educational activities also illustrate the importance of cultural encounters, and transnational and imperial connections to educational lives. Yonge's greatest enthusiasm was Anglican missionary activity in and beyond the British colonies, which she promoted by descriptions of such activity in her fiction and through her biography of Bishop Coleridge Patteson of Melanesia.[15] The MU spread in and beyond British colonies and dominions, with branches in Canada and New Zealand by 1888, in Australia, India, and Ceylon shortly afterwards, and in China, Japan, and South America by the end of the century.[16] A request to translate Mason's writing into Gujerati and Marathi demonstrates the transnational flows of Mason's thought as families following her curriculum moved regularly around the British Empire and back to England, leaving traces of her philosophy behind in local communities.

The chapter draws out three aspects of the educational lives of Yonge, Sumner, and Mason. The first section looks at the women's family and upbringing and touches on their informal and formal education (where the latter was in place). The second section extends Cremin's framework by focusing on some of the cultural encounters and transnational and imperial connections that transcended national physical and conceptual boundaries and were important to the three women's educational activism as they threaded imperial aspects into educational activities "at home." Rather than compiling a comparative account of the women's lives, the chapter highlights elements of significance in writing a life-history account. The conclusion argues that Cremin's framing of educational life histories and the importance he attributes to configurations touches on spatial understandings of individual lives in ways that resonate with Ballantyne and Burton's analysis of spatial logics through which the developing global order was being shaped during the nineteenth and early twentieth century.[17] It also argues that Cremin's framing resonates with Goodson's call for life histories that provide "stories of action within theories of context."[18] Goodson stresses the importance for life histories of how lives are "storied,"[19] which points to aspects of narrative and representation of concern to so-called new cultural histories of education.[20] Finally, the chapter highlights Maria Tamboukou's argument that the meaning that life histories generate is only accessible to the tellers and listeners of the stories, not to their protagonists, at least in the moment of action;[21] and that it is the assemblage of stories as life history that creates archives for historical understanding.

EARLY LIVES AND EDUCATION

Yonge (Figure 8.1) was born in the Hampshire village of Otterbourne, the daughter of two devout Anglicans, a retired army officer and a mother who, as well as running her household, taught her daughter and the children of the village poor. The upbringing and education Yonge received from her parents was to influence her educational experience, practice, and theory. Their Anglican faith was the center of her life. To Yonge, education was above all a medium for the teaching of religion, more precisely, the Anglican religion of the Church of England. In teaching for over seventy years (1830–1901) in her local village school, she followed her mother's example. Having been encouraged to read widely in her father's library, she both offered and promoted a similar informal education through her many novels and works of nonfiction, and through her magazine, *The Monthly Packet*. The intended audiences for her writing varied from the children of the rural working class to daughters of the gentry, and adult gentlefolk.

Mary Sumner (Figure 8.2) also had diverse formative experiences in girlhood, education, and cultural life, which she used in published material to assert her pedagogic credentials and to signal the knowledge and contingent codes of behavior that she prioritized and wished to transmit. Mary Sumner's parents were practicing Anglicans but had been prominent members of the influential Manchester Unitarian Cross Street Chapel, prior to the family's move in 1833 to Hope End, a country estate in Herefordshire. Mary Summer's "Account of Early Life at Hope End," a manuscript prepared in later life to inform her biography, provides evidence that she experienced what, in the context of the time, may be considered a privileged and relatively extensive home education.[22] Both parents took an interest in her education. As former Unitarians they came from a tradition that acknowledged women's intellect, valued their education, and acknowledged women as educators despite envisaging women's roles as being within family life.[23] Travel abroad with the family to European destinations, including Germany, France, Switzerland, and Italy, secured Sumner's command of languages, and together with literature taught by a governess, and training

FIGURE 8.1 Portrait of writer Charlotte Mary Yonge, 1880. Photograph by Mansell/ Mansell/The LIFE Picture Collection via Getty Images.

FIGURE 8.2 Photograph of Mary Sumner. Hampshire Record Office: Diocese of Winchester Mothers' Union Archive: 145M85/A3.

in operatic singing in the fashionable winter destination of Rome, illustrate a breadth of cultural education that Sumner noted in her memoir.[24]

The Heywoods prioritized the personal scrutiny of conscience and public witness of religion, much of which was realized through philanthropy and reflected the commitment to education for the betterment of society characteristic of both the Unitarian tradition and evangelical enthusiasm. In addition to daily Bible study for her own children, like Charlotte Yonge's mother, Mrs. Heywood taught village children at Sunday school, a project to which her son and daughters were expected to contribute. While "cottage visiting" was prohibited by Charlotte Yonge's parents and neither Charlotte nor her mother appear to have visited the schoolchildren when they became fathers and mothers,[25] Mary Sumner considered her parents' personal interventions and befriending the poor "were the means of transforming a wild district into a respectable community," and she recorded her father's philanthropy in building a church and school for the improvement of the working class.[26]

On July 26, 1848, Mary married George Sumner, a nephew of the Archbishop of Canterbury and son of Charles Sumner, the Bishop of Winchester. The formative experience of early married life spent in the household of an evangelical bishop, where George served as his father's chaplain, positioned Mary within a family that sought to uphold Anglicanism against the claims of rival denominations. Lessons learned in childhood on the prioritization of religion in daily life, the duty of philanthropy, and esteem for pious women were affirmed by the Sumners' conduct of family life. George Sumner's mother, Jennie (née Barnadine), was commended for efficient administration of charitable giving and eulogized publicly by diocesan clergy as a moral exemplar and spiritual helpmeet to her husband. Women possessing education were also valued by the Sumners. George's elder sister Louisanna taught him Latin and Greek to prepare him for schooling at Eton.[27]

Both Mary Sumner and Charlotte Yonge left autobiographical accounts that covered their childhood and early youth. These constituted particular self-presentations of the identity that each of the two women chose to present, along with a fabric of assumptions, values, ideas, and associations. These autobiographical fragments also implied the presence of an audience and provided a groundwork on which future biographers might draw.[28] Charlotte Yonge refused the idea of a biography during her lifetime, saying that "her mother would not have liked such a thing to be done";[29] but her biographer Christabel Coleridge notes that Yonge gave her pieces of information about her early days with a view to Coleridge making subsequent use of them in the biography that Yonge expected Coleridge would write after her death. As a friend and relative as well as Yonge's biographer, Coleridge drew on Yonge's correspondence and on the material Yonge had given her as she brought "love" to her struggle to balance the desire of friends for detail and the wish of the general reader for a more general picture of Yonge.[30] Although a large number of Charlotte Yonge's letters survive and are available digitally,[31] Georgina Battiscombe's 1943 biography of Yonge claims that Coleridge appeared to have destroyed all the "invaluable first hand material" that was available for Coleridge's biography.[32] The manuscripts of various kinds that Mary Sumner accumulated across her lifetime, which packed the attics of her Winchester house, were destroyed on her death. As a result, early versions of Sumner's life were written as celebratory organizational accounts with an MU audience in mind. As this chapter illustrates later, in these accounts the "foundress" tended to be equated with the organization.[33] The ambiguity in biographical writing around the "story" of Mason's life is worthy of further consideration in that (as in the case of Sumner) it illustrates Cremin's statement that "one of the most difficult problems in studying educational life histories is to differentiate between the external relationships involved in the patterning of educational institutions and the particular experience of the individual."[34]

The narrative of Charlotte Mason's (Figure 8.3) life first appeared in *The Story of Charlotte Mason* begun by her associate Elsie Kitching and completed by Essex Cholmondeley. *The Story* recounts a lonely experience of being an only child of only children, educated mainly at home by her parents with "some lessons from outside."[35] This analysis presents early educational life as one of self-reflection and observation. Kitching and Cholmondeley situated Mason's family background as securely middle class, the daughter of a Liverpool Merchant. *The Story* suggests that Mason's career decision came after an encounter with a teacher when she decided that "somehow I knew that teaching was the thing to do, and above all the teaching of poor children like those I had been watching."[36] These descriptions that might explain the origins of her methods that would suit children of all social classes came allegedly from "Memories" in *The Parents' Review* and "Recollections" from a manuscript "found after her death." According to Cholmondeley, Mason was acutely aware of the significance of childhood in creating the adult when she explained her rationale for recording her youth: "I shall try to seize those moments when such ideas dropped into me [...] as have since come into play in my educational work [...] the ideas one receives as a child, or rather those one selects, in a whimsical and unaccountable way produce extraordinary effects in after life."[37] An awareness of Mason's lonely childhood spent amongst adults might well explain her focus on the theory and practice of home education. It does not satisfactorily explain the importance of religion in her educational writing and in her reported daily life, or her emphasis on the education of children of all social classes. Mason's authority in later life as a single woman in late Victorian England was dependent upon an impeccable private life, family background, and a calling to teach from an early age. Any hint of irregularity, even as a child, would have compromised her legacy as the "pioneer of sane education" reported in her obituary in *The Times* (January 19, 1923).

Recent research by Margaret Coombs highlights the lengths to which Mason and her loyal biographers went in order to ensure that the "story" of her early life was fit for public consumption. Coombs failed to find any originals or records of "Memories" or "Recollections" and concluded that the early chapters of *The Story* "were an artificial reconstruction [...] to present an appropriate

FIGURE 8.3 Fred Yates's portrait of Charlotte Mason. Courtesy of the Armitt Trust, Ambleside.

background for the founder of the PNEU [...]. Other letters cited in the early chapters, were either unreferenced or actually altered."[38] Coombs describes the alleged documents as presenting a "confusing mixture of stereotype and realism," but notes the intensive attempts to regularize Mason's past do reflect the cultural and social mores of the time and the "traditional veneration for her cultured social standing."[39] Coombs's research revealed that Mason was the illegitimate child of her Quaker father, who already had twelve children, and a young Roman Catholic girl, whom he did eventually marry. As Coombs concludes, Mason's family background now offers a far better understanding of her motivations, the complex role that religion played in her educational philosophy, her financially expedient and Quaker-inspired capacity for hard work, and her insistence that "I do not wish my life to be written, it is the work that matters; it will live."[40] The example of Mason highlights the problem of researching the educational lives of Victorian women whose personal standing was so easily compromised by circumstances out of their control. Coombs suggests that it is unlikely that Mason had nothing to do with her father's family as they also lived in Birkenhead when she was growing up. Stories of her mother as an invalid appear to be accurate; she died at the age of forty, followed some months later by her father. Mason was orphaned by the age of seventeen, at which point Cholmondeley's account becomes less problematic and the record of Mason's educational life history is more straightforward. This conspiracy of silence around her family background was encouraged by Mason and then proliferated from *The Times* obituary to later biographers.

The inference that she was home educated suggests a typical middle-class Victorian experience that might shed light on Mason's determination to provide a sound liberal education for governesses and for the children in their charge. However, Coombs's research records Mason as attending a Church of England national school before becoming a pupil teacher at the age of twelve. The national schools provided a basic education for those lower down the social ladder and also, through the pupil-teacher system, offered a path to social mobility; they were also "synonymous with lower class status."[41] After work as a pupil teacher in Birkenhead, Mason took the Queen's Scholarship exam that provided entrance to teacher training in London at the Home and Colonial College, based on Pestalozzi's methods. Her vocation to teach from the "Memories" is somewhat modified as a necessity to find work that did not compromise aspirations to respectable femininity. It also chimes with her Quaker background and the Friends' adherence to the significance of education.[42] Her lifelong friendships with Selina Heelis (later Fleming) and Elizabeth Pendlebury (later Groveham) originated at the Home and Colonial, where their education not only prepared them as teachers but also gave them the gravitas to be introduced into the wider networks of contemporary women pioneer educators. Ann Jemima Clough employed Selina Heelis to take over her school in Ambleside, in the Lake District, when she moved to be principal of the new Newnham College in Cambridge. Mason's visits to Selina led to her decision to start her House of Education in Ambleside. Networks started at the Home and Colonial enabled Mason to engage later with Clough and Dorothea Beale who both contributed to her *Parents' Review*. Mason's health did not allow her to complete her training at the Home and Colonial, and she was found a teaching position at a church infant school in Worthing.

Correspondence with Pendlebury during this period reflected a spiritual as well as academic growth. Mason completed her teaching certificate in 1863, which gave her professional status as a headmistress.[43] Coombs observed that Mason's association with the local clergy and gentlemen helped her to develop "social graces and a pleasing manner facilitating her rise through the rigid social structures keeping elementary schoolteachers in their place."[44] From the Davison school and the completion of her first-class teaching certificate Mason became Lecturer in Hygiene and Physiology combined with Mistress of Method at Bishop Otter Training College for women in Chichester. The college trained young women to work in elementary schools; students came from relatively wealthy backgrounds and some were Queen's Scholars. While the original *Story* and the *In Memoriam* collection suggest that Mason's reticence and soft-spoken authority came naturally, Elizabeth Edwards observes that in addition to teaching subject knowledge and pedagogy the teacher training colleges were at pains to inculcate middle-class values and behaviors in their students.[45] This also suggests that her time on the staff at Bishop Otter Training College provided Mason with an informal education into the middle-class sociability that was as integral to her eventual success as a philosopher of education for middle- and upper-class families as her own origins were to her insistence that her theories equally applied to working-class families.

Charlotte Mason's educational life history after Bishop Otter follows the development of her philosophy of education and the founding of the PNEU, which she set up after a series of public lectures in Bradford at the request of one of her former college friends, Elizabeth Pendlebury (Mrs. Groveham). Initially the PNEU consisted of "parents of whatever class and others interested in education" who met together to "study the laws of education as they bear on the bodily development, the moral training, the intellectual life and the religious upbringing of children."[46] The role of home life as integral to the education of the child was central to Mason's philosophy. Her ideas on education both inside and outside the formal schoolroom were published in a series of six books under the broad title of "Home Education" from 1886 to the posthumous *Philosophy of Education* in 1923. Mason set up the House of Education in 1892 in Ambleside, a small institution that trained young women to be governesses, and teachers in elementary schools. *The Parents' Review,* containing articles by Mason and other leading educationalists, such as Oscar Browning and HMI T.G. Rooper, was circulated to all members and the Parents' Review School sent courses out to parents whose children were taught at home across Britain and the empire. Mason was clear that her philosophy included in equal parts physical, moral, intellectual, and religious education. Additionally, and unusually for her time, Mason considered her curriculum equally applicable to the home education of children of the middle and upper-middle classes and to working-class children in elementary schools. The constraints imposed upon Mason's own education by both her social class and her sex underpin her insistence that her educational philosophy applies to all children. According to Mason, education is "an atmosphere, a discipline and a life," and she insisted that "Education is the Science of Relations."[47] This approach ensured that children's learning was not confined to the formal schoolroom but permeated every aspect of their lives; their family life, their transition between home education overseas and school life back in Britain; and their Church.

LIFE HISTORIES AND THE TRANSNATIONAL

By 1907 children were following PNEU courses in both Britain and abroad.[48] PNEU courses were used in European countries such as Belgium, settler societies including Australia and South Africa, and for British children being educated in India rather than being sent to England for their schooling. Mason's work can be read as an imperial project, designed to ensure that children of families whose parents were posted overseas could be educated within an English curriculum, isolated from any local influences.[49] Mason also wrote a series of letters for *The Times* on the "Basis of National Strength."[50] However, PNEU pedagogy aimed to stimulate discussion and it appears that even if the children were retained within the boundaries of the home, Mason's ideas were more widely disseminated. Her work was translated, on request, into German and Gujerati, indicating that some discussion had already taken place within local communities. Understanding the role that spirituality rather than adherence to any one denomination played in Mason's educational life history is also significant for a transnational reading of her ideas that transcend national, physical, and conceptual boundaries. In her preface to the Home Education series Mason averred that we "must regard education not as a shut-off compartment, but as being as much a part of life as birth or growth, marriage or work; and it must leave the pupil attached to the world at many points of contact."[51] In the 1912 Winchester gathering of home-schooled children in Britain, those studying overseas were invited to send an account or drawing of their lives so that children at home and abroad would feel part of one school.

A transnational reading of Mason's educational life history highlights some tensions within her theory and practice. Her writing on Loyalty in *Ourselves* exhorts the reader that "our country claims our Loyalty. Let us not make a mistake. Benevolence is due to the whole world, Loyalty is due to *our own*; and however greatly we may value or become attached to alien kings or alien countries, the debt of Loyalty is due not to them but to our own."[52] She continues to explain that patriotism requires:

> some intelligent knowledge of [one's country's] history, laws and institutions; of her great men and her people; of her weaknesses and her strength; and is not to be confounded with the ignorant and impertinent attitude of the

Englishman or the Chinese who believes that to be born an Englishman or a Chinese puts him on a higher level than the people of all other countries.[53]

However, for Mason adherence to faith transcends geographical boundaries as "It is only to God that we can give the whole, and only from Him can we get the love we exact; a love which is like the air, an element to live in, out of which we gasp and perish."[54]

The GFS, with which Mary Sumner began a long-term association in 1875, also positioned itself as a transnational but patriotic organization that identified with the British Empire but also extended beyond it. Like the MU, the GFS had branches in British colonies, the dominions of Canada and Australia, and in contact zones beyond British imperial rule. The year 1877 saw the genesis of what was to become GFS America, and by 1888 there were continental European branches in Lisbon, Milan, and Naples, as well as in Malta. Members were also to be found in the Ottoman imperial capital of Constantinople,[55] Russia, China, and South America. Writing in 1912 on the occasion of the establishment of the GFS in Argentina, GFS founder Mrs. Mary Townsend noted, "it is not a colony: it is beyond the Empire, but it is not beyond the sphere of British influence."[56] In promoting a belief in "purity as the true standard for the womanhood of the world,"[57] the GFS took inspiration from the work of missionaries who were seen to exemplify the esteemed qualities of piety and service. Sumner became one of the GFS's founding organizers, serving as Vice President and then President of the Winchester Diocesan GFS (1887, 1888). By providing "respectable" leisure pursuits and educational opportunities such as Bible study, reading unions, and vocational training, Associates (the middle- and upper-class women who ran GFS local branches) sought to prevent loss of chastity amongst working-class girls and to protect them from exploitation by employers or the morally unscrupulous.[58] The GFS magazine *Friendly Leaves* kept members "at home" informed of news from overseas. The settler destinations of South Africa, Australia, and Canada were of particular interest to the GFS. A department for girls emigrating (later incorporated into the British Women's Emigration Association) was initiated in 1886.[59] Emigration was seen as an opportunity for members to better themselves and contribute to the imperial project by populating the empire with "the right sort of woman," Christian, chaste, domesticated, and (implicitly) white.[60]

In 1880, Mary and George Sumner, accompanied by a small party of friends and relations, took an extended tour to Egypt and the Holy Land, a popular destination amongst the upper and middle classes. A recurrent theme in Mary Sumner's published commemoration of the journey in *Our Holiday in the East* was her assertion of the superiority of (Protestant) Christianity concerning the treatment of women.[61] Muslim practice drew her strongest disapproval and affirmed her view that Christianity was the only religion to treat women fairly. She considered that the zenana system—where women lived in a secluded area of the home which she observed at first hand—symbolized the low social and spiritual status of women and condemned them to "a life of ignorance and practical imprisonment."[62] The Anglican Communion extended beyond British imperial borders and Protestant missionary work was celebrated wherever it occurred. *Our Holiday* records visits to mission schools in Egypt, Syria, and Lebanon.[63] Mary Sumner praised the "brave, indomitable" Miss Whatley and commended Mrs. Bowen Thompson for her work in Damascus where "the sphere is one of great difficulty and danger and requires much tact as well as Christian Courage." In "Beyrout," mothers at Mrs. Mott's school for girls "sent a kind message to the members of my Mothers' Meeting at home about which I had told them."[64] Exemplified by *Our Holiday in the East*, the identification in the GFS and the MU with a Christian sisterhood that transcended national borders and geographical distance was not incompatible with patriotic support of the British Empire. The empire, with the queen as head of both church and state, was identified as an Anglican Christian institution. For the MU and GFS the imperial project was justified as a benign civilizing cultural and religious mission. What did concern them was any failure to uphold Christian standards on the part of settlers, colonists, or imperial officials.

The establishment of a constitution in 1896 and the unopposed appointment of Mary Sumner as Central President gave her, and the MU, a national profile that was affirmed by the grant of royal patronage the following year. In positioning itself (like the GFS) as a transnational but patriotic organization, the MU drew on Queen Victoria as maternal icon and on the rhetoric of the "mother country" to assert the contribution of mothers to the imperial project.[65] For Mary Sumner, laudable "English" characteristics were attributable to the Christian identity of the nation. She exhorted "*all* English women" to set an example of the highest standards of Christian behavior because the English reputation and therefore the moral legitimacy of imperial rule were at stake.[66] Just as the Queen Empress embodied the empire, Mary Sumner was portrayed as personifying the MU. Her biographers eulogized "Mrs. Sumner's part in the world wide extension of the MU [through] her personal share by her pen, by her prayers and by that true mother's love that went out to all the daughter branches of her beloved union in far off lands."[67] In a letter to an overseas president, Mary Sumner was explicit on the need to spread Christian conduct: "We must get the members of our Mothers' Union to act as missionaries amongst their relations and friends, helping to bring the Christian life into the darkened homes where as yet our dear Lord is not loved and honoured."[68] In addition to correspondence the magazines *MIC* (aimed at middle- and upper-class readers) and *The Mothers Union Journal* (*MUJ*) (for working-class mothers) offered channels of communication whereby intelligence from overseas branches could be relayed "home" and "home" news and values exported, thereby providing members, especially those separated by distance, with a sense of contact and unity of purpose.[69]

The activity of missionaries was used to inspire, affirm identity, and enhance MU claims to religious authority in the metropole. Cooperation with Anglican missionary societies and the financial support of women missionary workers, organized through its Overseas Committee, strengthened the identification of the MU (and its members) with the Church and thereby sanctified mothering as work to uphold its sacraments and moral code. Mary Sumner's enthusiasm for the work of overseas missions as expressed in *Our Holiday in the East* was reflected in the 1898 Winchester Diocesan MU Committee resolution that members should be reminded of the duty of the MU to assist via the Society for the Propagation of the Gospel (SPG), or the Church of England Zenana Society, in sending women medical missionaries "to try to raise home life in zenanas and harems,"[70] a message repeated in the MU magazines. In the October 1898 edition of *MIC,* Mary Sumner advocated support for missions by prayer and subscription and suggested that MU members might be mission workers themselves.

Mary Sumner's personal touch was applied to indigenous members of the MU as well as to expatriates in settler colonies nostalgic for the "mother country." As was the case with missionaries, contact with them served a pedagogic function by signaling desirable conduct and the rewards of faith. Correspondence with indigenous members was shared with the wider membership via the MU magazines and given prominence in Mary Sumner's biography. Chinese members' expressed gratitude to "the foundress" for teaching them "good methods of carefully bringing up and educating our children," and missionary worker Miss Rix noted that Mary Sumner's letter to mothers had been translated into Tamil.[71] The MU branch established in Madagascar (then under French colonial rule) and notable as the earliest in Africa[72] was lauded as a particular success. When writing to Malagasy members, Mary Sumner addressed them as "dear daughters" and signed her letters, "your loving white mother."[73]

Indigenous members were welcomed into the MU on the understanding that they complied with the cultural and religious preferences of the society. Although perceived from Mary Sumner's maternalistic metropolitan perspective as a category needing to be led by example toward social, cultural, educational, and religious enlightenment, indigenous mothers were also drawn on to inspire religious enthusiasm. For Mary Sumner, their uninhibited "innocent" joy at conversion confirmed the "liberating" message of Christianity. In 1908 The Pan-Anglican Conference of bishops provided the MU with the opportunity to make a conspicuous demonstration of their presence alongside the church overseas. Many wives of delegates were MU Associates, and following the conference, an MU "mass meeting" at London's Royal Albert Hall was addressed by Mary Sumner. She noted that: "They had now nearly covered the Empire with their number of over a quarter of a million members [...] their objects and their rules had been translated into twelve different languages and they were winning a way in other countries."[74]

The meeting also marked the achievement of access to the organizational hierarchy of the MU by indigenous women. Mrs. Oluwole, the "wife of the African Bishop of Lagos," spoke from the platform to express "the deep appreciation felt by her fellow countrywomen in Western Equatorial Africa for the Mothers' Union and of the help it brought to Christian mothers of every race and colour uniting them in an unbreakable bond of fellowship and prayer."[75] Mary Sumner's life in education reflects an assemblage of traditions of philanthropy, religious faith, and transactions. An organization that currently numbers four million members worldwide sustains her memory and continues her pedagogic work. It emerged from connections that stretched across Britain, British imperial networks, and French colonial spaces such as Madagascar, in addition to China, Japan, South America, and a range of European countries.

Charlotte Yonge's writings on cultural encounters were also negotiated around her conviction that Christian mission was the ideal transnational contact. Yonge's particular transnational interest in mission, the evangelization of the indigenous peoples of the British Empire and of peoples where Bishops "governed persons not under English government,"[76] was fostered by the influential High Churchman, John Keble, her parish priest and mentor, who prepared her for confirmation as a full member of the Church of England. To Yonge the mission field was a place of education, where missionaries learned to accept and carry on despite disappointment and disillusion, and their converts were educated to love one another, which meant giving up cruel (in her view) customs and welcoming white missionaries as teachers and helpers.

Yonge's interest in mission was first aroused in 1838, the year of her confirmation, when John Keble organized a subscription to the SPG and regularly invited missionary speakers to meetings. Her interest was not translated into action until the 1850s, when Yonge had her own magazine, *The Monthly Packet*, to edit and her own money to spend, thanks to her authorial success. Over the years she supported and enabled mission by personal financial contributions from the sale of her books, through her authorship, both of fiction and nonfiction, and through her journalism as editor of *The Monthly Packet*. Her fictional characters take up mission work abroad, promote the work of the SPG and give money to missions. Yonge's nonfiction included a biography of the missionary Bishop John Coleridge Patteson of Melanesia (1827–71) and a collection of short missionary biographies, including the life of Bishop Charles Mackenzie of Central Africa. *The Monthly Packet* included articles by correspondents on foreign missions. When writing about foreign missions Yonge and her informants seldom mentioned empire. Theirs was a narrative of service, not of power. Yet they could not ignore the fact that missionaries were protected by British arms. When she did mention empire, the emphasis was on the colonists' duty to "uphold England's name for truth, for justice and for mercy" and, still more importantly, "not put to shame [Christ's] name."[77] Nevertheless, Huffman Traver suggests that Yonge herself interwove the narrative of imperial power implicitly with that of missionary service in *The Daisy Chain*, her novel of 1856.[78]

In Yonge's view the mission stage was peopled by three groups of actors: white missionaries and their supporters, indigenous peoples (divided into converts and potential converts), and finally white colonists (divided into those who were merely hostile to indigenous peoples on one hand, and on the other hand those who exploited them). She saw white missionaries as responding to the indigenous peoples' own desire for education in Christianity by English priests, saving them from self-inflicted harm (cannibalism among the South Pacific Islanders, slave-trading in Africa, and female infanticide in China) or harm done by whites. Yonge's representation of white missionaries and choice of mission field to support were initially shaped by her friends and family, just as her Anglican beliefs had been in her childhood and youth.[79] George Selwyn (1809–78), Bishop of New Zealand, was a family friend, and his missionary chaplain, John Coleridge Patteson, (later to become Bishop of Melanesia) was her cousin. In 1854 Yonge gave Selwyn the proceeds of her recent bestseller, *The Heir of Redclyffe*, to buy a missionary ship in which Patteson was to visit the Melanesian islands (Vanuatu and the Solomon Islands, about 2,000 miles north of New Zealand) and convert the islanders.[80] Yonge shows in Patteson's biography how missionaries could face a conflict between power and service. Having invited Pacific islanders to come, with the Elders' permission, 2,000 miles south to New Zealand to be trained as Christian ministers, Patteson was responsible for them. He then inflicted suffering on them; they were "exceedingly fragile [...] continually catching cold or getting disordered,"[81] and then, in 1863, many died of dysentery in the crowded premises of St. Andrew's.[82]

Yonge's representation of white missionaries was further influenced by the life and death of Bishop Charles Mackenzie of Central Africa (1825–62), whose sister Anne was a friend of Yonge. Mackenzie first arrived in South Africa in 1855, where he found that he was not to evangelize the indigenous peoples but instead was to serve the white colonists of Durban in the then-British colony of Natal. His disappointment at this decision was to affect Yonge's portrayal of white missionaries. She took care to warn her readers through her fictional characters' experiences that the reality of mission might not match their hopes. They must be prepared to struggle on through difficulties. Real-life missionaries could make serious mistakes that would affect the whole purpose of their presence. Mackenzie agreed to carry arms and free slaves from local slave-traders; this meant that he became involved in local disputes and finally burnt the (empty) huts of a village whose inhabitants had captured two of his men.[83]

For Yonge, indigenous peoples could be disappointing too. Once converted, they might be rewarding recipients of ministry, but the difficulty was to convert them in the first place. In her first novel in which mission plays a significant part,

The Daisy Chain, serialized in *The Monthly Packet* between 1853 and 1855, she sidesteps this issue by introducing South Pacific islanders who have already been converted. As *Daisy Chain* character Harry May tells his family about the Christian chief who cared for him after shipwreck: "You must not think of him like a savage, for he is my friend, and a far more perfect gentleman than I ever saw anyone [...] coming to me with little easy first questions about the Belief, like what we used to ask mamma [...] but those islanders have been dying off since Europeans came among them."[84] Harry's remark reflects the ambivalence of white missionaries toward their role. For all his praise of the island's chief, Harry's portrayal of him as a child in religion emphasizes the islanders' supposed initial need of teaching from a white priest. His observation that Europeans bring death to the islanders does not prevent him from encouraging his brother Norman to go to New Zealand and the South Pacific as a missionary.

Letters from New Zealand, published in *The Monthly Packet* from 1853 to 1855, also contributed to the promotion of mission in the South Pacific, a process that also brought the empire "home."[85] The letters painted a rosy picture of the success of Selwyn's missionary efforts. An important part of his policy, carried on by Patteson, was to train indigenous priests and pastors. He founded St. John's College, an Anglican school in New Zealand for both the sons of colonists and Maori converts. Here they were educated and trained for missionary work among their own people. They were introduced to "civilized" customs, received basic Christian teaching, learned the three Rs, and farming and craft skills. One letter describes a Maori deacon and his missionary work in a Maori community. The emphasis is on the Maori desire for Christian teaching: "The native people welcomed him amongst them very heartily" ... "There are now four or five in his district most anxious to come [to St John's College]."[86] While Patteson supported the idea of training converts away from home, he did not think it was necessary to teach the islanders in their homes to wear clothes and adopt European customs in order to Christianize them. Yonge, on the other hand, thought that wearing clothes was a necessary part of Christianity and describes fictional African converts happily wearing European-style dress and living in European-style dwellings.[87]

Later accounts were to affect Yonge's portrayal of indigenous peoples. After Patteson had sailed to the South Pacific in 1856, his letters told another story from Selwyn's. Yonge pointed to evidence of cannibalism, noting that the islanders' reactions varied from welcoming through hostility to lack of interest. According to Yonge, in Central Africa Bishop Mackenzie had needed to use his guns to frighten African slave-traders into releasing their captives.[88] Yonge herself, as a novelist, was not above painting a dark picture of non-Christians to make her story more exciting and inspiring. In her 1900 novel set in China, *The Making of a Missionary,* Mabel, the missionary's sister-in-law, is killed by a gang of fanatical anti-Christians as she tries to protect the Chinese children at her missionary school.[89]

While Yonge did not pretend there were no problems, she preferred to accentuate the positive. In *The Monthly Packet* she published an account of a happy community of missionaries and converts at the consecration of the mission church on Norfolk Island,[90] whose organ she had funded with the proceeds of her biography of Patteson. Less positive was her attitude to white colonists, who were "hindrances and drawbacks, first and foremost in [...] almost uniform hostility [...] [They] are used to consider the dark races as subjects for servitude."[91] What did impress Yonge, as she almost reluctantly acknowledged, was the self-reliance of colonists and their families.[92] Her 1868 novel of South Africa, *New Ground*, portrayed white colonists less dismissively—crude, uncultivated, and as ever, hostile to the indigenous peoples but fundamentally goodhearted. But for Yonge, far worse than colonists were labor-recruiters for plantations in the South Pacific, some of whom corrupted, exploited, and killed local people.[93] On these wicked white men, or on Portuguese slavers in Africa, could be blamed many of the shortcomings of Pacific islanders or Africans, including the most shocking (to Yonge and her circle) murder of Patteson on Nukapu Island on September 20, 1871. Hovdhaugen and Kolshus have reassessed the reasons for Patteson's death, but his murder was said to be in revenge for the kidnapping of five islanders.[94] The murder's aftermath was problematic for Yonge. A Royal Navy vessel sailed to Nukapu to make enquiries, whereupon the members of the mission drew up a formal protest against punishing the people of Nukapu for Patteson's death. This protest was ignored. According to Yonge, the islanders fired arrows at the British flag, an attack that was "severely chastised with British firearms."[95] In fact, a village was destroyed by shelling and up to thirty islanders were killed.[96] Yonge glossed over the link between mission and the coercive power of the British Empire, to which Nukapu was not formally subject until 1893. Patteson's death was the supreme example of service in Yonge's missionary narrative. He died in the service of God and of the Nukapu islanders whom he wanted to convert. They were chastised not for his death, she wrote, but for shooting at the British flag. Thus, by maintaining her conviction that Christian mission was the ideal transnational contact, Yonge's educative messages exonerated missionary efforts from responsibility for imperial reprisals.

CONCLUSION: ASSEMBLING EDUCATIONAL LIVES

When the lives of Yonge, Sumner, and Mason are considered "with educational matters uppermost in mind,"[97] commonalities thread through their life histories but also some "variegations." While Yonge and Sumner left accounts of their early lives, Mason's reluctance to disclose her familial background points to how early education in familial spaces, together with familial networks, played into notions of feminine respectability on which future educational activities could depend. In this light, Yonge and Sumner's autobiographical fragments can be read as retrospective presentations of "respectable" credentials that prefigure the basis for their future educational work. Whereas Mason considered her curriculum to be applicable to both children of the middle and upper classes being educated at home and to working-class children in elementary schools, under Sumner's leadership the MU developed a distinction between middle-class Associates and working-class members, and differentiated the audience for their journals. The educational lives of all three women illustrate how cultural and transnational elements of educational activities were negotiated around a Christian belief. But in contrast to Yonge's and Sumner's adherence to Anglicanism, for Mason it was the role of spirituality in her educational life history rather than adherence to any one denomination that is significant for a reading of how her educational ideas transcended national, physical, and conceptual boundaries. When it came to patriotism, Mason also distinguished benevolence due to the world from loyalty due to "our own,"[98] whereas in the MU and the GFS the relation between patriotism and empire hinged around the queen as head of both church and state, and the view that the Anglican Communion extended beyond imperial borders. As with Yonge, what was problematic for Sumner and the MU was any failure to uphold Christian standards.

The three women's responses point to the importance of the relational aspects of educational institutions for educational life histories, including relationships among households, churches, schools, journals, and popular culture. An important configuration was the mission field as place of education for and by missionaries. Like Mason's promotion of an English curriculum in an education that isolated children from local influences, Yonge's and Sumner's negotiation in print of asymmetrical relations of power around colonial/missionary encounters were responses to the spatial and temporal co-presence in "contact zones" of subjects previously separated by geographic and historical disjunctures.[99] The cultural assumptions underpinning Sumner's account of *Our Holiday* and the transnational flows around the MU held together metropole and colony in ways that resonate with Hall and Rose's analysis of how empire became part of everyday, taken-for-granted ideas at "home,"[100] as did Yonge's inclusion of missionary letters in *The Monthly Packet*. Although Yonge glossed over the link between mission and the coercive power of the British Empire in the aftermath of Patteson's death in Melanesia, her writings at this point illustrate Hall and Rose's comment that "at particular historical moments, everyday taken-for-granted ideas [might] be questioned or consciously underlined."[101]

The women's educational lives highlight the importance of geographical spaces for educational life histories. At times, the women's interactions with educational configurations played into the kind of "cartographic imagination" that Ballantyne and Burton argue was central to the emergence of how the global was understood during the nineteenth and twentieth centuries.[102] While their educational lives demonstrate "variegations" in personal mobility, the three women's educational life histories demonstrate transnational circulations of texts across a range of national and imperial boundaries and a complex web of European connections, and intercolonial, imperial, and inter-imperial flows that fostered the growth of the organizations with which they were associated. Taken together these highlight aspects of the spatial dimensions through which the developing global order was being shaped during the nineteenth and early twentieth centuries.

Cremin's notion of configurations also resonates with what Goodson terms "genealogies of context."[103] These pay close attention to social context and social processes, which he maintains are needed to move anecdotal life *stories* toward life *histories*. Drawing on Passerini,[104] Goodson maintains that "genealogies of context" enable researchers to unpack how people tell life stories through preexisting story lines and ways of telling stories, even if these are in part modified by circumstances. Mary Sumner, for example, composed *Our Holiday in the East* along the lines of a narrative of pilgrimage, and Yonge's extensive writings deployed a narrative of service not of power when writing about foreign missions. Portrayals of Mason and Sumner that entangle with how the PNEU and the MU were depicted demonstrate the challenge to which Cremin pointed around untangling lives and institutions as well as Goodson's argument that how we "story" our lives (and those of others) is deeply connected to storylines derived from elsewhere.[105] Goodson's discussion of story lines raises questions about the relation between subjectivity, representation, and narrative that align with a focus in "new" cultural histories of education on how knowledge as a field of practice intervenes as part of social life.[106] Mason's obfuscation of her early life and Yonge's and Sumner's autobiographical fragments together with their approaches to material for future biographies indicate how individuals deploy narrative in accounts of their lives to portray themselves for different purposes and with different audiences in mind.[107] This points, as Scott suggests, to a search for the performative qualities of discourses and materialities that together produce a particular way of seeing the constructed subject.[108]

But, as Tamboukou argues, narratives express only a limited set of lines of thought interwoven around moments of "being" temporarily crystallized into narrative forms.[109] As actualized narratives they create conditions of possibility for more stories to emerge. From this perspective storytelling expresses contingency and the potentiality for change. Furthermore, writes Tamboukou, because human beings live fragmented lives, the meaning that life histories generate is only accessible to the tellers and listeners of the stories, not to their protagonists, at least in the moment of action.[110] Stories take up the role of congealing the fleeting meaning of moments and actions. It is through their assemblage into life histories, as Tamboukou argues, that archives for historical understanding are created.

NOTES

Preface

1. Burke 2019.
2. Geertz 1973: 42.
3. Williams 1961: 145.
4. See, for example, Boyd 1947; Bowen 1972.
5. McCulloch 2011.
6. See, for example, Goodman, McCulloch, and Richardson 2009b; McCulloch, Goodson, and Gonzalez-Delgado 2020.
7. Giorgetti, Campbell, and Arslan 2017: 1.
8. See also McCulloch 2019.
9. Bailyn 1960: 53.
10. Ibid.: 14.
11. For example, Butts 1947, 1953.
12. Cremin 1976: 27.
13. Ibid.: 29.
14. Cremin 1970, 1980, 1988.
15. Church, Katz, and Silver 1989: 419–20; Veysey 1990: 285; see also Cohen 1998.
16. Silver 1983: xxiv.
17. See, for example, Burke 1997, 2019.
18. For example, Cohen 1999; Popkewitz, Peyrera, and Franklin 2001; Fendler 2019.
19. Fendler 2019: 15.
20. Graff 1995.
21. Burke 2000, 2011.
22. For example, O'Neill 2014.
23. Ariès 1962; see, for example, Foyster and Marten 2010b.
24. See, for example, in relation to learners and learning, McCulloch and Woodin 2010b; on teachers and teaching, Tyack and Cuban 1995.
25. For example, Godfrey et al. 2017.
26. See, for example, Said 1993; Davidann and Gilbert 2019.

Introduction

1. Quote from Tröhler 2020: 4.
2. Hobsbawm 1962, 1975, 1987.
3. Hall and Rose 2006b: 6.
4. Ibid.
5. Goodman, McCulloch, and Richardson 2009a.
6. Depaepe 2009.
7. Akami 2013; Löhr and Wenzlhuemer 2013; Fuchs 2014.
8. Tröhler 2016.
9. Ibid.: 281.
10. Ibid.: 293.
11. Brockliss and Sheldon 2012.
12. Brockliss and Sheldon 2012.
13. Cremin 1976.
14. Ibid.: 29.
15. Goodman and Martin 2002; Cortina and San Román 2006; Goodman 2011; Jöns 2017; Jöns, Meusberger, and Heffernan 2017.
16. Brockliss and Sheldon 2012.
17. Ibid.: 251.
18. Barcan 1980.
19. Axelrod 1997.
20. Raftery and Relihan 2012.
21. Harik and Schilling 1984: 4.
22. For example, Scott 1938.
23. Harik and Schilling 1984.
24. Nóvoa 1995.
25. Anzaldua 1999: 239 cited in Goodman, McCulloch, and Richardson 2009a: 701.
26. Bagchi, Fuchs, and Rousmaniere 2014; Bush 2014.
27. Brockliss and Sheldon 2012.
28. Abdelkader 2000; Holzwarth 2014; Ikhlef 2014.
29. Harik and Schilling 1984.
30. Depaepe 2009, 2014.
31. Kumar 2012.
32. Bagchi 2009, 2010, 2014.
33. Heathorn 2000; Goodman, McCulloch, and Richardson 2009a.
34. Mill 1817: viii.
35. Greenblatt 2006.
36. Colley 2002.
37. Ibid.: 1.
38. Heathorn 2000; English 2006; Bartie et al. 2017.
39. Disraeli 1845: 76.
40. On parallels with ancient Rome, see Hagerman 2005; on the cult of athleticism, see Mangan 2012.
41. Ellis 2012.
42. Mackenzie 2012.
43. Khan 1997.
44. Tipton 2002: 60.
45. Cited in Horio 1990: 80.
46. Stamp 1973; Watts 2009.

47. Moruzi and Smith 2014.
48. Walther 2001.
49. Goodman, McCulloch, and Richardson 2009a.
50. Ibid.: 696.
51. Akami 2013: 178.
52. Eklof 2012.
53. Berg 2012: 186.
54. Chapman 1990; Cavalier 2011.
55. Pombo de Barros 2016.
56. Cicek 2012.
57. Elman and Woodside 1994.
58. Borthwick 1983 cited in Brockliss and Sheldon 2012.
59. Ibid.: 25.
60. Löhr and Wenzlhuemer 2013: 8.
61. Bagchi, Fuchs, and Rousmaniere 2014: 2.
62. Ballantyne and Burton 2005; Lambert and Lester 2006.
63. Pietsch 2013.
64. Anderson 1992; Francis 1994; Kearns 1997.
65. Craig 1984; Välimaa 2004.
66. Anderson 2004, 2006.
67. Butlin 2009: 5.
68. Cooper 2005: 109.
69. Butlin 2009: 41.

Chapter 1

Translations from French, Italian, and Spanish are my own.
 1. Wilkinson 2015: 16–25.
 2. Ferrer 2011.
 3. Chadwick 1975: 229.
 4. Clarke and Kaiser 2003.
 5. Archer 1984: 61–72.
 6. Papenheim 2003.
 7. D'Agostino 2004.
 8. Braster 2011.
 9. Archer 1984: 65.
10. Aldrich 1979: 1.
11. Rudé 1985.
12. Cremin 1980: 148.
13. Pepperman Taylor 2010: 7.
14. Roberts 2004: 96.
15. Brown 2009: 25.
16. Patriarca 2013.
17. Dolan 1985: 128.
18. Ibid.: 129.
19. Choate 2008: 4.
20. Cremin 1980: 172.
21. Chadwick 1970a: 338.
22. Cremin 1988: 175.
23. Arthur 2019: 6–7.

24. Braster 2011: 4.
25. Ferrer 2011: 18–20.
26. Sanderson 1991: 34–5; Arthur 2019: 2.
27. Zeldin 1977; Genua 2012; Wright 2018.
28. Zeldin 1977: 983.
29. Bruneau 1990: 11.
30. Ibid.: 9.
31. McGreavy 2016: 77–97.
32. Fraser 2016: 41.
33. Gutek 1995: 458.
34. Cremin 1988.
35. Ibid.: 127.
36. Dolan 1985: 269.
37. Fraser 2016: 57.
38. Langlois 1984: 9; Scaraffia 1999: 259.
39. Rogers 2005: 63; Soldani 2010: 62.
40. Rogers 2005: 161.
41. Soladani 2010: 63.
42. McGreevy 2016.
43. Raftery, Delaney, and Bennett 2018.
44. Williams 2015.
45. Norman 1985: 6.
46. Cruikshank 1963: 190.
47. D'Agostino 2004: 44.
48. Cremin 1988: 127.
49. Dolan 1985: 277.
50. Ibid.: 263.
51. Ibid.: 293.
52. Aldrich 1979: 1.
53. Martin 2013: 74.
54. Cruickshank 1963: 190.
55. Chadwick 1970b: 186.
56. Smith 2009: 47–69.
57. Chadwick 1970b: 307.
58. Olekhnovitch 2007: 32.
59. Vinard 2004.
60. Olekhnovitch 2007: 33.
61. Chadwick 1970a: 338.
62. Cruikshank 1963: 190.
63. Cremin 1980: 170–1.
64. Ibid.: 180.
65. Elias 2002: 161.
66. Fraser 2016: 57.
67. Ibid.: 109.
68. Ibid.: 84–5.
69. D'Agostino 2004: 43.
70. Olekhnovitch 2007: 4.
71. Zeldin 1980a: 150.
72. Wright 2018.

73. Arthur 2019: 6.
74. Ibid.: 9.
75. Simon 1985: 88.
76. Arthur 2019: 9.
77. Galton 1904: 5.
78. Cruickshank 1963: 190.
79. Olekhnovitch 2007: 34.
80. Pruneri 2006: 41–2.
81. Smith 2009: 158–60.
82. Rogers 2011.
83. Choate 2008: 6–7.
84. Williams 2018.
85. Braster 2011: 4.
86. Chadwick 1997: 11.
87. Bruneau 1990; Genua 2012; Wright 2018.
88. Wright 2018: 221.
89. Bruneau 1990: 13.
90. Raftery 2012: 47–8.
91. Watkins [1845] 1969: 18–19.
92. Martins 2013: 80.
93. Wright 2018: 222.
94. Casulleras [1917] 2018: 113.
95. Ibid.
96. Gordon 1983.
97. Ibid.: 21.
98. Canfield Fisher 1912: 11.
99. Ibid.
100. Wright 2004: 140.
101. O'Donoghue 2001: 133.
102. Coldrey 1992.
103. Chadwick 1997: 11.
104. Erskine Stuart 1911.
105. Ibid.: 41.
106. Simon 1985: 77–105.
107. Ibid.: 37–8.
108. Ibid.: 37.
109. Ibid.: 38.
110. Rocca 1999; Rogers 2005.
111. Rocca 1999: 438.
112. Rocca 2019: 78.
113. De Giorgi 2018: 61.
114. Martin 2013: 79.
115. Williams 2018: 244.
116. Canfield Fisher 1912: 23.
117. Montessori [1939] 2013: 145; emphasis in the original.
118. Williams 2018: 335.
119. Vojtáš 2018.
120. Zeldin 1980b: 339.
121. Watkins [1845] 1969: 20.

122. Bartie et al. 2018.
123. Watkins [1845] 1969: 20.
124. De Giorgi 2013: 37.
125. Pinckaers 2001: 32–41.
126. Ibid.: 25–31.
127. Ibid.: 60.
128. Wright 2004: 110–72.
129. Cremin 1988: 21.
130. Ibid.
131. Chadwick 1970b: 469.
132. Rev. 3:20.
133. Arthur 2019: 12.

Chapter 2

 1. Mann 2004; May et al. 2014.
 2. Viswanathan 1989; Kumar 1991; Seth 2007.
 3. Cooper and Stoler 1997; Bhattacharya 1998; Hall 2000; Chavan 2013; Rao 2014.
 4. Curtis 1988; Fischer-Tiné 2001; Maier 2006.
 5. Roldán Vera 1999; Caruso and Roldán Vera 2005.
 6. Sinha 1995.
 7. Möller and Wischmeyer 2013; Allender 2016.
 8. Adanir 1991; Mahrung and Naumann 2014; Kamenov 2020.
 9. Brehony 2004; Mann 2015.
10. Archer 1984; Miller 1998.
11. Roldán Vera and Caruso 2007a.
12. Ressler 2010, 2013.
13. Boli and Thomas 1999; Iriye 2002.
14. Kaviraj and Khilnani 2003.
15. Caruso and Roldán Vera 2005; Schriewer and Caruso 2005; Caruso 2015.
16. On the British-imperial circuit, see May et al. 2014; Tschurenev 2019; on the transatlantic liberal circuit, see Roldán Vera and Schupp 2005; Roldán Vera 2007.
17. Bojčeva 1991.
18. Bartle 1991.
19. Jones and Williamson 1979.
20. Miller 1998: 143.
21. BFSS 1815: 66.
22. Ibid.: 14.
23. Sedra 2011.
24. Basak 1959; Tschurenev 2019: 203–90.
25. Roldán and Schupp 2005.
26. Kaestle 1973; Greene 2007.
27. Curtis 1988, 2005.
28. Roldán Vera and Caruso 2007b; Caruso 2010b.
29. Adanir 1991; Gecev 1995; Trenkov 2014.
30. Ressler 2010: 141–64; Caruso and Moritz 2018.
31. Caruso 2015.
32. Ressler 2010, 2013.
33. Real Sociedad Económica de Amigos del País de Cádiz 1818; Molesworth 1825; Pearson 1830; Bartle 1990.

34. Ressler 2010, 2013.
35. Hamilton 1980; Hogan 1989.
36. Curtis 2012; Tschurenev 2019.
37. Miller 1998: 144–7; Greene 2007: 20.
38. Mill [1812] 1995: 72; emphasis in original; cf. Jones and Williamson 1979: 73.
39. Marshman et al. 1816; Kaestle 1976.
40. Caruso 2005; Schriewer 2007.
41. Shahidullah 1987; Kumar 1991; Bara 1998.
42. Marshman et al. 1816; Pearson 1830.
43. Bell 1797.
44. McCann 1988; Babu 2012; Tschurenev 2014.
45. Roldán Vera 2007.
46. Hilton 2014.
47. May et al. 2014.
48. Wollons 2000b; Allen 2017; Powell 2017.
49. Cavallo 1976: 150.
50. Allen 1982: 321–2; Steedman 1985: 154.
51. Münchow 2006.
52. Allen 1988: 23.
53. Ibid.
54. The IKU is the institutional predecessor of today's Association for Childhood Education International, a nongovernmental organization with consultative status at the United Nations.
55. Cavallo 1976: 151.
56. Reeves-Ellington 2010; Kamenov 2020.
57. Kulichev 2008: 255–8.
58. Allen 2006: 178.
59. Fröbel quoted in Steedman 1985: 149.
60. Allen 1982: 319.
61. Tyrrell 2010.
62. Midgley 2000; May et al. 2014: 131–9.
63. On promotion by American missionaries, see Allen 2018; and by female kindergarten experts, see Allender 2016: 218–28; Powell 2017.
64. There were remarkable overlaps between the NAI and the British Fröbel movement. Adelaide Manning (1828–1905) established the NAI's London chapter in 1871, and was also a founding member of the Fröbel Society in 1874.
65. Allender 2016: 228.
66. Allen 2018.
67. Burton 1995; Chakravarti 1998; Kosambi 1998, 2016.
68. Jayawardena 1994.
69. Allen 2018.
70. Chakravarti 1998; Tschurenev 2018.
71. Ramabai Association 1898: 31–2.
72. Wollons 2000b.
73. Allender 2016: 218–28.
74. Cunningham 2000; Kersting 2008.
75. Böllert and Gogolin 2002.
76. Imber 1982.
77. Tyack and Thomas 1985: 514.

78. Cook 1993: 252.
79. Tyack and Thomas 1985: 533.
80. On US civic education, see Tyack and Thomas 1985; on Eugenics education in Australia, see Rodwell 2000; on hygiene instruction in Uruguay, see Little 1975.
81. Blocker et al. 2003; Eisenbach-Stangl 2004; Große et al. 2014; Kamenov 2020.
82. Hunt 1897; Zimmerman 1999.
83. Donovan 2006.
84. "The Kindergarten Department was adopted by the National W.C.T.U. in 1878, and by the World's W.C.T.U. and a Superintendent appointed at the first Convention held in Boston in 1891" (Bessie Locke, Executive Secretary of the *National Kindergarten Association* to Lucretia H. Little, WCTU, December 15, 1938 [Manuscript, Willard Archives, Evanston, IL]).
85. *Union Signal*, March 27, 1890: 8, quoted in Allen 2006: 180.
86. *Union Signal*, January 11, 1900: 12.
87. Tyrrell 1991.
88. Tyrrell 2010.
89. On "imperial community," see Bunkle 1980; Cook 1993; Grimshaw 2000; Smitley 2002; on the exception of Japan, see Ogawa 2007.
90. Ramabai Association 1898: 33.
91. Zimmerman 1992: 2.
92. Mezvinsky 1961: 50.
93. Tyack and Thomas 1985: 519.
94. Chitambar 1926; Rodwell 2000.
95. Lohmann 1923.
96. Scientific Temperance Federation (Boston) 1923: 5. The US-American opponents to STI would have heartily agreed with that assessment. "In the ensuing battle surrounding Progressive education, a movement of experts devoted to curbing 'lay influence' in schools, STI's women warriors would continue to hold down the fort-and to wield 'influence,' against all odds, in American schools" (Zimmerman 1992: 12).
97. Schall-Kassowitz 1923: 5–6.
98. Caruso 2010a.
99. Allen and Women's Christian Temperance Union of India, n.d.
100. Billings et al. 1903: 44.
101. Zimmerman 1992: 29.
102. Olsen 2012.
103. Zimmerman 1992: 19.
104. Tyack 1985: 518.
105. Bunkle 1980: 69.
106. Zimmerman 1992: 15–18, 27–8.
107. Brehony 2009: 593.
108. Zimmerman 1992: 18.
109. Babini 2000: 45.
110. Smuts 2006; Brehony 2009: 601.
111. Siegel and White 1982: 253.
112. Brehony 2009.
113. British Child Study Association quoted in Brehony 2009: 594–5.
114. Siegel and White 1982.
115. Babini 2000.

116. Little 1975; Karlekar 1986, Babini 2000: 48.
117. Babini 2000: 47–8.
118. Little 1975; Lengwiler 2014.
119. Montessori with George and Holmes 1912; Brehony 2009: 601.
120. Babini 2000: 45.
121. Brehony 2009: 593.
122. Ibid.: 598–601.
123. Siegel and White 1982: 250–1.
124. Brehony 2009: 599.
125. On locally defined "useful knowledge," see Marshman et al. 1816.
126. Rousmaniere et al. 2013: 3.
127. Viswanathan 1989; Kumar 1991; Twells 1995; Bhattacharya 1998; Rao 2014.
128. Hamilton 1980; Hogan 1989.
129. Kumar 1991.

Chapter 3

1. Swartz 2019: 2.
2. Sandin 2014: 91.
3. Marten 2018: 71.
4. Heywood 2010.
5. Foyster and Marten 2010a: 3.
6. Sen 2005: 3.
7. Swartz 2019: 1.
8. Eitler, Olsen, and Jensen 2014: 4–5.
9. Olsen 2014b: 140.
10. For more on this, see Swartz 2019.
11. Biswas and Agrawal 1986: 835, cited in Eitler, Olsen, and Jensen 2014: 3–5.
12. Pomfret 2014: 194.
13. Stoler 2001: 851.
14. Vallgårda, Alexander, and Olsen 2015: 12–34. The concept of emotional formation was developed in our bid to understand how emotions are shaped in childhood and youth in different global contexts. "Emotional formation" designates on the one hand the emotional codes or prescriptions that structure a given society, culture, or subculture, and on the other hand, the processes through which children learn and adapt these codes. The structure and the process are dynamically related: the structure is affected by the activities of individuals and collectives; those activities or practices are framed by the structural delimitation of meaningful feeling. While "formation" refers to the culturally specific codes of affective comportment and expression, and the process through which the individual incorporates and embodies these codes, the concept of "emotional frontiers" designates the boundary between different affective formations or else of dealing with divergences or apparent contradictions within the same emotional formation. An emotional frontier may be perceived in various ways, either individually or relationally. An individual may be so habituated to traversing emotional frontiers that they do not notice them at all; or else the existence of a frontier might be registered through a sense of unease, of a shift in emotional register that requires a conscious adaptation, or through the socially compromising experience of getting the emotional codes wrong.
15. For the German context, see Bowersox 2013: 21; and Donson 2010; for the British context, see Olsen 2014b: 4, 52.

16. Bowersox 2013: 14–15.
17. Ibid.: 59.
18. Roberts [1971] 1990: 133.
19. Ibid.: 134.
20. For more on English public school education, see Newsome 1961; Mangan 1981; Boddice 2009; Ellis 2010; Olsen 2014b.
21. On brutal emotional and physical conditioning, see Hamlett 2015b.
22. Swartz 2019: 1.
23. Bowersox 2013: 56.
24. Seth 2008: 2.
25. Swartz 2019: 5.
26. Said 1993: 101.
27. Swartz 2019: 2.
28. Bowersox 2013: 12.
29. Sen 2005: 1.
30. Olsen 2014b.
31. Sen 2005: 2.
32. Caruso 2015: 154.
33. Cf. Whitehead 2003 and Swartz 2019.
34. Carl Ochs quoted in Vallgårda 2014: 42n13.
35. Vallgårda 2014: 43.
36. Ibid.: 44.
37. Ibid.: 45.
38. In recent years historians have contributed greatly to knowledge on the background and functioning of these schools and their predecessors, as well as their impact on children and on societies. See, for example, Milloy 1999; de Leeuw 2009; Carleton 2011, 2017; McCallum 2014; Fraser and Mosby 2015; Fraser 2019.
39. For example, Miller 2006: 9.
40. Truth and Reconciliation Commission 2015: 145.
41. Ibid.: 58.
42. Sir John A. Macdonald, Canada, House of Commons Debates (May 9, 1883), 1107–8, quoted in Truth and Reconciliation Commission 2015: 2.
43. Library and Archives Canada, RG10, Volume 6810, file 470-2-3, Volume 7, Evidence of D. C. Scott to the Special Committee of the House of Commons Investigating the Indian Act amendments of 1920, (L-2)(N-3) quoted in Truth and Reconciliation Commission 2015: 3.
44. See de Leeuw 2009, for an analysis of the impact of these reports and more on the foundations of nineteenth-century residential schools.
45. Marten 2018: 75.
46. For more on industrial and ragged schools, see Mahood 1995; Gear 1999; Mair 2019; Swartz 2019.
47. Truth and Reconciliation Commission 2015: 154.
48. Ibid.
49. Miller 2006: 7–8.
50. Key 1909.
51. Olsen 2014b: 4
52. Kelley 1905: 3–57.
53. Marten 2018: 77–8.

Chapter 4

1. *Minutes of the Juvenile Literary Society* (hereafter *Minutes*), November 6, 1874.
2. *Annual Monitor for 1912*, 1912.
3. Cleall et al. 2013.
4. Gunn 2012.
5. Davidoff and Hall 2002.
6. Dodd 1986; Heathorn 2000.
7. Roldán Vera and Fuchs 2019.
8. Pietsch 2013; Alexander 2017.
9. Dyhouse 1981; Roach 1986; Tosh 1999.
10. Burton 1994; Hall 2002.
11. Goodman, Albisetti, and Rogers 2010; Ricardo López and Weinstein 2012.
12. Holloway et al. 2010.
13. Olsen 2015.
14. Cleall et al. 2013.
15. French and Rothery 2012: 40; Wright 2012; Sutherland 2015.
16. Anderson 1985.
17. Shefrin and Hilton 2009; de Bellaigue 2016.
18. Grenby 2011; Cohen 2015.
19. Hilton 2007: 87–108.
20. Leach 2002; Cohen 2015.
21. Bailey 2012.
22. *Minutes*, 1875.
23. *Catalogue of the Library of the Boys' Juvenile Literary Society* 1858.
24. Fyfe 1999; Shefrin and Hilton 2009; Grenby 2011.
25. Leach 2002; Bailey 2012.
26. Grenby 2011; Gleadle 2016.
27. Caruso 2012.
28. Amies 1985.
29. Schultz 1999; Roldán Vera 2017.
30. Vincent 1997; Fyfe 1999.
31. Schultz 1999; O'Connor 2010: 1–28.
32. Duff 2013.
33. de Bellaigue 2016.
34. Scotland Census 1871, 467/4/17.
35. Grenby 2011: 37–42.
36. Vincent 1997: 141–79; Humphries 2010; Pooley 2015.
37. Amies 1982; Gorham 1982: 20.
38. Amies 1982; Duff 2012, 2013.
39. Legge 1884.
40. Johnson 2003; Fass 2013.
41. Heathorn 2000; Sobe 2010.
42. Fitzgerald 2001; Twells 2006.
43. Amies 1985; Lerner 2018.
44. Millions 2017.
45. Banerjee 2010.
46. Roldán Vera 2017.
47. Lee 2010.

48. Bonner 1877.
49. Pooley 2015.
50. Alexander 2005; Gleadle 2019.
51. Yamaguchi 2014.
52. Sánchez-Eppler 2005; Matthews-Schlinzig 2018.
53. Rappaport 2004: 233; Buettner 2004.
54. England Census, Class: RG10; Piece: 2665; Folio: 67: 12.
55. Gillis 1981: 95–105.
56. *Parliamentary Papers* 1868: 1:349.
57. *Annual Monitor* 1910.
58. Crone 2015; de Bellaigue 2019.
59. Humphries 2010; Crone 2015; de Bellaigue 2019.
60. Tosh 1999: 116.
61. Rubinstein and Jolles 2011.
62. Chambers 1842: 7.
63. Carter 2018.
64. Elliott and Daniels 2005.
65. Vincent 1997; Rose 2001.
66. Shapin and Barnes 1976.
67. Shuttleworth 2013.
68. Brehony 1998.
69. Bourke 1994; McDermid 2013.
70. Fitzgerald 2001; Krishnan 2017.
71. Schultz 1999; Davis 2014: 55–6; Carter 2018.
72. Fitzgerald 2001; Walsh 2008; Sobe 2010; de Leeuw and Greenwood 2014; May, Kaur, and Prochner 2014; Griffith 2015.
73. Swartz 2019.
74. Sen 2005.
75. Wollons 2000a; Roldán Vera and Caruso 2007a.
76. *Minutes*, April 12, 1876.
77. Griffith 2015: 97.
78. Tosh 1999: 117–18.
79. *Examination of Classes*, January 20, 1872.
80. French and Rothery 2012.
81. Honey 1977: 1–46; Woodley 2009.
82. Ellis 2014.
83. Deslandes 2005: 71–80; Hamlett 2015a: 62–110.
84. Honey 1977; Dyhouse 1981: 41–44; Gorham 1982; Tosh 1999.
85. Pedersen 1987; McDermid 2013.
86. England Census, Class: RG10; Piece: 1453; Folio: 42: 19.
87. de Bellaigue 2007: 135.
88. de Bellaigue 2007: 16; Hamlett 2015a.
89. French and Rothery 2012.
90. Ibid.
91. N.B. 1874.
92. Hurst 1849.
93. Stack 1963.
94. Simon 1960: 105–7.
95. Davis 2014: 59–60.

96. Roach 1986.
97. Pietsch 2013: 5.
98. Vincent 1997: 173.
99. Macías-González 2012.
100. Buettner 2004: 130–9.
101. Millions 2017: 255–71.
102. Wollons 2000a.
103. O'Neill 2014: 161–89; de Bellaigue 2016: 202–16.
104. O'Neill 2014.
105. Duff 2013.
106. Bourke 1994; Vincent 1997.
107. Gaitskell 2017; see also Millions 2017: 134.
108. Swartz 2019.
109. Griffith 2015: 35.
110. Duff 2013.
111. Rose 2001: 58–91; de Bellaigue 2016.
112. Part Minute Book of the Society for Arts (1870–82), ERO, D/Q 49/F2/b2.
113. Wiener 1981; Holt 2008.
114. Deslandes 2005; Whyte 2015: 152.
115. Whyte 2003; Gamsu 2016.
116. Wiener 1981; Mangan 1986; Roach 1986.
117. Honey 1977; Holt 2008.
118. *Annual Monitor* 1910.
119. *Annual Reports (Printed) of the Juvenile Literary Society of the Boys' School Croydon*, June 1876.
120. Prochaska 1978; Gleadle 2016.
121. Sutherland 2015; Kumbhat 2017.
122. Rubinstein, Jolles, and Rubinstein 2011: 292.
123. Pietsch 2013; Roldán Vera and Fuchs 2019.
124. Cohen 2017.
125. Ryan 1981: 136–43.
126. Morris 1990; Rose 2001.
127. Elleray 2011; McAllister 2015.
128. Weaver 2004; Ellis 2014.
129. "Correspondence" 1873: 30–1; "Letters" 1898: 57.
130. French and Rothery 2012: 41–4.
131. Sloan 2017.
132. Whyte 2003.
133. Whyte 2003, 2015; Weaver 2004; Deslandes 2005; Sloan 2017.
134. Mangan 1986; Hulme 2015.
135. "The Conversazione" 1898: 11.
136. Naturalization Certificates and Declarations, 1870–1916, Class: HO 334; Piece: 23; Certificate: 8601.
137. Millions 2017.
138. Deslandes 2005; Boehmer and Mukherjee 2011.
139. Hulme 2015.
140. Livshin 1990.
141. Krishnan 2017.
142. "The Conversazione" 1898.

143. Adi 1997; Mukherjee 2009.
144. Adi 1997: 15.
145. Legge 1884.
146. Fitzgerald 2001; Przystupa 2018.
147. Gleason 2018.
148. O'Connor 2010; Duff 2012.
149. "Letters to the Editor" 1915: 89–90.
150. Sinn 2017.
151. Sutherland 2015; Alexander 2017.
152. Alexander 2017: 38–41.
153. Martin 2016.
154. Hawkins and Morgan 2006: 1–34.
155. Sinn 2017: 71–2.
156. Wu 2015.

Chapter 5

1. Porter 2001.
2. Rose 2001; McCulloch and Woodin 2010a.
3. For instance, Hall 2002.
4. Horlacher 2011.
5. Lilley 1967.
6. Israel 2001.
7. Humphrey [1801] 1962; French 2000.
8. On literacy in general, see Vincent 1989.
9. Thompson 1968: 24.
10. Blake n.d.
11. Cooper 1872; see also Vincent 1981.
12. Lovett and Collins [1840] 1969.
13. Balmforth 1902: 42.
14. Habermas 1989; Negt and Kluge 1993.
15. Harrison 1969b; also Harrison 1969a.
16. Holyoake 1900; Claeys 1989.
17. Johnson 1979.
18. Uglow 2002.
19. Edgeworth and Edgeworth 1815: 193.
20. Ibid.
21. Osborne 1964: 7.
22. Ibid.: 8, 10.
23. Mill 1874: 8.
24. Casalini 2019.
25. Burke 2014: 80.
26. Hansard, House of Commons, HC Deb June 13, 1807, Volume 9, cc798–806. Available online: https://api.parliament.uk/historic-hansard/commons/1807/jun/13/parochial-schools-bill (accessed April 20, 2020).
27. Woodin 2017.
28. Chambliss 2019.
29. Tolstoy 1967.
30. Hobsbawm 1994.
31. See Ardao 1963: 518.

32. See Pycior 2013: 37–8; see also Zoraida Vázquez 2019.
33. Fortna 2002.
34. Miller 1989.
35. Tyack and Cuban 1995.
36. Simon 2005.
37. Corrigan and Sayer 1985; Woodin, McCulloch, and Cowan 2013.
38. Lockeridge 1974.
39. Vinovskis 1992.
40. Rawick 1972; Williams 2005.
41. See, for instance, Coleman 1996.
42. Kaestle 1983; Katznelson and Weir 1985; Rose 2001; Woodin 2018.
43. Bayly 2004: 67–8; Anderson 2016.
44. See Ramirez and Boli 1987.
45. Rose 2001.
46. de Amicis 2005: 17.
47. Russell 1898.
48. Youmans 2003: esp. 64–9.
49. Miss Beer, headmistress of Birley-house open air school, *The Times*, January 8, 1908.
50. Williams, Ivin, and Morse 2001.
51. Simon 1985.
52. Davis 2000.
53. Kropotkin [1902] 1987.
54. Newman 1873.
55. Goldman 1995.
56. Mehl 2001, 2000; Taylor and Taylor 2014; Tsujimoto and Yamasaki 2017.
57. Snow 1938; Schram 1967; Kirkes 1976.
58. Goodman, McCulloch, and Richardson 2009a.
59. Hall 2002.
60. Macaulay [1848] 1906.
61. Dalrymple 2019.
62. Nurullah and Naik 1951; Whitehead 2005b.
63. Pruess 1983; Cross 1986.
64. Little 1948.
65. Bayly 2004: 349.
66. Boampong 2013.
67. Leach 2008.
68. Whitehead 2005b.
69. See, for instance, Harris 2007; Joliffe and Bruce 2019.
70. For example, Fry and Bi 2005.

Chapter 6

1. Iriye 1989; Burke 2004.
2. Smith and Ward 2000; Randeria 2009.
3. Randeria 2009.
4. Wolf 1982; Smith and Ward 2000.
5. Greenblatt 2010: 5.
6. Sardar and Van Loon 1994.
7. Yun Casalilla 2014.
8. On the notion of entanglement, see Randeria 2009.

 9. Szasz 1994; Gaul 2014.
10. Weaver 1998: 21.
11. Groves 1936: 46.
12. Graham 1971: xi.
13. Miller 1996.
14. Barman, Hébert, and McCaskill 1987; Huhndorf and Huhndorf 2014.
15. Minogue 1965; Cleverley 1971; Higginson 1974; Seccombe 1993; Wyman 1995; Harper 2010.
16. Minogue 1965; Seccombe 1993; Langton 2008; Whitehead and Wilkinson 2008.
17. Harper 2010.
18. Seccombe 1993.
19. Commission 1861; Vincent 1981; Seccombe 1993; Langton 2008.
20. Quoted in Wyman 1995: 32.
21. Commission 1861; Hodgins 1894.
22. Murphy 2000; Pawlikova-Vilhanova 2007; Pankhurst 2018.
23. Carpenter 1960: 192.
24. Quoted in Van der Walt 1992: 81.
25. Wayland Carpenter 1960; Van der Walt 1992; Pawlikova-Vilhanova 2007; Pankhurst 2018.
26. Pawlikova-Vilhanova 2007: 255.
27. Wayland Carpenter 1960; Pawlikova-Vilhanova 2007.
28. Jacobs 2010.
29. Goodyear-Kaōpua 2014.
30. McLoughlin 1986.
31. Coleman 1994.
32. Martin 2001.
33. Mt. Pleasant 2014.
34. Quoted in McLoughlin 1994: 116.
35. Murphy 2000; Pankhurst 2018.
36. Goodyear-Kaōpua 2014.
37. Quoted in Wyatt 1994: 192.
38. Gaul 2014.
39. Anderson 2014.
40. Brown 2014: 105.
41. Gaul 2014: 6–7.
42. Szasz 1994; Gaul 2014.
43. Gaul 2014: 21.
44. Curtis 1988; Larsen 2011.
45. Larsen 2011.
46. Platt 2004: 173.
47. Wang Jiang 2010.
48. Evered 2012: 197.
49. Larsen 2011.
50. Austin 1972; Ghosh 1995; Larsen 2011.
51. Cubberley 1947; Tyack 1974.
52. Larsen 2011.
53. La Volpa 1980; Albisetti 1988.
54. Evered 2012: 199.
55. Evered 2012.

56. Larsen 2011.
57. Cubberley 1947; Harper 1970; Larsen 2011.
58. Wang Jiang 2010; Yu 2013.
59. Platt 2004.
60. Ibid.
61. Larsen 2011.
62. Ibid.
63. Bell 1797.
64. Lancaster 1803.
65. Bell 1797; Lancaster 1803.
66. Cleverley 1971; Graham 1971; Kaestle 1973; Caruso and Roldán Vera 2005; Roldán Vera and Schupp 2005; Caruso 2009, 2013.
67. Kaestle 1973: 39–40.
68. Kaestle 1973.
69. Kaestle 1973; Caruso 2013.
70. Caruso 2013: 40.
71. Kaestle 1973; Caruso 2009, 2013.
72. Caruso and Roldán Vera 2005; Roldán Vera and Schupp 2005; Caruso 2009.
73. Kaestle 1973.
74. Graham 1971.
75. Keefer 2019: xi.
76. Graham 1971; Kaestle 1973; Keefer 2019.
77. Kazamias 1966.
78. Kaestle 1973: 33.
79. Kaestle 1973.
80. Roldán and Schupp 2005: 69.
81. Barnard 1859; Pestalozzi 1894.
82. Barnard 1859; Pestalozzi 1894.
83. Barnard 1859; Pestalozzi 1894.
84. Pinoche 1901: 289.
85. Ibid.: 307.
86. Brown 1986.
87. Langton 2008.
88. Silber 1960; Elson 1964.
89. Rich 1933; Larsen 2011.
90. Mayo 1830.
91. Mayo 1890.

Chapter 7

1. Vincent 1989; Brooks 1985: xii.
2. Barton 1994: 127.
3. Vincent 1989: xi.
4. Street 1994.
5. Cook-Gumpertz [1986] 2006: 26.
6. Crain 2020: 971.
7. Williams 1983: 188.
8. Gordon and Gordon 2003: xv.
9. Barton 1994: 21.
10. Duncan 2012: 39.

11. Burton 2014.
12. Graff 2011/13: 107–8.
13. Street 1990: 4–5.
14. Graff 2010: 639.
15. Stephens 1987: 14.
16. Vincent 2000: 8–9.
17. Stone 1969: 69–139; see also, for example, McCulloch and Richardson 2000: esp. ch. 6.
18. Stephens 1987: 3.
19. Stephens 1990: 554.
20. Stone 1969; Stephens 1987: esp. ch. 1.
21. Stephens 1987: 264.
22. Vincent 1989: 18.
23. Ibid.: 22–3.
24. Mitch 1992.
25. Johansson 2009.
26. Nilsson 1999.
27. Frago 1990.
28. Quiroca 2003.
29. Hately-Broad 2008: 23–4.
30. Brooks 1985: 20.
31. Soltow and Stevens 1981: 117.
32. Gordon and Gordon 2003: 273.
33. Rubinger 1990.
34. Mironov 1991; see also Mironov 1986.
35. Rose 2001; see also Rose 2007.
36. Vincent 1989: xi.
37. Vincent 1981.
38. Vincent 2000: 4.
39. Kaestle 1988. See also Kaestle 1985; Kaestle et al. 1991.
40. Frago 1990.
41. Fussell [1975] 2000: 157.
42. Ibid.: 158.
43. Ibid.: 170.
44. Ibid.: 173.
45. See, for example, Sutcliffe 2016.
46. Mace 2001, 2002; Burton 2014.
47. Dickens 1865: ch. 16.
48. Burton 2014.
49. Stephens 1998: 82.
50. Smelser 1991: 294–5.
51. Hurt 1979: 4.
52. Brooks 1985.
53. Graff 2011/13: 93.
54. Vincent 1989: 67.
55. Vincent 1999: 191.
56. Howard 2012: 192.
57. Soltow and Stevens 1981: 96.
58. Graff 1979: 330.

59. Ibid.: 316.
60. Gaskell [1866] 1996: ch. 46.
61. Altick 1957: 4; Vincent 1989; Stephens 1998.
62. Burton 2014.
63. Webb 1955: 15.
64. Mitch 2009: 197.
65. Burton 2014: 132.
66. Vincent 1989: 35.
67. Soltow and Stevens 1981.
68. Trollope [1875] 1994: ch. 18, pp. 169–70.
69. Howard 1991: 93–4.
70. Martin 1991: 190.
71. Stephens 1998: 39.
72. Howard 1991: 81.
73. Burton 2014: 131.
74. Purvis 1985: 198.
75. Long and Long 1999: 5.
76. Gordon and Gordon 2003: xix.
77. Blouet 1990.
78. Jenkins 1994.
79. Berg 2007: 123.
80. Song 2012: 542.
81. Ibid.: 546.
82. Stevens 1995: 4–5.
83. Walker 2016.
84. Ibid.: 149.
85. Keane 1988: 171.
86. Berg 2007: 124–5; and Mokyr 2003.
87. Jacob 1997.
88. Hilaire-Pérez 2002.

Chapter 8

1. Cremin 1980: 588.
2. Cremin 1976: 30–6.
3. Cremin 1976: 27.
4. Cohen 1999: 284, 287, 295.
5. Rousmaniere 2015.
6. Franklin 1979.
7. Lagemann 1979.
8. Blakeway 2018.
9. Anderson-Faithful 2018: 60–1.
10. Sumner 1895: 1–8.
11. Mason 1886: 6, 1989: preface.
12. PNEU 1923; de Bellaigue 2015.
13. Anderson-Faithful 2018.
14. Coombs 2015.
15. Yonge 1875.
16. Porter, Woodard, and Erskine 1921: 36.
17. Ballantyne and Burton 2012.

18. Goodson 1995.
19. Ibid.: 15.
20. Cohen 1999; Popkewitz, Franklin, and Pereyra 2001.
21. Tamboukou 2016.
22. Sumner n.d.-a.
23. Watts 1998.
24. Sumner n.d.-a.
25. Romanes 1908: 8.
26. Sumner n.d.-a.
27. Sumner 1876.
28. On implied presence of an audience, see Collini 1993: 3.
29. Coleridge 1903: viii.
30. Coleridge 1903: vii.
31. Letters of Charlotte Mary Yonge, n.d.
32. Battiscombe 1943.
33. Anderson-Faithful 2018.
34. Cremin, 1976: 41.
35. Chomondeley 1960: 4.
36. Mason quoted in Chomondeley 1960: 4–5.
37. Mason quoted in Chomondeley 1960: 3.
38. Coombs 2015: 11.
39. Ibid.: 13.
40. Kitching quoted in Cholmondeley 1960: ix.
41. Coombs 2015: 69.
42. Ibid.: 68.
43. Ibid.: 105
44. Ibid.: 107.
45. Edwards 2001.
46. Chlomondeley 1960: 17.
47. Mason 1886: 6, 1989: preface.
48. de Bellaigue 2015: 515.
49. Buettner 2004: 87.
50. *The Times*, March 5, 1912; May 6, 1912; June 6, 1912; January 17, 1923.
51. Mason [1905] 1989: preface.
52. Ibid.:119; emphasis in the original.
53. Ibid.: 121.
54. Ibid.: 176.
55. Heath Stubbs 1926: 140–5, 173.
56. Ibid.: 161.
57. Ibid.: 8.
58. Heath-Stubbs 1926.
59. Money 1902.
60. Bush 1994: 395.
61. Sumner 1881.
62. Ibid.: 226.
63. Pitman 1895.
64. Sumner 1881: 302.
65. Moyse 2009.
66. Sumner 1910: 51–2, emphasis in the original.

67. Porter, Woodard, and Erskine 1921: 36.
68. Ibid.: 41.
69. *MUJ*, January 1901: 22–3; Mary Sumner *MIC*, October 1898: 211–13.
70. Winchester Diocesan Mothers' Union Committee February 24, 1898.
71. Porter, Woodard, and Erskine 1921: 39.
72. Prevost 2010.
73. Porter, Woodard, and Erskine 1921: 37.
74. Ibid.: 113.
75. *MIC*, October 1908: 74.
76. Yonge [1871] 2015: loc. 179015.
77. Yonge [1868] 2006: 129.
78. Traver 2010.
79. Walton 2010.
80. Yonge 1854.
81. Yonge 2015: loc. 304967.
82. Yonge 2015.
83. Yonge 2015.
84. Yonge [1856] 1899: 473.
85. Thorne 2006: 147.
86. Anonymous 1855: 400.
87. Yonge [1868] 2006.
88. Yonge 2015.
89. Ibid.
90. Lush 1881.
91. Yonge 2015: loc. 291081.
92. Yonge 2015.
93. Bass 1996.
94. Hovdhaugen and Kolshus 2010.
95. Yonge 2015: loc. 313318.
96. Anonymous 1872.
97. Cremin 1980: 588.
98. Mason [1905] 1989: 119.
99. On contact zones, see Pratt 1992: 6.
100. Hall and Rose 2006a.
101. Ibid.: 23.
102. Ballantyne and Burton 2012.
103. Goodson 1995: 12.
104. Passerini 1987.
105. Goodson 1995: 8.
106. Popkewitz, Franklin, and Pereyra 2001.
107. Goodman and Martin 2000.
108. Scott 1992.
109. Tamboukou 2016.
110. Tamboukou 2016.

BIBLIOGRAPHY

Archival sources

Annual Reports (Printed) of the Juvenile Literary Society of the Boys' School Croydon (1850–87), Essex Record Office (ERO), D/Q 49/F1/c1.
Catalogue of the Library of the Boys' Juvenile Literary Society (1858), ERO, D/Q 49/F1/d1.
Examination of Classes (1814–82), ERO, D/Q 49/E2/a1.
Minutes of the Juvenile Literary Society (1870–95), ERO, D/Q 49/F1/a4.
Parliamentary Papers (1868), Schools Inquiry Commission, volume 1.
Society of Arts: Part Minute Book of the Society of Arts (1870–82), ERO, D/Q 49/F2/b2.

Abdelkader, Yamna (2000), "Guérir la Folie? Les Enjeux de la Thématique Médicale dans le Roman Maghrebin des Années Soixante-Dix," in Jean-Louis Cabanès (ed.), *Littérature et Medicine II*: *Eidôlon*, 401–12, Bordeaux: Université de Michel de Montaigne.
Adanır, Fikret (1991), "Die Schulbildung in Griechenland (1750–1830) und in Bulgarien (1750–1878). Im Spannungsfeld von Bewahrung der ethnisch-konfessionellen Identität, Entstehung der bürgerlichen Gesellschaft und Herausbildung des Nationalbewusstseins," in Wolfgang Schmale, Nan L. Dodde, and Fikret Adanir (eds), *Revolution des Wissens? Europa und seine Schulen im Zeitalter der Aufklärung (1750–1825)*, 433–68, Bochum: Winkler.
Adi, Hakim (1997), *West Africans in Britain 1900–1960: Nationalism, Pan-Africanism and Communism*, London: Lawrence & Wishart.
Akami, Tomoko (2013), "The Nation-State/Empire as a Unit of Analysis in the History of International Relations: A Case Study in Northeast Asia, 1868–1933," in Isabella Löhr and Roland Wenzlhuemer (eds), *The Nation State and Beyond: Governing Globalization Processes in the Nineteenth and Early Twentieth Centuries*, 177–208, Heidelberg: Springer Verlag.
Albisetti, James C. (1988), *Schooling: German Girls and Women*, Princeton, NJ: Princeton University Press.
Aldrich, Richard (1979), *Sir John Pakington and National Education*, Leeds: University of Leeds.

Alexander, Christine (2005), "Play and Apprenticeship: The Culture of Family Magazines," in Christine Alexander and Juliet McMaster (eds), *The Child Writer from Austen to Woolf*, 31–50, Cambridge: Cambridge University Press.

Alexander, Kristine (2016), "Childhood and Colonialism in Canadian History," *History Compass*, 14 (9): 397–406.

Alexander, Kristine (2017), *Guiding Modern Girls: Girlhood, Empire, and Internationalism in the 1920s and 1930s*, Vancouver: University of British Columbia Press.

Allen, Ann Taylor (1982), "Spiritual Motherhood: German Feminists and the Kindergarten Movement, 1848–1911," *History of Education Quarterly*, 22 (3): 319–39.

Allen, Ann Taylor (1988), "'Let Us Live with Our Children': Kindergarten Movements in Germany and the United States, 1840–1914," *History of Education Quarterly*, 28 (1): 23–48.

Allen, Ann Taylor (2006), "The Kindergarten in Germany and the United States, 1840–1914: A Comparative Perspective," *History of Education*, 35 (2): 173–88.

Allen, Ann Taylor (2017), *The Transatlantic Kindergarten: Education and Women's Movements in Germany and the United States*, New York: Oxford University Press.

Allen, Ann Taylor (2018), "Indian and American Women in the International Kindergarten Movement, 1880s–1930s," *Südasien-Chronik/South Asia Chronicle*, 8: 53–78.

Allen, Maud and Women's Christian Temperance Union of India (n.d.), *Ten Things Every One Should Remember About …* Lucknow: Printed by K.O. Banerjee, at A.O. Press [Educational booklet, WCTU Archives, Evanston, IL].

Allender, Tim (2016), *Learning Femininity in Colonial India, 1820–1932*, Manchester: Manchester University Press.

Altick, Richard D. (1957), *The English Common Reader*, Chicago: University of Chicago Press.

Amies, Marion (1982), "Schooling at Home in Nineteenth Century Australian Fiction," *Discourse: Studies in the Cultural Politics of Education*, 3 (1): 40–56.

Amies, Marion (1985), "Amusing and Instructive Conversations: The Literary Genre and its Relevance to Home Education," *History of Education*, 14 (2): 87–99.

Anderson, Benedict (2016), *Imagined Communities: Reflections on the Origin and Spread of Nationalism*, London: Verso.

Anderson, Jon W. (1992), "Colonial Ethnography in British Afghanistan," in Richard Brown (ed.), *Writing the Social Text: Essays on the Poetics and Politics of Social Science Discourse*, 91–116, New York: Aldine de Gruter.

Anderson, Michael (1985), "The Emergence of the Modern Life Cycle in Britain," *Social History*, 10 (1): 69–87.

Anderson, Robert D. (2004), *European Universities from the Enlightenment to 1914*, Oxford: Oxford University Press.

Anderson, Robert D. (2006), *British Universities: Past and Present*, London: Hambledon Continuum.

Anderson, Rufus (2014), "Memoir of Catherine Brown, a Christian Indian of the Cherokee Nation (1825)," in Catharine Brown, *Cherokee Sister: The Collected Writings of Catharine Brown 1818–1823*, edited by Theresa Strouth Gaul, 163–258, Lincoln: University of Nebraska Press.

Anderson-Faithful, Sue (2018), *Mary Sumner, Mission, Education and Motherhood: Thinking a Life with Bourdieu*, Cambridge: Lutterworth.

The Annual Monitor for 1911 (1910), London: Headley Brothers.

The Annual Monitor for 1912: Being an Obituary of the Members of the Society of Friends in Great Britain and Ireland, From October 1, 1910, to September 30, 1911 (1912), Gloucester: John Bellows, Eastgate.

The Annual Monitor for 1913 (1912), Gloucester: John Bellows.

Anonymous (1855), "New Zealand; The Maori Deacon," *The Monthly Packet*, May: 396–400.

Anonymous (1872), *Nukapu Expedition*, February 15, 1872. Available online: https://en.wikipedia.org/wiki/Nukapu_Expedition (accessed March 12, 2019).

Anzaldua, Gloria (1999), *Borderlands/La Frontera: The New Mestiza*, San Francisco: Spinsters/Aunt Lute.

Archer, Margaret S. (1984), *Social Origins of Educational Systems*, university edition, London: Sage.

Ardao, Arturo (1963), "Assimilation and Transformation of Positivism in Latin America," *Journal of the History of Ideas*, 24 (4): 515–22.

Ariès, Philippe (1962), *Centuries of Childhood*, London: Cape.

Arthur, James (2019), "Christianity and the Character Education Movement 1897–1914," *History of Education*, 48 (1): 60–76.

Austin, A.G. (1972), *Australian Education 1788–1900: Church, State and Public Education in Colonial Australia*, Westport, CT: Greenwood Press.

Axelrod, Paul (1997), *The Promise of Schooling: Education in Canada, 1800–1914*, Toronto: University of Toronto Press.

Babini, Valeria (2000), "Science, Feminism and Education: The Early Work of Maria Montessori," *History Workshop Journal*, 49: 45–68.

Babu, D.S. (2012), "Indigenous Traditions and the Colonial Encounter: A Historical Perspective on Mathematics Education in India," in R. Ramanujam and K. Subramaniam (eds), *Mathematics Education in India: Status and Outlook*, 37–62, Mumbai: Homi Bhabha Centre for Science.

Bagchi, Barnita (2009), "Towards Ladyland: Rokeya Sakhawat Hossain and the Movement for Women's Education in Bengal, *c*. 1900–*c*. 1932," *Paedagogica Historica*, 45 (6): 743–55.

Bagchi, Barnita (2010), "Two Lives: Voices, Resources, and Networks in the History of Female Education in Bengal and South Asia," *Women's History Review*, 19 (1): 51–69.

Bagchi, Barnita (2014), "Connected and Entangled Histories: Writing Histories of Education in the Indian Context," *Paedagogica Historica*, 50 (6): 813–21.

Bagchi, Barnita, Eckhardt Fuchs, and Kate Rousmaniere, eds (2014), *Connecting Histories of Education: Transnational and Cross-cultural Exchanges in (Post-) Colonial Education*, New York: Berghahn.

Bailey, Joanne (2012), *Parenting in England 1760–1830: Emotion, Identity, and Generation*, Oxford: Oxford University Press.

Bailyn, Bernard (1960), *Education in the Forming of American Society: Needs and Opportunities for Study*, Chapel Hill: University of North Carolina Press.

Ballantyne, Tony and Antoinette Burton (2012), "Empires in the Reach of the Global," in Emily S. Rosenberg (ed.), *A World Connecting 1870–1945*, 285–434, London: Belknap Press.

Ballantyne, Tony and Antoinette Burton, eds (2005), *Bodies in Contact: Rethinking Colonial Encounters in World History*, London: Duke University Press.

Balmforth, Ramsden (1902), *Some Social and Political Pioneers of the Nineteenth Century*, London: Swan Sonnenschein.

Banerjee, Swapna M. (2010), "Debates on Domesticity and the Position of Women in Late Colonial India," *History Compass*, 8 (6): 455–73.

Bara, Joseph (1998), "Colonialism and Educational Fragmentation in India," in Sabyasachi Bhattacharya (ed.), *The Contested Terrain: Perspectives on Education in India*, 125–170, Hyderabad: Orient Longman.

Barcan, Alan (1980), *A History of Australian Education*, Oxford: Oxford University Press.

Barman, Jean, Yvonne Hébert, and Don McCaskill (1987), "The Challenge of Indian Education: An Overview," in Jean Barman, Yvonne Hébert, and Don McCaskill (eds), *Indian Education in Canada*, volume 2, *The Challenge*, 1–21, Vancouver: University of British Columbia Press.

Barnard, Henry (1859), *Pestalozzi and Pestalozzianism*, New York: F.C. Brownell.

Bartie, Angela, Linda Fleming, Mark Freeman, Tom Hulme, and Paul Readman (2017), "Commemoration Through Dramatic Performance: Historical Pageants and the Age of Anniversaries, 1905–1920," in Thomas G. Otte (ed.), *The Age of Anniversaries: The Cult of Commemoration, 1895–1925*, 195–218, London: Routledge.

Bartie, Angela, Linda Fleming, Mark Freeman, Tom Hulme, Alexander Hutton, and Paul Readman (2018), "'History Taught in the Pageant Way': Education and Historical Performance in Twentieth-Century Britain," *History of Education*, 48 (2): 156–79.

Bartle, George F. (1990), "The Teaching Manuals and Lesson Books of the British and Foreign School Society," *History of Education Society Bulletin*, 46: 22–33.

Bartle, George F. (1991), "Benthamites and Lancasterians—The Relationship between the Followers of Bentham and the British and Foreign School Society During the Early Years of Popular Education," *Utilitas*, 3 (2): 275–88.

Bartle, George F. (1994), "The Role of the British and Foreign School Society in Elementary Education in India and the East Indies 1813–75," *History of Education*, 23 (1): 17–33.

Barton, David (1994), *Literacy: An Introduction to the Ecology of Written Language*, Oxford: Blackwell.

Basak, N.L. (1959), "Origin and Role of the Calcutta School Book Society in Promoting the Cause of Education in India, Especially Vernacular Education in Bengal," *Bengal Past and Present*, 77: 30–69.

Bass, Cecila (1996), "The Melanesian Mission and The Monthly Packet," *Newsletter of the Charlotte M Yonge Fellowship*, 3: 8.

Battiscombe, Georgina (1943), *Charlotte Mary Yonge: The Story of an Uneventful Life, with an Introduction by E.M. Delafield*, London: Constable.

Bayly, C.A. (2004), *The Birth of the Modern World 1780–1914*, Oxford: Blackwell.

Bell, Andrew (1797), *An Experiment in Education, Made at the Male Asylum of Madras, Suggesting a System by Which a School or Family May Teach Itself under the Superintendence of the Master or the Parent*, London: Cadell and Davies.

Berg, Ellen L. (2012), "'To Become Good Members of Civil Society and Patriotic Americans': Mass Education in the United States, 1870–1930," in Laurence Brockliss and Nicola Sheldon (eds), *Mass Education and the Limits of State Building, c. 1870–1930*, 177–201, Basingstoke: Palgrave Macmillan.

Berg, Maxine (2007), "The Genesis of 'Useful Knowledge'," *History of Science*, 45: 123–33.

Bhattacharya, Sabyasachi, ed. (1998), *The Contested Terrain: Perspectives on Education in India*, New Delhi: Orient Longman.

Billings, John S. et al., eds (1903), *Physiological Aspects of the Liquor Problem: Investigations Made by and Under the Direction of John O. Atwater, John S. Billings and Others. Sub-Committee of the Committee of Fifty to Investigate the Liquor Problem*, Boston: Houghton, Mifflin.

Biswas, Arabinda and Surendra Prasad Agrawal (1986), *Development of Education in India: A Historical Survey of Educational Documents before and after Independence*, New Delhi: Concept Publishing Company.

Blake, William (n.d.), "London," Poetry Foundation. Available online: https://www.poetryfoundation.org/poems/43673/london-56d222777e969 (accessed April 20, 2020).

Blakeway, Alys (2018), "Charlotte Yonge The Educator," Winchester Heritage Open Day, September 15.

Blocker, Jack S., David M. Fahey, and Ian R. Tyrrell, eds (2003), *Alcohol and Temperance in Modern History: An International Encyclopedia*, Santa Barbara, CA: ABC-CLIO.

Blouet, Olwyn M. (1990), "Slavery and Freedom in the British West Indies: The Role of Education," *History of Education Quarterly*, 30 (4): 625–43.

Boampong, Cyrelene Amoah (2013), "Rethinking British Colonial Policy in the Gold Coast: The Language Factor," *Transactions of the Historical Society of Ghana*, n.s.s., 15: 137–57.

Boddice, Rob (2009), "In Loco Parentis? Public-School Authority, Cricket and Manly Character, 1855–62," *Gender and Education*, 21 (2): 159–72.

Boehmer, Elleke and Sumita Mukherjee (2011), "Re-making Britishness: Indian Contributions to Oxford University, c. 1860–1930," in Catherine McGlynn, Andrew Mycock, and James McAuley (eds), *Britishness, Identity and Citizenship: The View From Abroad*, 95–112, Oxford: Peter Lang.

Böllert, Karin and Ingrid Gogolin (2002), "Stichwort: Professionalisierung," *Zeitschrift für Erziehungswissenschaft*, 5 (3): 367–83.

Bojčeva, Vera (1991), "La France et la dissémination du système d'enseignement mutuél dans les pays Balkaniques," *Études balkaniques*, 1: 118–20.

Boli, John and George M. Thomas, eds (1999), *Constructing World Culture: International Nongovernmental Organizations since 1875*, Stanford, CA: Stanford University Press.

Bonner, Violet (1877), "The Scornful Monkey," *Little Folks*, February 1: 125.

Borthwick, Sally (1983), *Education and Social Change in China: The Beginnings of the Modern Era*, Stanford, CA: Hoover Institute Press.

Bourke, Joanna, (1994), "Housewifery in Working-class England 1860–1914," *Past & Present*, 143: 167–97.

Bowen, James (1972), *A History of Western Education*, 3 volumes, New York: St. Martin's Press.

Bowersox, Jeff (2013), *Raising Germans in the Age of Empire: Youth and Colonial Culture, 1871–1914*, Oxford: Oxford University Press.

Boyd, William (1947), *The History of Western Education*, 4th edition, London: Adam and Charles Black.

Braster, Sjaak (2011), "The People, the Poor, and the Oppressed: The Concept of Popular Education Through Time," *Paedagogica Historica*, 47 (1–2): 1–14.

Brehony, Kevin J. (1998), "'Even far distant Japan' is 'showing an interest': The English Froebel Movement's Turn to Sloyd," *History of Education*, 27 (3): 279–95.

Brehony, Kevin J. (2004), "A New Education for a New Era: The Contribution of the Conferences of the New Education Fellowship to the Disciplinary Field of Education 1921–1938," *Paedagogica Historica*, 40 (5–6): 733–55.

Brehony, Kevin J. (2009), "Transforming Theories of Childhood and Early Childhood Education: Child Study and the Empirical Assault on Froebelian Rationalism," *Paedagogica Historica*, 45 (4–5): 585–604.

British and Foreign School Society (BFSS) (1815), *Report of the British and Foreign School Society*, London: Longman.

Brockliss, Laurence and Nicola Sheldon, eds (2012), *Mass Education and the Limits of State Building, c. 1870–1930*, Basingstoke: Palgrave Macmillan.

Brooks, Jeffrey (1985), *When Russia Learned to Read: Literacy and Popular Literature 1861–1917*, Princeton, NJ: Princeton University Press.

Brown, Callum G. (2009), *The Death of Christian Britain: Understanding Secularisation 1800–2000*, London: Routledge. Available online: http://www.evolbiol.ru/docs/docs/large_files/secular.pdf (accessed January 10, 2019).

Brown, Catharine (2014), *Cherokee Sister: The Collected Writings of Catherine Brown 1818–1823*, edited by Theresa Strouth Gaul, Lincoln: University of Nebraska Press.

Brown, J.A. (1986), "British Pestalozzianism in the Nineteenth Century: Pestalozzi and His Influence on British Education," PhD diss., University of Wales.

Bruneau, William A. (1990), "The 'New' Social History and the History of Moral Education," *Paedagogica Historica*, 26 (1): 7–33.

Buettner, Elizabeth (2004), *Empire Families: Britons and Late Imperial India*, Oxford: Oxford University Press.

Bunkle, Phillida (1980), "The Origins of the Women's Movement in New Zealand: The Women's Christian Temperance Union 1885–1895," in Phillida Bunkle and B. Hughes (eds), *Women in New Zealand Society*, 52–76, Auckland: George Allen, Unwin.

Burke, Edmund (2014), *Reflections on the Revolution in France*, in Iain Hampsher-Monk (ed.), *Burke: Revolutionary Writings*, 1–250, Cambridge: Cambridge University Press.

Burke, Peter (1997), *Varieties of Cultural History*, Cambridge: Polity Press.

Burke, Peter (2000–11), *A Social History of Knowledge*, 2 volumes, Cambridge: Polity Press.

Burke, Peter (2004), *What is Cultural History?* Cambridge: Polity Press.

Burke, Peter (2019), *What is Cultural History?*, 3rd edition, Cambridge: Polity Press.

Burton, Antoinette M. (1994), *Burdens of History: British Feminists, Indian Women, and Imperial Culture*, Chapel Hill: University of North Carolina Press.

Burton, Antoinette M. (1995), "Colonial Encounters in Late-Victorian England: Pandita Ramabai at Cheltenham and Wantage 1883–1886," *Feminist Review*, 49: 29–49.

Burton, Maxine (2014), *Illiteracy in Victorian England: "Shut out from the world,"* Leicester: National Institute of Adult Continuing Education (NIACE).

Bush, Barbara (2014), *Imperialism and Postcolonialism*, London: Routledge.

Bush, Julia (1994), "'The Right Sort of Woman': Female Emigrators and Emigration to the British Empire, 1890–1910," *Women's History Review*, 3 (3): 385–40.

Butlin, Robin (2009), *Geographies of Empire: European Empires and Colonies c. 1880–1960*, Cambridge: Cambridge University Press.

Butts, R. Freeman (1947), *A Cultural History of Education*, New York: McGraw-Hill.

Butts, R. Freeman (1953), *A Cultural History of Western Education: Its Social and Intellectual Foundations*, New York: McGraw-Hill.

Canfield Fisher, Dorothy (1912), *A Montessori Mother*, New York: Henry Holt and Co.

Carleton, Sean (2011), "Colonizing Minds: Public Education, the 'Textbook Indian,' and Settler Colonialism in British Columbia, 1920–1970," *BC Studies*, no. 169: 101–30.

Carleton, Sean (2017), "Settler Anxiety and State Support for Missionary Schooling in Colonial British Columbia, 1849–1871," *Historical Studies in Education/Revue d'histoire de l'éducation*, 29 (1) (Spring): 57–76.

Carter, Sarah (2018), *Object Lessons: How Nineteenth-Century Americans Learned to Make Sense of the Material World*, Oxford: Oxford University Press.

Caruso, Marcelo (2005), "The Persistence of Educational Semantics: Patterns of Variation in Monitorial Schooling in Colombia (1821–1844)," *Paedagogica Historica*, 41 (6): 721–44.

Caruso, Marcelo (2009), "Imperial Connections, Entangles Peripheries: Cadiz and the Latin American Monitorial Schools," in Linda Chisholm and Gita Steiner-Khamsi (eds), *South-South Cooperation in Education and Development*, 17–38, New York: Teachers College Press.

Caruso, Marcelo (2010a), *Geist oder Mechanik: Unterrichtsordnungen als kulturelle Konstruktionen in Preussen, Dänemark (Schleswig-Holstein) und Spanien 1800–1870*, Komparatistische Bibliothek, volume 19, Frankfurt: Peter Lang.

Caruso, Marcelo (2010b), "Latin American Independence: Education and the Invention of New Polities," *Paedagogica Historica*, 46 (4): 409–17.

Caruso, Marcelo (2012), "Learning and New Sociability: Schooling and the Concept of the Child in the Spanish Enlightenment," *Paedagogica Historica*, 48 (1): 85–98.

Caruso, Marcelo (2013), "Cheap, Suitable, Promising: Monitorial Schooling and the Challenge of Mass Education in Early Liberal Spain (1808–1823)," *Bordón*, 65 (4): 33–45.

Caruso, Marcelo (2015), "Emotional Regimes and School Policy in Colombia, 1800–1835," in Stephanie Olsen (ed.), *Childhood, Youth and Emotions in Modern History: National, Colonial and Global Perspectives*, 139–57, Basingstoke: Palgrave.

Caruso, Marcelo, ed. (2015), *Classroom Struggle: Organizing Elementary School Teaching in the 19th Century*, Frankfurt: Peter Lang.

Caruso, Marcelo and Maria Moritz (2018), "The Indian Female Pupil-Teacher: Social Technologies of Education and Gender in the Second Half of the Nineteenth Century," *Südasien-Chronik/South Asia Chronicle*, 8: 21–52.

Caruso, Marcelo and Eugenia Roldán Vera (2005), "Pluralizing Meanings: The Monitorial System of Education in Latin America in the Early Nineteenth Century," *Paedagogica Historica*, 41 (6): 645–54.

Casalini, Chrstiano (2019), "Rise, Character, and Development of Jesuit Education: Teaching the World," *The Oxford Handbook of the Jesuits*. https//:dx.doi.org/10.1093/oxfordhb/9780190639631.013.7.

Casulleras, Antonio ([1917] 2018), "Appendice: Rapporto di Antonio Casulleras a Joaquín de Llevanteras sul sistema Montessori" (Appendix: Report from Antonio Casulleras to Joaquín de Llevanteras on the Montessori System), in Erica Moretti, "Alejandro Mario Dieguez- i progetti di Maria Montessori" (Alejandro Mario Dieguez-Maria Montessori's Projects), *Annali di storia dell'educazione e delle istituzioni scholastiche*, 25: 89–114.

Cavalier, Christine (2011), "Sentimental Ideology, Women's Pedagogy, and American Indian Women's Writing: 1815–1921," PhD diss., Washington University, St. Louis.

Cavallo, Dom (1976), "From Perfection to Habit: Moral Training in the American Kindergarten, 1860–1920," *History of Education Quarterly*, 16 (2): 147–61.

Chadwick, Owen (1970a), *The Victorian Church*, Part 1, *1829–1859*, 2nd edition, London: Adam and Charles Black.

Chadwick, Owen (1970b), *The Victorian Church*, Part 2, *1860–1901*, London: Adam and Charles Black.

Chadwick, Owen (1975), *The Secularisation of the European Mind*, Cambridge: Cambridge University Press.

Chadwick, Priscilla (1997), *Shifting Alliances: Church and State in English Education*, London: Cassell.

Chakravarti, Uma (1998), *Rewriting History: The Life and Times of Pandita Ramabai*, New Delhi: Kali for Women.

Chambers, William and Robert Chambers (1842), *Introduction to English Composition*, London: Chambers's Educational Course.

Chambliss, J.J. (2019), "Education: Russia," *Encyclopaedia Brittanica*. Available online: https://www.britannica.com/topic/education/Development-of-state-education (accessed April 20, 2020).

Chapman, Bernadine S. (1990), "Northern Philanthropy and African-American Adult Education in the Rural South: Hegemony and Resistance in the Jeanes Movement," EdD diss., North Illinois University.

Chavan, Dilip (2013), "Politics of Patronage and the Institutionalization of Language Hierarchy in Colonial Western India," in Deepak Kumar, Joseph Bara, Nandita Khadria, and Ch. R. Gayatri (eds), *Education in Colonial India: Historical Insights*, 187–226, New Delhi: Manohar.

Chitambar, Satyavati S. (1926), "Systematic Scientific Teaching on Temperance in Indian Schools" [Pamphlet], Howrah.

Choate, Mark (2008), *Emigrant Nation*, Cambridge, MA: Harvard University Press.

Cholmondeley, Essex (1960), *The Story of Charlotte Mason (1842–1943)*, London: Dent.

Church, Robert L., Michael B. Katz, and Harold Silver (1989), "Forum Review of Cremin 1988," *History of Education Quarterly*, 29 (3): 419–46.

Cicek, Nazan (2012), "The Role of Mass Education in Nation-Building in the Ottoman Empire and the Turkish Republic, 1870–1930," in Laurence Brockliss and Nicola Sheldon (eds), *Mass Education and the Limits of State Building, c. 1870–1930*, 224–50, Basingstoke: Palgrave Macmillan.

Claeys, Gregory (1989), *Citizens and Saints: Politics and Anti-Politics in Early British Socialism*, Cambridge: Cambridge University Press.

Clark, Christopher and Wolfram Kaiser, eds (2003), *Culture Wars: Secular-Catholic Conflict in Nineteenth-Century Europe*, Cambridge: Cambridge University Press.

Cleall, Esme, Laura Ishiguro, and Emily J. Manktelow (2013), "Imperial Relations: Histories of Family in the British Empire," *Journal of Colonialism and Colonial History* 14 (1). https://dx.doi.org/10.1353/cch.2013.0006.

Cleverley, John F. (1971), *The First Generation: School and Society in Early Australia*, Sydney: Sydney University Press.

Cohen, Benjamin (2017), *In the Club: Associational Life in Colonial South Asia*, Manchester: Manchester University Press.

Cohen, Michèle (2015), "The Pedagogy of Conversation in the Home: 'familiar conversation' as a Pedagogical Tool in Eighteenth and Nineteenth-Century England," *Oxford Review of Education*, 41 (4): 447–63.

Cohen, Sol (1998), "Lawrence A. Cremin: Hostage to History," *Historical Studies in Education*, 10: 180–204.

Cohen, Sol (1999), *Challenging Orthodoxies: Toward a New Cultural History of Education*, New York: Peter Lang.

Coldrey, Barry (1992), "'A most unenviable reputation': The Christian Brothers and School Discipline over Two Centuries," *History of Education*, 21 (3): 277–89.

Coleman, Michael C. (1994), "American Indian School Pupils as Cultural Brokers: Cherokee Girls at Brainerd Mission, 1828–1829," in Margaret Connell Szasz (ed.), *Between Indian and White Worlds: The Cultural Broker*, 122–35. Norman: University of Oklahoma Press.

Coleman, Michael C. (1996), "The Symbiotic Embrace: American Indians, White Educators and the School, 1820s–1920s," *History of Education*, 25 (1): 1–18.

Coleridge, Christabel (1903), *Charlotte Mary Yonge, Her Life and Letters*, London: Macmillan.

Colley, Linda (2002), *Captives: Britain, Empire and the World, 1600–1850*, London: Jonathan Cape.

Collini, Stefan (1991), *Public Moralists: Political Thought and Intellectual Life in Britain, 1850–1930*, Oxford: Clarendon Press.

Collini, Stefan (1993), *Public Moralists: Political Thought and Intellectual Life in Britain, 1850–1930*, Oxford: Oxford University Press.

Commission, Newcastle (1861), "Evidence of Assistant Commissioners Code and Cumin, vol. ii," London.

"The Conversazione" (1898), *Ulula*, February: 11.

Cook-Gumpertz, Jenny ([1986] 2006), *The Social Construction of Literacy*, Cambridge: Cambridge University Press.

Cook, Sharon A. (1993), "Educating for Temperance: The Woman's Christian Temperance Union and Ontario Children, 1880–1916," *Historical Studies in Education/Revue d'histoire de l'éducation*, 5 (2): 251–77.

Coombs, Margaret (2015), *Charlotte Mason: Hidden Heritage and Educational Influence*, Cambridge: James Clarke.

Cooper, Frederick (2005), *Colonialism in Question*, Berkeley: University of California Press.

Cooper, Frederick and Ann L. Stoler, eds (1997), *Tensions of Empire: Colonial Cultures in a Bourgeois World*, Berkeley: University of California Press.

Cooper, Thomas (1872), *The Life of Thomas Cooper, Written by Himself*, London: Hodder and Stoughton.

"Correspondence" (1873), *Ulula*, July: 30–1.

Corrigan, Philip and Derek Sayer (1985), *The Great Arch: English State Formation as Cultural Revolution*, Oxford: Blackwell.

Cortina, Regina and Sonsoles San Román, eds (2006), *Women and Teaching: Global Perspectives on the Feminization of a Profession*, Basingstoke: Palgrave Macmillan.

Craig, John E. (1984), *Scholarship and Nation-Building: The Universities of Strasbourg and Alsatian Society, 1870–1939*, Chicago: University of Chicago Press.

Crain, Patricia (2020), "New Histories of Literacy," in Simon Eliot and Jonathan Rose (eds), *Companion to the History of the Book*, Chichester: John Wiley & Sons.

Cremin, Lawrence A. (1970–88), *American Education*, 3 volumes, New York: Harper and Row.

Cremin, Lawrence A. (1976), *Public Education*, New York: Basic Books.

Cremin, Lawrence A. (1980), *American Education: The National Experience 1783–1876*, New York: Harper and Row.

Cremin, Lawrence A. (1988), *American Education: The Metropolitan Experience 1876–1980*, New York: Harper and Row.

Crone, Rosalind (2015), "Education in the Working-Class Home: Modes of Learning as Revealed by Nineteenth-Century Criminal Records," *Oxford Review of Education*, 41 (4): 482–500.

Cross, Michael (1986), "A Historical Review of Education in South Africa: Towards an Assessment," *Comparative Education*, 22 (3): 185–200.

Cruickshank, Marjorie (1963), *Church and State in English Education 1870 to the Present Day*, London: Macmillan.

Cubberley, Ellwood P. (1947), *Public Education in the United States: A Study and Interpretation of American Educational History*, Cambridge, MA: Houghton Mifflin.

Cunningham, Peter (2000), "The Montessori Phenomenon: Gender and Internationalism in Early Twentieth-Century Innovation," in Mary Hilton and Pam Hirsch (eds), *Practical Visionaries: Women, Education, and Social Progress, 1790–1930*, 203–20, Harlow: Longman.

Curtis, Bruce (1988), *Building the Educational State: Canada West, 1836–1871*, London, ONT: Althouse Press.

Curtis, Bruce (2005), "Joseph Lancaster in Montreal (bis): Monitorial Schooling and Politics in a Colonial Context," *Historical Studies in Education/Revue d'histoire de l'éducation*, 17 (1): 1–27.

Curtis, Bruce (2012), *Ruling by Schooling Quebec: Conquest to Liberal Governmentality; A Historical Sociology*, Toronto: University of Toronto Press.

D'Agostino, Peter (2004), *Rome in America*, Chapel Hill: University of North Carolina Press.

Dalrymple, William (2019), *The Anarchy: The Relentless Rise of the East India Company*, London: Bloomsbury.

Davidann, Jon and Marc Jason Gilbert ([1453] 2019), *Cross-Cultural Encounters in Modern History 1453–Present*, 2nd edition, New York: Routledge.

Davidoff, Leonore and Catherine Hall (2002), *Family Fortunes: Men and Women of the English Middle Class, 1780–1850*, London: Routledge.

Davis, John R. (2014), "Higher Education Reform and the German Model: A Victorian Discourse," in Heather Ellis and Ulrike Kirchberger (eds), *Anglo-German Scholarly Networks in the Long Nineteenth Century*, 39–62, Leiden: Brill Nijhoff.

Davis, Mary (2000), *Fashioning a New World: A History of the Woodcraft Folk*, Manchester: Holyoake Books.

de Amicis, Edmondo (2005), *Cuore: The Heart of a Boy*, London: Peter Owen.

de Bellaigue, Christina (2007), *Educating Women: Schooling and Identity in England and France, 1800–1867*, Oxford: Oxford University Press.

de Bellaigue, Christina (2015), "Charlotte Mason, Home Education and the Parents' National Educational Union in the Late Nineteenth Century," *Oxford Review of Education*, 41 (4): 501–17.

de Bellaigue, Christina (2019), "Great Expectations? Childhood, Family, and Middle-Class Social Mobility in Nineteenth-Century England," *Cultural & Social History* 16 (1): 29–46.

de Bellaigue, Christina, ed. (2016), *Home Education in Historical Perspective*, Abingdon: Routledge.

De Giorgi, Fulvio, ed. (2013), *Montessori, Dio e il bambino e altri scritti inediti* (Montessori, God and the Child and Other Unpublished Writings), Brescia: Editrice La Scuola.

De Giorgi, Fulvio (2018), "Maria Montessori tra modernisti, anti-modernisti e Gesuiti" (Maria Montessori Between Modernists, Anti-Modernistas and Jesuits), *Annali di storia dell'educazione e delle istituzioni scholastiche*, 25: 27–73.

de Leeuw, Sarah (2009), "'If Anything Is to Be Done with the Indian, We Must Catch Him Very Young': Colonial Constructions of Aboriginal Children and the Geographies of Indian Residential Schooling in British Columbia, Canada," *Children's Geographies*, 7 (2): 123–40.

de Leeuw, Sarah and Margo Greenwood (2014), "History Lessons: What Empire, Education, and Indigenous Childhoods Teaches Us," in Helen May, Baljit Kaur, and Larry Prochner (eds), *Empire, Education, and Indigenous Childhoods: Nineteenth-Century Missionary Infant Schools in Three British Colonies*, xv–xxii, Farnham: Ashgate.

Depaepe, Marc (2009), "Belgian Images of the Psycho-Pedagogical Potential of the Congolese During the Colonial Era, 1908–1960," *Paedagogica Historica*, 45 (6): 707–25.

Depaepe, Marc (2014), "Writing Histories of Congolese Colonial and Post-Colonial Education: A Historiographical View from Belgium," in Barnita Bagchi, Eckhardt Fuchs, and Kate Rousmaniere (eds), *Connecting Histories of Education: Transnational and Cross-cultural Exchanges in (Post)Colonial Education*, 41–60, New York: Berghahn.

Deslandes, Paul (2005), *Oxbridge Men: British Masculinity and the Undergraduate Experience, 1850–1920*, Bloomington: Indiana University Press.

Dickens, Charles (1865), *Our Mutual Friend*, London: Chapman and Hall.

Disraeli, Benjamin (1845), *Sibyl: Or, The Two Nations*, New York: George Routledge and Sons.

Dodd, Philip (1986), "Englishness and the National Culture," in Robert Colls and Philip Dodd (eds), *Englishness: Politics and Culture, 1880–1920*, 1–24, London: Croom Helm.

Dolan, Jay (1985), *The American Catholic Experience*, New York: Doubleday.

Donovan, Brian (2006), *White Slave Crusades: Race, Gender, and Anti-Vice Activism, 1887–1917*, Urbana: University of Illinois Press.

Donson, Andrew (2010), *Youth in the Fatherless Land: War Pedagogy, Nationalism, and Authority in Germany, 1914–1918*, Cambridge, MA: Harvard University Press.

Doyle, William (2017), *Napoleon Bonaparte: Emperor*, New York: Cavendish Square.

Duff, Sarah Emily (2012), "'Education for Every Son and Daughter of South Africa': Race, Class, and the Compulsory Education Debate in the Cape Colony," in Laurence Brockliss and Nicola Sheldon (eds), *Mass Education and the Limits of State Building, c. 1870–1930*, 261–82, London: Palgrave Macmillan.

Duff, Sarah Emily (2013), "'Unto Children's Children': Clerical Families and Childrearing Advice in the Cape Colony," *Journal of Colonialism and Colonial History* 14 (1). https://dx.doi.org/10.1353/cch.2013.0009.

Duncan, Sam (2012), *Reading Circles, Novels and Adult Reading Development*, London: Continuum.

Dunkley, Charles (1885), *The Official Report of the Church Congress, held at Portsmouth: On October 6th, 7th, 8th, and 9th, 1885*, London: Bemrose & Sons.

Dyhouse, Carol (1981), *Girls Growing Up in Victorian and Edwardian England*, London: Routledge & Kegan Paul.

Edgeworth, Maria and Richard Lovell Edgeworth (1815), *Practical Education*, Boston: J. Francis Lippitt and T.B. Wait and Sons.

Edwards, Elizabeth (2001), *Women in Teacher Training Colleges, 1900–1960: A Culture of Femininity*, London: RoutledgeFalmer.

Edwards, Elizabeth (2004), *Women in Teacher Training Colleges, 1900–1960: A Culture of Femininity*, London: Routledge.

Eisenbach-Stangl, Irmgard (2004), "From Temperance Movements to State Action: An Historical View of the Alcohol Question in Industrialised Countries," in Richard Müller and Harald Klingemann (eds), *From Science to Action? 100 Years Later— Alcohol Policies Revisited*, 15–28, Dordrecht: Springer.

Eitler, Pascal, Stephanie Olsen, and Uffa Jensen (2014), "Introduction," in Ute Frevert, Pascal Eitler, Stephanie Olsen, Uffa Jensen, Margrit Pernau, Daniel Bruckenhaus, Magdalena Beljan, Benno Gammerl, and Anja Laukotter, *Learning How to Feel: Children's Literature and Emotional Socialization, 1870–1970*, 1–20, Oxford: Oxford University Press.

Eklof, Ben (2012), "Russia and the Soviet Union: Schooling, Citizenship and the Reach of the State, 1870–1945," in Laurence Brockliss and Nicola Sheldon (eds), *Mass Education and the Limits of State Building, c. 1870–1930*, 140–66, Basingstoke: Palgrave Macmillan.

Elias, John L. (2002), *A History of Christian Education*, Malabar, FL: Kreiger Publishing.

Elleray, Michelle (2011), "Little Builders: Coral Insects, Missionary Culture, and the Victorian Child," *Victorian Literature and Culture*, 39 (1): 223–38.

Elliott, Paul and Stephen Daniels (2005), "Pestalozzianism, Natural History and Scientific Education in Nineteenth-Century England: The Pestalozzian Institution at Worksop, Nottinghamshire," *History of Education* 34 (3): 295–313.

Ellis, Heather (2010), "Corporal Punishment in the English Public School in the Nineteenth Century," in Laurence Brockliss and Heather Montgomery (eds), *Childhood, Violence and the Western Tradition*, 141–6, Oxford: Oxbow Books.

Ellis, Heather (2012), "Elite Education and the Development of Mass Elementary Schooling in England, 1870–1930," in Laurence Brockliss and Nicola Sheldon (eds), *Mass Education and the Limits of State Building, c. 1870–1930*, 46–70, Basingstoke: Palgrave Macmillan.

Ellis, Heather (2014), "Thomas Arnold, Christian Manliness and the Problem of Boyhood," *Journal of Victorian Culture*, 19 (4): 425–41.

Elman, Benjamin A. and Alexander Woodside, eds (1994), *Education and Society in Late Imperial China, 1600–1900*, Berkeley: University of California Press.

Elson, Ruth Miller (1964), *Guardians of Tradition, American Schoolbooks of the Nineteenth Century*, Lincoln: University of Nebraska Press.

English, Jim (2006), "Empire Day in Britain, 1904–1958," *Historical Journal*, 49 (1): 247–76.

Erskine Stuart, Janet (1911), *The Education of Catholic Girls*, Charlotte, NC: Tan Books.

Evered, Emine Ö. (2012), *Empire and Education under the Ottomans: Politics, Reform, and Resistance from the Tanzimat to the Young Turks*, London: I.B. Tauris.

Fass, Paula (2013), "Introduction," in Paula Fass (ed.), *The Routledge History of Childhood in the Western World*, 1–13, Abingdon: Routledge.

Fendler, Lynn (2019), "New Cultural Histories," in Tanya Fitzgerald (ed.), *Handbook of Historical Studies in Education*, Singapore: Springer.

Ferrer, Alejandro Tiana (2011), "The Concept of Popular Education Revisited—or What do We Talk about When We Speak of Popular Education," *Paedagogica Historica*, 47 (1–2): 15–31.

Fischer-Tiné, Harald (2001), "The Only Hope for Fallen India, the Gurukul Kangri as an Experiment in National Education (1902–22)," in George Berkemer (ed.), *Explorations in History of South Asia: Essays in Honour of Dietmar Rothermund*, 277–99, New Delhi: Manohar.

Fitzgerald, Tanya (2001), "Jumping the Fences: Maori Women's Resistance to Missionary Schooling in Northern New Zealand, 1823–1835," *Paedagogica Historica*, 37 (1): 175–92.

Fortna, Benjamin C. (2002), *Imperial Classroom: Islam, the State, and Education in the Late Ottoman Empire*, Oxford: Oxford University Press.

Foyster, Elizabeth and James Marten (2010a), "Introduction," in Elizabeth Foyster and James Marten (eds), *A Cultural History of Childhood and Family in the Age of Enlightenment*, volume 4, 1–13, New York: Berg Publishers.

Foyster, Elizabeth and James Marten, eds (2010b), *A Cultural History of Childhood and Family*, 6 volumes, London: Bloomsbury.

Frago, Antonio Viñao (1990), "The History of Literacy in Spain: Evolution, Traits, and Questions," *History of Education Quarterly*, 30 (4): 573–99.

Francis, Mark (1994), "Anthropology and Social Darwinism in the British Empire: 1870–1900," *Australian Journal of Politics and History*, 40 (1): 203–15.

Franklin, Vincent P. (1979), *The Education of Black Philadelphia: The Social and Educational History of a Minority Community, 1900–1950*, Philadelphia: University of Pennsylvania Press.

Fraser, Crystal (2019), *"T'aih k'iighe' tth'aih zhit dìidìch'ùh* (By Strength, We Are Still Here): Indigenous Northerners Confronting Hierarchies of Power at Day and Residential Schools in Nanhkak Thak (the Inuvik Region, Northwest Territories), 1959 to 1982," PhD thesis, University of Alberta.

Fraser, Crystal and Ian Mosby (2015), "Setting Canadian History Right?: A Response to Ken Coates' 'Second Thoughts about Residential Schools'," *Active History*. Available online: http://activehistory.ca/papers/paper-20/ (accessed October 15, 2019).

Fraser, James W. (2016), *Between Church and State Religion and Public Education in Multicultural America*, Baltimore: John Hopkins University Press.

French, Henry and Mark Rothery (2012), *Man's Estate: Landed Gentry Masculinities, c.1660–c.1900*, Oxford: Oxford University Press.

French, J.E. (2000), "Itard, Jean-Marie-Gaspard," in Alan E. Kazdin (ed.), *Encyclopedia of Psychology*, Oxford: Oxford University Press.

Fry, Gerald W. and Hui Bi (2005), "The Evolution of Educational Reform in Thailand: The Thai Educational Paradox," *Journal of Educational Administration*, 51 (3): 290–319.

Fuchs, Eckhardt (2014), "History of Education Beyond the Nation? Trends in Historical and Educational Scholarship," in Barnita Bagchi, Eckhardt Fuchs, and Kate Rousmaniere (eds), *Connecting Histories of Education: Transnational and Cross-Cultural Exchanges in (Post)Colonial Education*, 11–26, New York: Berghahn.

Fussell, Paul ([1975] 2000), *The Great War and Modern Memory*, New York: Oxford University Press.

Fyfe, Aileen (1999), "How the Squirrel Became a Squgg: The Long History of a Children's Book," *Paradigm*, 27: 25–37. Available online: http://faculty.ed.uiuc.edu/westbury/paradigm/fyfe2.html (accessed October 12, 2018).

Gaitskell, Deborah (2017), "Leadership (with Fun and Games) Instead of Domestic Service: Changing African Girlhood in a Johannesburg Mission, 1907–1940," in Hugh Morrison and Mary Clare Martin (eds), *Creating Religious Childhoods in Anglo-World and British Colonial Contexts, 1800–1950*, 134–54, London: Routledge.

Galton, Francis (1904), "Eugenics: Its Definition, Scope, and Aims," *American Journal of Sociology*, 10 (1): 1–25.

Gamsu, Sol (2016), "Moving Up and Moving Out: The Re-location of Elite and Middle-class Schools from Central London to the Suburbs," *Urban Studies*, 53 (14): 2921–38.

Gaskell, Elizabeth ([1866] 1996), *Wives and Daughters*, London: Penguin Classics.

Gaul, Theresa Strouth (2014), "Editor's Introduction," in Catharine Brown, *Cherokee Sister: The Collected Writings of Catharine Brown 1818–1823*, edited by Theresa Strouth Gaul, 1–57, Lincoln: University of Nebraska Press.

Gear, Gillian Carol (1999), "Industrial Schools in England, 1857–1933," PhD thesis, University of London.

Gecev, Minko [Гечев, Минко] (1995), *Огнища на народната свяст: Взаимните училища в България*. София: Изд. авт.

Geertz, Clifford (1973), *The Interpretation of Cultures: Selected Essays*, New York: Basic Books.

Geuna, Andrea (2012), "Educare l'uomo, il cittadino, il patriota: l'insegnamento delle 'prime nozioni dei doveri dell'uomo' nell'età della Sinistra (1872–1894)" (Educating the Man, the Citizen, the Patriot: The Teaching of the First Notions of the Duties of Man in the Age of the Left [1872–1894]), *Rivista storia del Cristianesimo*, 9 (1): 161–81.

Ghosh, Suresh C. (1995), "Bentinck, Macaulay and the Introduction of English Education in India," *History of Education*, 24 (1): 17–24.

Gillis, John R. (1981), *Youth and History: Tradition and Change in European Age Relations, 1770–Present*, New York: Academic Press.

Giorgetti, Filiz Meseci, Craig Campbell, and Ali Arslan (2017), "Introduction—Culture and Education: Looking Back to Culture Through Education," *Paedagogica Historica*, 53 (1–2): 1–6.

Gleadle, Kathryn (2016), "The Juvenile Enlightenment: British Children and Youth during the French Revolution," *Past and Present*, 233 (1): 143–84.

Gleadle, Kathryn (2019), "Magazine Culture, Girlhood Communities, and Educational Reform in Late Victorian Britain," *English Historical Review*, 134 (570): 1169–95.

Gleason, Mona (2018), "Metaphor, Materiality, and Method: The Central Role of Embodiment in the History of Education," *Paedagogica Historica*, 54 (1–2): 4–19.

Godfrey, Barry, Pamela Cox, Heather Shore, and Zoe Alker (2017), *Young Criminal Lives: Life Chances and Life Courses from 1850*, Oxford: Oxford University Press.

Goldman, Lawrence (1995), *Dons and Workers: Oxford Adult Education since 1850*, Oxford: Clarendon.

Goodman, Joyce (2011), "International Citizenship and the International Federation of University Women before 1939," *History of Education*, 40 (6): 701–21.

Goodman, Joyce and Jane Martin (2000), "Reforming Lives? Progressivism, Leadership and Educational Change," *History of Education*, 30 (5): 409–12.

Goodman, Joyce and Jane Martin, eds (2002), *Gender, Colonialism and Education: The Politics of Experience*, London: Woburn Press.

Goodman, Joyce, James Albisetti, and Rebecca Rogers (2010), *Girls' Secondary Education in the Western World: From the 18th to the 20th Century*, Basingstoke: Palgrave Macmillan.

Goodman, Joyce, Gary McCulloch, and William Richardson (2009a), "'Empires Overseas' and 'Empires at Home': Postcolonial and Transnational Perspectives on Social Change in the History of Education," *Paedagogica Historica*, 45 (6): 695–706.

Goodman, Joyce, Gary McCulloch, and William Richardson, eds (2009b), "'Empires Overseas' and 'Empires at Home': Postcolonical and Transnational Perspectives on Social Change in the History of Education," special issue of *Paedagoca Historica*, 65 (6).

Goodson, Ivor F. (1995), "The Story So Far: Personal Knowledge and the Political," in J. Amos Hatch and Richard Wisniewski (eds), *Life History and Narrative*, 89–98, London: Falmer.

Goodyear-Kaōpua, Noelani (2014), "Domesticating Hawaiians: Kamehameha Schools and the 'Tender Violence' of Marriage," in Brenda J. Child and Brian Klopotek (eds), *Indian Subjects: Hemispheric Perspectives on the History of Indigenous Education*, 16–47, Santa Fe, NM: School for Advanced Research Press.

Gordon, Edward E. and Elaine H. Gordon (2003), *Literacy in America: Historic Journey and Contemporary Solutions*, Westport, CT: Praeger.

Gordon, Peter (1983), "The Writings of Edmund Holmes: A Reassessment and Bibliography," *History of Education*, 12 (1): 15–24.

Gorham, Deborah (1982), *The Victorian Girl and the Feminine Ideal*, London: Croom Helm.

Graff, Harvey J. (1979), *The Literacy Myth: Literacy and Social Structure in the Nineteenth Century City*, New York: Academic Press.

Graff, Harvey J. (1995), *The Labyrinths of Literacy: Reflections on Literacy Past and Present*, revised edition, Pittsburgh, PA: University of Pittsburgh Press.

Graff, Harvey J. (2010), "The Literacy Myth at Thirty," *Journal of Social History*, 43 (3): 635–61.

Graff, Harvey J. (2011/13), *Literacy Myths, Legacies and Lessons: New Studies on Literacy*, New Brunswick, NJ: Transaction Publishers.

Graham, Charles Kwesi (1971), *The History of Education in Ghana: From Earliest Times to the Declaration of Independence*, London: Frank Cass and Company.

Greenblatt, Miriam (2006), *Napoleon Bonaparte and Imperial France*, Tarrytown, NY: Marshall Cavendish Benchmark.

Greenblatt, Stephen (2010), *Cultural Mobility: A Manifesto*, Cambridge: Cambridge University Press.

Greene, Maxine ([1965] 2007), *The Public School and the Private Vision: A Search for America in Education and Literature*, New York: New Press.

Grenby, Matthew O. (2011), *The Child Reader, 1700–1840*, Cambridge: Cambridge University Press.

Griffith, Jane (2015), "News from School: Language, Time, and Place in the Newspapers of 1890s Indian Boarding Schools in Canada," PhD thesis, University of York, Toronto.

Grimshaw, Patricia (2000), "Settler Anxieties, Indigenous Peoples, and Women's Suffrage in the Colonies of Australia, New Zealand, and Hawaii: 1888 to 1902," *Pacific Historical Review*, 69 (4): 553–72.

Große, Judith, Francesco Spöring, and Jana Tschurenev, eds (2014), *Biopolitik und Sittlichkeitsreform: Kampagnen gegen Alkohol, Drogen und Prostitution 1880–1950*, Frankfurt: Campus.

Groves, William C. (1936), *Native Education and Culture-Contact in New Guinea*, Melbourne: Melbourne University Press.

Gunn, Simon (2012), "Between Modernity and Backwardness: The Case of the English Middle Class," in A. Ricardo López and Barbara Weinstein (eds), *The Making of the Middle Class: Toward a Transnational History*, 58–74, Durham, NC: Duke University Press.

Gutek, Gerald Lee (1995), *A History of the Western Educational Experience*, 2nd edition, Prospect Heights, IL: Waveland Press.

Habermas, Jürgen (1989), *The Structural Transformation of the Public Sphere*, Cambridge: Polity Press.

Hagerman, Christopher A. (2005), "Muse of Empire? Classical Education, the Classical Tradition and British Attitudes to Empire, 1757–1902," PhD diss., University of Toronto.

Hall, Catherine (2002), *Civilizing Subjects: Colony and Metropole in the English Imagination, 1830–1867*, Chicago: University of Chicago Press.

Hall, Catherine, ed. (2000), *Cultures of Empire: Colonizers in Britain and the Empire in Nineteenth and Twentieth Centuries; A Reader*, Manchester: Manchester University Press.

Hall, Catherine and Sonya O. Rose (2006a), "Introduction: Being at Home with the Empire," in Catherine Hall and Sonya O. Rose (eds), *At Home with the Empire: Metropolitan Culture and the Imperial World*, 1–31, Cambridge: Cambridge University Press.

Hall, Catherine and Sonya O. Rose, eds (2006b), *At Home with the Empire: Metropolitan Culture and the Imperial World*, Cambridge: Cambridge University Press.

Hamilton, David (1980), "Adam Smith and the Moral Economy of the Classroom System," *Journal of Curriculum Studies*, 12 (4): 281–98.

Hamlett, Jane (2015a), *At Home in the Institution*, London: Palgrave Macmillan.

Hamlett, Jane (2015b), "Space and Emotional Experience in Victorian and Edwardian English Public School Dormitories," in Stephanie Olsen (ed.), *Childhood, Youth and Emotions in Modern History: National, Colonial and Global Perspectives*, 119–38, Basingstoke: Palgrave.

Harik, Elsa. M. and Donald G. Schilling (1984), *The Politics of Education in Colonial Algeria and Kenya*, Athens: Centre for International Studies, Ohio University.

Harper, Charles Athiel (1970), *A Century of Public Teacher Education*, Westport, CT: Greenwood Press.

Harper, Elizabeth P. (2010), "Dame Schools," in Thomas C. Hunt, James C. Carper, Thomas J. Lasley II, and C. Daniel Raisch (eds), *Encyclopedia of Educational Reform and Dissent*, 259–60. Thousand Oaks, CA: Sage. https://doi.org/10.4135/9781412957403.

Harris, Ian, ed. (2007), *Buddhism, Power and Political Order*, London: Routledge.

Harrison, John F.C. (1969a), *Robert Owen and the Owenites in Britain and America: The Quest for the New Moral World*, London: Routledge.

Harrison, John F.C., ed. (1969b), *Utopianism and Education: Robert Owen and the Owenites*, New York: Teachers College.

Hately-Broad, Barbara (2008), "Today We Have Naming of Parts: The Development of Basic Education in the British Army in the Twentieth Century," *RaPAL Journal*, 65: 23–31.

Hawkins, Sean and Philip D. Morgan, eds (2006), *Black Experience and the Empire*, Oxford: Oxford University Press.

Heath-Stubbs, Mary (1926), *Friendships Highway: Being the History of the Girls' Friendly Society*, London: Girls' Friendly Society.

Heathorn, Stephen J. (2000), *For Home, Country and Race: Constructing Gender, Class and Englishness in the Elementary School 1880–1914*, Toronto: University of Toronto Press.

Heywood, Colin (2010), "Centuries of Childhood: An Anniversary—and an Epitaph?," *Journal of the History of Childhood and Youth*, 3 (3): 341–65.

Heywood, Colin (2018), *A History of Childhood*, 2nd edition, Cambridge: Polity.

Heywood, Colin, ed. (2014), *A Cultural History of Childhood and Family in the Age of Empire*, London: Bloomsbury.

Higginson, J.H. (1974), "Dame Schools," *British Journal of Educational Studies*, 22 (2): 166–81.

Hilaire-Pérez, Liliane (2002), "Cultures techniques et pratiques de l'échange, entre Lyon et le Levant: inventions et réseaux au XVIIIe siècle," *Revue d'histoire moderne et contemporaine*, 49 (1): 89–114.

Hilton, Mary (2007), *Women and the Shaping of the Nation's Young: Education and Public Doctrine in Britain 1750–1850*, Farnham: Ashgate.

Hilton, Mary (2014), "A Transcultural Transaction: William Carey's Baptist Mission, the Monitorial Method and the Bengali Renaissance," in Barnita Bagchi, Eckhardt Fuchs, and Kate Rousmaniere (eds), *Connecting Histories of Education: Transnational and Cross-Cultural Exchanges in (Post-)Colonial Education*, 85–104, New York: Berghahn Books.

Hobsbawm, Eric (1962), *The Age of Revolution, 1789–1848*, New York: New American Library.

Hobsbawm, Eric (1975), *The Age of Capital, 1848–1875*, London: Cardinal.

Hobsbawm, Eric (1987), *The Age of Empire, 1875–1914*, London: Cardinal.

Hobsbawm, Eric (1994), *Age of Extremes: The Short Twentieth Century 1914–1991*, London: Abacus.

Hodgins, J. George (1894), *Documentary History of Education in Upper Canada from the Passing of the Constitutional Act of 1791 to the Close of Rev. Ryerson's Administration of the Education Department in 1876*, 28 volumes, Toronto: Warwick Bros. & Rutter.

Hogan, David (1989), "The Market Revolution and Disciplinary Power: Joseph Lancaster and the Psychology of the Early Classroom System," *History of Education Quarterly*, 29 (3): 381–417.

Holloway, Sarah L., Phil Hubbard, Heike Jöns, and Helena Pimlott-Wilson (2010), "Geographies of Education and the Significance of Children, Youth and Families," *Progress in Human Geography*, 34 (5): 583–600.

Holt, Jenny (2008), *Public School Literature, Civic Education and the Politics of Male Adolescence*, Farnham: Ashgate.

Holyoake, George Jacob (1900), *A History of the Rochdale Pioneers*, London: Swan Sonnenschein.

Holzwarth, Simone (2014), "A New Education for 'Young India': Exploring Nai Talim from the Perspective of a Connected History," in Barnita Bagchi, Eckhardt Fuchs, and Kate Rousmaniere (eds), *Connecting Histories of Education: Transnational and Cross-Cultural Exchanges in (Post)Colonial Education*, 123–39, New York: Berghahn.

Honey, John (1977), *Tom Brown's Universe: The Development of the Victorian Public School*, London: Millington.

Horio, Teruhisa (1990), *Educational Thought and Ideology in Modern Japan: Authority, and Intellectual Freedom*, Tokyo: Tokyo University Press.

Horlacher, Rebekka (2011), "Schooling as a Means of Popular Education: Pestalozzi's Method as a Popular Education Experiment," *Paedagogica Historica*, 47 (1–2): 65–75.

Howard, Ursula (1991), "Self, Education and Writing in Nineteenth Century English Communities," in David Barton and Roz Ivanic (eds), *Writing in the Community*, 78–108, Newbury Park, CA: Sage.

Howard, Ursula (2012), *Literacy and the Practice of Writing in the 19th Century: A Strange Blossoming of Spirit*, Leicester: National Institute of Adult Continuing Education (NIACE).

Huhndofr, Roy M. and Shari M. Huhndorf (2014), "Worlds Apart: A History of Native Education in Alaska," in Brenda J. Child and Brian Klopotek (eds), *Indian Subjects: Hemispheric Perspectives on the History of Indigenous Education 2*, 133–47, Santa Fe, NM: School for Advanced Research Press.

Hulme, Tom (2015), "'A Nation Depends on its Children': School Buildings and Citizenship in England and Wales, 1900–1939," *Journal of British Studies*, 54 (2): 406–32.

Humphrey, George ([1801] 1962), "Introduction," in Jean Marc Gaspard Itard, *The Wild Boy of Aveyron*, New York: Appleton-Century-Crofts.

Humphries, Jane (2010), *Childhood and Child Labour in the British Industrial Revolution*, Cambridge: Cambridge University Press.

Hunt, Mary (1897), *An Epoch of the Nineteenth Century: An Outline of the Work for Scientific Temperance Education in the Public Schools of the United States*, Boston, MA: Foster.

Hurst [Hertz], Arthur (1949), *A Twentieth Century Physician*, London: Edward Arnold.

Hurt, John S. (1979), *Elementary Schooling and the Working Classes 1860–1918*, London: Routledge and Kegan Paul.

Ikhlef, Hakim (2014), "Constructive Orientalism: Debates on Languages and Educational Policies in Colonial India, 1830–1880," in Barnita Bagchi, Eckhardt Fuchs, and Kate Rousmaniere (eds), *Connecting Histories of Education: Transnational and Cross-Cultural Exchanges in (Post)Colonial Education*, 156–74, New York: Berghahn.

Imber, Michael (1982), "Toward a Theory of Curriculum Reform: An Analysis of the First Campaign for Sex Education," *Curriculum Inquiry*, 12 (4): 339–62.

Inkster, Ian (1975), "Science and the Mechanics' Institutes, 1820–1850: The Case of Sheffield," *Annals of Science*, 32 (5): 451–74.

Iriye, Akira (1989), "The Internationalization of History," *American Historical Review*, 94 (1): 1–10.

Iriye, Akira (2002), *Global Community: The Role of International Organizations in the Making of the Contemporary World*, Berkeley: University of California Press.

Israel, Jonathan I. (2001), *Radical Enlightenment: Philosophy and the Making of Modernity, 1650–1750*, Oxford: Oxford University Press.

Jacob, Margaret C. (1997), *Scientific Culture and the Making of the Industrial West*, Oxford: Oxford University Press.

Jacobs, Sylvia M. (2010), "Three African American Women Missionaries in the Congo, 1887–1899," in Barbara Reeves-Ellington, Kathryn K. Sklar, and Connie A. Shemo (eds), *Competing Kingdoms: Women, Mission, Nation, and the American Protestant Empire, 1812–1960*, 318–41, Durham, NC: Duke University Press.

Jayawardena, Kumari (1994), "Going for the Jugular of Hindu Patriarchy: American Fundraisers for Ramabai," in Vicki L. Ruiz and Ellen C. DuBois (eds), *Unequal Sisters: A Multicultural Reader in U.S. Women's History*, 197–204, New York: Routledge.

Jenkins, Edgar W. (1994), "Public Understanding of Science and Science Education for Action," *Journal of Curriculum Studies*, 26 (6): 601–11.

Jensz, Felicity (2012), "Missionaries and Indigenous Education in the 19th-Century British Empire: Part I; Church-State Relations and Indigenous Actions and Reactions," *History Compass*, 10 (4): 294–305.

Johansson, Egil (2009), "The History of Literacy in Sweden," in Harvey J. Graff, Alison Mackinnon, Bengt Sandin, and Ian Winchester (eds), *Understanding Literacy in its Historical Contexts: Socio-Cultural History and the Legacy of Egil Johansson*, 28–59, Lund: Nordic Academic Press.

Johnson, Richard (1979), "'Really useful knowledge': Radical Education and Working-Class Culture, 1790–1848," in John Clarke, Chas Critcher, and Richard Johnson (eds), *Working-Class Culture: Studies in History and Theory*, 75–102, London: Hutchinson.

Johnson, Walter (2003), "On Agency," *Journal of Social History*, 37 (1): 113–24.

Joliffe, Pia Maria and Thomas Richard Bruce, eds (2019), *Southeast Asian Education in Modern History: Schools, Manipulation and Contest*, London: Routledge.

Jones, Karen and Kevin Williamson (1979), "The Birth of the Schoolroom—A Study of the Transformation in the Discursive Conditions of English Popular Education in the First Half of the 19th Century," *Ideology & Consciousness*, 19 (6): 59–110.

Jöns, Heike (2017), "The University of Cambridge, Academic Expertise, and the British Empire: 1885–1962," in Heike Jöns, Peter Meusberger, and Michael Heffernan (eds), *Mobilities of Knowledge*, 185–210, Cham: Springer.

Jöns, Heike, Peter Meusberger, and Michael Heffernan, eds (2017), *Mobilities of Knowledge*, Cham: Springer.

Kaestle, Carl F. (1973), *Joseph Lancaster and the Monitorial School Movement: A Documentary History*, New York: Teachers College Press.

Kaestle, Carl F. (1976), "'Between the Scylla of Brutal Ignorance and the Charybdis of a Literary Education': Elite Attitudes toward Mass Schooling in Early Industrial England and America," in Lawrence Stone (ed.), *Schooling and Society*, 177–91, Baltimore: Johns Hopkins University Press.

Kaestle, Carl F. (1983), *Pillars of the Republic: Common Schools and American Society 1780–1860*, New York: Hill and Wang.

Kaestle, Carl F. (1985), "The History of Literacy and the History of Readers," *Review of Research in Education*, 12: 11–53.

Kaestle, Carl F. (1988), "Literacy and Diversity: Themes from a Social History of the American Reading Public," *History of Education Quarterly*, 28 (4): 523–49.

Kaestle, Carl F., Helen Damon-Moore, Lawrence C. Stedman, Katherine Tinsley, and William Vance Trollinger Jr. (1991), *Literacy in the United States: Readers and Reading Since 1880*, New Haven, CT: Yale University Press.

Kamenov, Nikolay (2020), *Global Temperance and the Balkans: American Missionaries, Swiss Scientists and Bulgarian Socialists, 1870–1940*, New York: Palgrave Macmillan.

Karlekar, Malavika (1986), "Kadambini and the Bhadralok: Early Debates over Women's Education in Bengal," *Economic and Political Weekly*, 21 (17): 25–31.

Katznelson, Ira and Margaret Weir (1985), *Schooling for All: Class, Race, and the Decline of the Democratic Ideal*, New York: Basic Books.

Kaviraj, Sudipta and Sunil Khilnani, eds (2003), *Civil Society: History and Possibilities*, Cambridge: Cambridge University Press.

Kazamias, Andreas M. (1966), *Education and the Quest for Modernity in Turkey*, London: George Allen & Unwin.

Keane, Patrick (1988), "Priorities and Resources in Adult Education: The Montreal Mechanics' Institute (1828–1843)," *McGill Journal of Education*, 23 (2): 171–88.

Kearns, Gerry (1997), "The Imperial Subject: Geography and Travel in the Work of Mary Kingsley and Halford Mackinder," *Transactions of the Institute of British Geographers*, 22 (4): 450–72.

Keefer, Katrina (2019), *Children, Education and Empire in Early Sierra Leone*, London: Routledge.

Kelley, Florence (1905), *Some Ethical Gains Through Legislation*, New York: MacMillan.

Kersting, Christa (2008), "Weibliche Bildung und Bildungspolitik: Das International Council of Women und seine Kongresse in Chicago (1893), London (1899) und Berlin (1904)," *Paedagogica Historica*, 44 (3): 327–46.

Key, Ellen (1909), *The Century of the Child*, New York: G.P. Putnam's Sons.

Khan, Yoshimitsu (1997), *Japanese Moral Education: Past and Present*, London: Associated University Presses.

Kirkes, Stephanie (1976), "Mao as Library User and Worker: How Early Experiences in Traditional Chinese Libraries Contributed to Mao's Revolutionary Ideas," *American Libraries*, 7 (10): 628–31.

Kolshus, Thorgeir and Even Hovdhaugen (2010), "Reassessing the Death of Bishop John Coleridge Patteson," *Journal of Pacific History*, 45 (3): 331–5.

Kosambi, Meera (1998), "Multiple Contestations: Pandita Ramabai's Educational and Missionary Activities in Late Nineteenth-Century India and Abroad," *Women's History Review*, 7 (2): 193–208.

Kosambi, Meera (2016), *Pandita Ramabai: Life and Landmark Writings*, A Routledge India Original, London: Taylor & Francis.

Krishnan, Sneha (2017), "Anxious Notes on College Life: The Gossipy Journals of Eleanor McDougall," *Journal of the Royal Asiatic Society*, 27 (4): 575–89.

Kropotkin, Peter ([1902] 1987), *Mutual Aid: A Factor of Evolution*, London: Freedom Press.

Kulicev, Kristo [Куличев, Кристо] (2008), *Заслугите на протестантите за българския народ*. Izd. 1. София: Университетско изд. "Свети Климент Охридски."

Kumar, Krishna (1991), *Political Agenda of Education: A Study of Colonialist and Nationalist Ideas*, New Delhi: Sage.

Kumar, Nita (2012), "India's Trials with Citizenship, Modernisation and Nationhood," in Laurence Brockliss and Nicola Sheldon (eds), *Mass Education and the Limits of State Building, c. 1870–1930*, 283–304, Basingstoke: Palgrave Macmillan.

Kumbhat, Christine Pushpa (2017), "Working Class Adult Education in Yorkshire 1918–1939," PhD thesis, University of Leeds.

La Volpa, A.J. (1980), *Prussian School Teachers: Profession and Office, 1763–1848*, Chapel Hill: University of North Carolina Press.

Lagemann, Ellen Condliffe (1979), *A Generation of Women: Education in the Lives of Progressive Reformers*, Cambridge, MA: Harvard University Press.

Lambert, David and Alan Lester (2006), *Colonial Lives Across the British Empire: Imperial Careering in the Long Nineteenth Century*, Cambridge: Cambridge University Press.

Lancaster, Joseph (1803), *Improvements in Education, as It Respects the Industrious Classes of the Community*, London: Darton and Harvey.

Langlois, Claude (1984), *Le catholicisme au féminin: les congrégations françaises à supérieure générale au xix e siècle* (The Feminization of Catholicism: French Congregations with Superior Generals in the XIX Century), Paris: Cerf.

Langton, Anne (2008), *A Gentlewoman in Upper Canada: The Journals, Letters and Art of Anne Langton*, edited by Barbara Williams, Toronto: University of Toronto Press.

Larsen, Marianne A. (2011), *The Making and Shaping of the Victorian Teacher: A Comparative New Cultural History*, New York: Palgrave Macmillan.

Leach, Camilla (2002), "Advice for Parents and Books for Children: Quaker Women and Educational Texts for the Home, 1798–1850," *History of Education Researcher*, 69 (2002): 49–58.

Leach, Fiona (2008), "African Girls, Nineteenth-Century Mission Education and the Patriarchal Imperative," *Gender and Education*, 20 (4): 335–47.

Lee, Christopher J. (2010), "Children in the Archives: Epistolary Evidence, Youth Agency, and the Social Meanings of 'Coming of Age' in Interwar Nyasaland," *Journal of Family History*, 35 (1): 25–47.

Legge, Anna (1884), "Women in China," *Oxford High School Magazine*, April: 642–64.

Lengwiler, Martin (2014), "Im Zeichen der Degeneration: Psychiatrie und internationale Abstinenzbewegungen im ausgehenden 19. Jahrhundert," in Judith Große, Francesco Spöring, and Jana Tschurenev (eds), *Biopolitik und Sittlichkeitsreform: Kampagnen gegen Alkohol, Drogen und Prostitution 1880–1950*, 85–110, Frankfurt: Campus.

Lerner, Loren (2018), "The Manipulation of Indigenous Imagery to Represent Canadian Childhood and Nationhood in 19th Century Canada," in Jane Eva Baxter and Meredith Ellis (eds), *Nineteenth Century Childhoods in Interdisciplinary and International Perspectives*, 15–33, Oxford: Oxbow Books.

Letters of Charlotte Mary Yonge (n.d.). Available online: https://c21ch.newcastle.edu.au/yonge/ (accessed May 5, 2020).

"Letters to the Editor" (1915), *Dollar Magazine*, June: 89–90.

"Letters to Ulula" (1898), *Ulula*, March: 57.

Lilley, Irene M., ed. (1967), *Friedrich Froebel: A Selection from his Writings*, Cambridge: Cambridge University Press.

Little, Cynthia J. (1975), "Moral Reform and Feminism: A Case Study," *Journal of Interamerican Studies and World Affairs*, 17 (4): 386–97.

Little, Kenneth L. (1948), "The Poro Society as an Arbiter of Culture," *African Studies*, 7 (1): 1–15.

Livshin, Rosalyn (1990), "The Acculturation of the Children of Immigrant Jews in Manchester, 1890–1930," in David Cesarini (ed.), *The Making of Modern Anglo-Jewry*, 79–96, Oxford: Basil Blackwell.

Lockeridge, Kenneth A. (1974), *Literacy in Colonial New England: An Enquiry into the Social Context of Literacy in the Early Modern West*, New York: Norton.

Lohmann, Wilhelmine (1923), "Zur Entwicklung des Nüchternheitsunterrichtes in Deutschland," in Scientific Temperance Federation (Boston) (ed.), *Der wissenschaftliche Nüchternheits-Unterricht: Begründung und Entwicklung*, 49–51, Bielefeld: Zentrale f. Nüchternheits-Unterricht; Wien: Bund Abstinenter Frauen.

Löhr, Isabella and Roland Wenzlhuemer, eds (2013), *The Nation State and Beyond: Governing Globalization Processes in the Nineteenth and Early Twentieth Centuries*, Heidelberg: Springer Verlag.

Long, Delbert H. and Roberta A. Long (1999), *Education of Teachers in Russia*, Westport, CT: Greenwood Press.

Lovett, William and John Collins ([1840] 1969), *Chartism, a New Organisation of the People*, Leicester: Leicester University Press.

Lush, Annie [Aroha, Te] (1881), "A Trip to Norfolk Island," *Monthly Packet*, January–June: 486–97.

Macaulay, Thomas Babington ([1848] 1906), *History of England from the Accession of James II*, London: Dent.

Mace, Jane (2001), "Signatures and the Lettered World," in Jim Crowther, Mary Hamilton, and Lyn Tett (eds), *Powerful Literacies*, 45–55, Leicester: National Institute of Adult Continuing Education (NIACE).

Mace, Jane (2002), *The Give and Take of Writing. Scribes, Literacy and Everyday Life*, Leicester: National Institute of Adult Continuing Education (NIACE).

Macías-González, Víctor (2012), "Learning the Rules of the Game: Informal Empire and the Mexican Experience at Stonyhurst College, 1805–1920," in Martin Hewitt (ed.), *The Victorian World*, 691–707, London: Routledge.

Mackenzie, John M. (2012), *European Empires and the People: Popular Responses to Imperialism in France, Britain, the Netherlands, Belgium, Germany and Italy*, Manchester: Manchester University Press.

Mahood, Linda (1995), *Policing Gender, Class and Family in Britain, 1800–1940*, London: Routledge.

Maier, Charles S. (2006), "Transformations of Territoriality, 1600–2000," in Gunilla Budde, Sebastian Conrad, and Oliver Janz (eds), *Transnationale Geschichte: Themen, Tendenzen Und Theorien*, 32–55, Göttingen: Vandenhoeck & Ruprecht.

Mair, Laura M. (2019), *Religion and Relationships in Ragged Schools: An Intimate History of Educating the Poor, 1844–1870*, London: Routledge.

Mangan, James A. (1981), *Athleticism in the Victorian and Edwardian Public School: The Emergence and Consolidation of an Educational Ideology*, Cambridge: Cambridge University Press.

Mangan, James A. (1986), "'The grit of our forefathers': Invented Traditions, Propaganda and Imperialism," in James MacKenzie (ed.), *Imperialism and Popular Culture*, 113–39, Manchester: Manchester University Press.

Mangan, James A. (2012), *Athleticism in the Victorian and Edwardian Public School: The Emergence and Consolidation of an Educational Ideology*, London: Routledge.

Mann, Michael (2004), "'Torchbearers Upon the Path of Progress': Britain's Ideology of 'Moral and Material Progress' in India," in Harald Fischer-Tiné and Michael Mann (eds), *Colonialism as Civilizing Mission: Cultural Ideology in British India*, 1–28, Anthem South Asian Studies, London: Anthem Press.

Mann, Michael, ed. (2015), *Shantiniketan—Hellerau: New Education in the "Pedagogic Provinces" of India and Germany*, Heidelberg: Draupadi.

Marshman, Joshua, William Carey, and William Ward (1816), *Hints Relative to Native Schools together with an Outline of an Institution for Their Extension and Management*, Serampore: Mission Press.

Marten, James (2018), *The History of Childhood A Very Short Introduction*, Oxford: Oxford University Press.

Martin, Jane (1991), "Hard-Headed and Large-Hearted: Women and the Industrial Schools, 1870–1855," *History of Education*, 20 (3): 187–201.

Martin, Joel W. (2001), *The Land Looks After Us: A History of Native American Religion*, New York: Oxford University Press.

Martin, Mary Clare (2013), "Church, School and Locality: Revisiting the Historiography of 'State' and 'Religious' Educational Infrastructures in England and Wales, 1780–1870," *Paedagogica Historica*, 49 (1): 70–81.

Martin, Mary Clare (2016), "Race, Indigeneity and the Baden-Powell Girl Guides: Age, Gender and the British World, 1908–1920," in Simon Sleight and Shirleen

Robinson (eds), *Children, Childhood and Youth in the British World*, 161–79, London: Palgrave Macmillan.

Marung, Steffi and Katja Naumann, eds (2014), *Vergessene Vielfalt: Territorialität und Internationalisierung in Ostmitteleuropa seit der Mitte des 19. Jahrhunderts*, 1st edition, Transnationale Geschichte v.2, Göttingen: Vandenhoeck & Ruprecht.

Mason, Charlotte (1886), *Home Education: A Course of Lectures to Ladies; Delivered in Bradford in the Winter of 1885–1886*, London: Kegan Paul, Trench.

Mason, Charlotte ([1905] 1989), *Ourselves: Improving Character and Conscience*, Wheaton, IL: Tyndale House.

Matthews-Schlinzig, Marie Isabel (2018), "Collaboration and Imagination in Letters Between Parents and their Children: The Herder Family Correspondence 1788–89," in Marie Isabel Matthews-Schlinzig and Caroline Socha (eds), *Was ist ein Brief? Aufsätze zu epistolarer Theorie und Kultur/What is a Letter? Essays on Epistolary Theory and Culture*, 235–54, Würzburg: Königshausen & Neumann.

May, Helen, Baljit Kaur, and Larry Prochner, eds (2014), *Empire, Education, and Indigenous Childhoods: Nineteenth-Century Missionary Infant Schools in Three British Colonies*, Farnham: Ashgate.

Mayo, Elizabeth (1830), *Lessons on Objects as Given in a Pestalozzian School at Cheam, Surrey*, London: R.B. Seeley & W. Burnside.

Mayo, Elizabeth (1890), *Pestalozzi and His Principles*, London: Home and Colonial Training College.

McAllister, Annemarie (2015), "Onward: How a Regional Temperance Magazine for Children Survived and Flourished in the Victorian Marketplace," *Victorian Periodicals Review*, 48 (1): 42–66.

McCallum, Mary Jane Logan (2014), "'I Would Like the Girls at Home': Domestic Labour and the Age of Discharge at Canadian Indian Residential Schools," in Victoria Haskins and Claire Lowry (eds), *Colonization and Domestic Service: Historical and Contemporary Perspectives*, 191–209, New York: Routledge.

McCann, Phillip (1988), "The Indian Origins of Bell's Monitorial System," in Peter Cunningham and Colin Brock (eds), *International Currents in Education*, 29–40, Leicester: History of Education Soicety.

McCulloch, Gary (2011), *The Struggle for the History of Education*, London: Routledge.

McCulloch, Gary (2019), "Consensus and Revisionism in Educational History," in John L. Rury and Eileen H. Tamura (eds), *The Oxford Handbook of the History of Education*, 19–32, Oxford: Oxford University Press.

McCulloch, Gary and William Richardson (2000), *Historical Research in Educational Settings*, Maidenhead: Open University Press.

McCulloch, Gary and Tom Woodin (2010a), "Introduction: Towards a Social History of Learners and Learning," *Oxford Review of Education*, 36 (2): 133–40.

McCulloch, Gary and Tom Woodin, eds (2010b), "Histories of Learning in the Modern World," special issue of *Oxford Review of Education*, 36 (2).

McCulloch, Gary, Ivor Goodson, and Mariano Gonzalez-Delgado, eds (2020), *Transnational Perspectives on Curriculum History*, London: Routledge.

McDermid, Jane (2013), *The Schooling of Girls in Britain and Ireland, 1800–1900*, New York: Routledge.

McGreevy, John T. (2016), *American Jesuits and the World: How an Embattled Religious Order Made Catholicism Global*, Princeton, NJ: Princeton University Press.

McLoughlin, William G. (1986), *Cherokee Renascence in the New Republic*, Princeton, NJ: Princeton University Press.

McLoughlin, William G. (1994), "An Alternative Missionary Style: Evan Jones and John B. Jones Among the Cherokees," in Margaret Connell Szasz (ed.), *Between Indian and White Worlds: The Cultural Broker*, 98–121, Norman: University of Oklahoma Press.

Mehl, Margaret (2000), "Chinese Learning (kangaku) in Meiji Japan (1868–1912)," *History: Journal of the Historical Association*, 85 (277): 48–66.

Mehl, Margaret (2001), "Women Educators and the Confucian Tradition in Meiji Japan (1868–1912): Miwada Masako and Atomi Kakei," *Women's History Review*, 10 (4): 579–602.

Mezvinsky, Norton (1961), "Scientific Temperance Instruction in the School," *History of Education Quarterly*, 1 (1): 48–56.

Midgley, Clare (2000), "Female Emancipation in an Imperial Frame: English Women and the Campaign Against Sati (Widow-Burning) in India, 1813–30," *Women's History Review*, 9 (1): 95–121.

Mill, James ([1812] 1995), *Schools for All, in Preference to Schools for Churchmen Only: or, the State of the Controversy between the Advocates for the Lancasterian System of Universal Education, and Those, Who Have Set Up an Exclusive and Partial System under the Name of the Church and Dr. Bell*, reprint edited by Jeffrey Stern, Bristol: Thoemmes Press.

Mill, James (1817), *The History of British India*, volume 1, London: Baldwin, Cradock and Joy.

Mill, John Stuart (1874), *Autobiography*, 3rd edition, London: Longmans, Green, Reader and Dyer.

Miller, James Rodger (1996), *Shingwauk's Vision: A History of Native Residential Schools*, Toronto: University of Toronto Press.

Miller, Jim ([1996] 2006), *Shingwauk's Vision: A History of Native Residential Schools*, Toronto: University of Toronto Press.

Miller, Pavla (1989), "Historiography of Compulsory Schooling: What is the Problem?," *History of Education*, 18 (2): 123–44.

Miller, Pavla (1998), *Transformations of Patriarchy in the West: 1500–1900*, Bloomington: Indiana University Press.

Millions, Erin (2017), "'By education and conduct': Educating Trans-Imperial Indigenous Fur-Trade Children in the Hudson's Bay Company Territories and the British Empire, 1820s to 1870s," PhD thesis, University of Manitoba, Winnipeg.

Milloy, John (1999), "When a Language Dies," *Index on Censorship*, 28 (3): 54–64.

Milloy, John S. and Mary Jane Logan McCallum (2017), *A National Crime: The Canadian Government and the Residential School System, 1879 to 1986*, Anniversary edition, Winnipeg: University of Manitoba Press.

Minogue, W.J.D. (1965), "Education in a Dependent Culture-New Zealand: Some Problems Relating to the British Influence in New Zealand Education," *Comparative Education*, 1 (3): 203–9.

Mironov, Boris N. (1986), "Literacy in Russia, 1797–1917," *Soviet Studies in History*, 25 (3): 86–117.

Mironov, Boris N. (1991), "The Development of Literacy in Russia and the USSR from the Tenth to the Twentieth Centuries," *History of Education Quarterly*, 31 (2): 229–52.

Mitch, David (1992), *The Rise of Popular Literacy in Victorian England: The Influence of Private Choice and Public Policy*, Philadelphia: University of Pennsylvania Press.

Mitch, David (2009), "How Did the Illiterates Fare?," in Harvey J. Graff, Alison Mackinnon, Bengt Sandin, and Ian Winchester (eds), *Understanding Literacy in its Historical Contexts: Socio-Cultural History and the Legacy of Egil Johansson*, 197–218, Lund: Nordic Academic Press.

Mokyr, Joel (2003), "Why Was the Industrial Revolution a European Phenomenon?," *Supreme Court Economic Review*, 10: 27–63.

Molesworth, J. (1826), *Shallapundhuttee, or, A Treatise of the Management of Schools According to the Lancasterian System of Education*, Bombay: Bombay Native Education Society [in Marathi].

Möller, Esther and Johannes Wischmeyer, eds (2013), *Transnationale Bildungsräume: Wissenstransfers im Schnittfeld von Kultur, Politik und Religion*, Göttingen: Vandenhoeck & Ruprecht.

Money, Agnes Louisa (1902), *History of the Girls' Friendly Society*, London: Wells Gardner, Darton.

Montessori, Maria ([1939] 2013), *Dio e il bambino* (God and the Child), in Fulvio De Giorgi (ed.), *Montessori, Dio e il bambino e altri scritti inediti* (Montessori, God and the Child and Other Unpublished Writings), 105–46, Brescia: Editrice La Scuola.

Montessori, Maria, with Anne George and Henry W. Holmes (1912), *The Montessori Method: Scientific Pedagogy as Applied to Child Education in "The Children's Houses": with Additions and Revisions by the Author*, London: Heinemann.

The Monthly Packet (1851–99), edited by Charlotte Yonge.

Moretti, Erica (2018), "Alejandro Mario Dieguez—I Progetti di Maria Montessori" (Alejandro Mario Dieguez—the Projects of Maria Montessori), *Annali di storia dell'educazione e delle istituzioni scholastiche*, 25: 89–114.

Morris, Robert J. (1990), *Class, Sect and Party: The Making of the British Middle Class, Leeds 1820–1850*, Manchester: Manchester University Press.

Moruzi, Kristine (2012), *Constructing Girlhood through the Periodical Press, 1850–1915*, Farnham: Ashgate.

Moruzi, Kristine and Michelle J. Smith, eds (2014), *Colonial Girlhood in Literature, Culture and History, 1840–1950*, Basingstoke: Palgrave Macmillan.

Moyse, Cordelia (2009), *A History of the Mothers' Union: Women Anglicanism and Globalisation, 1876–2008*, Woodbridge: Boydell Press.

Mt Pleasant, Alyssa (2014), "Guswenta and the Debate over Formal Schooling at Buffalo Creek, 1800–1811," in Brenda J. Child and Brian Klopotek (eds), *Indian Subjects: Hemispheric Perspectives on the History of Indigenous Education*, 114–32, Santa Fe, NM: School for Advanced Research Press.

Mukherjee, Sumita (2009), *Nationalism, Education and Migrant Identities: The England-Returned*, London: Routledge.

Münchow, Katja (2006), "The Relationship between the Kindergarten Movement, the Movement for Democracy and the Early Women's Movement in the Historical Context of the Revolution of 1848–49, as reflected in Die Frauen-Zeitung," *History of Education*, 35 (2): 283–92.

Murphy, Daniel (2000), *A History of Irish Emigrant and Missionary Education*, Dublin: Four Courts Press.

N.B. (1874), "Town Schools," *Ulula*, 1 (2): 162.

Negt, Oskar and Alexander Kluge (1993), *Public Sphere and Experience: Towards an Analysis of the Bourgeois and Proletarian Public Sphere*, Minneapolis: University of Minnesota Press.

Newman, John Henry (1873), *The Idea of a University*, London: Basil Montagu Pickering.

Newsome, David (1961), *Godliness and Good Learning: Four Studies on a Victorian Ideal*, London: John Murray.

Nilsson, Anders (1999), "What Do Literacy Rates in the 19th Century Really Signify?: New Light on an Old Problem from Unique Swedish Data," *Paedagogica Historica*, 35 (2): 274–96.

Norman, Edward (1985), *Roman Catholicism in England*, Oxford: Oxford University Press.

Nóvoa, António (1995), "On History, History of Education, and History of Colonial Education," in António Nóvoa, Marc Depaepe, and Erwin V. Johanningmeier (eds), *The Colonial Experience in Education: Historical Issues and Perspectives*, 23–61, Ghent: C.H.S.P.

Nurullah, Syed and J.P. Naik (1951), *A History of Education in India (During the British Period)*, London: Macmillan.

O'Connor, Maura (2010), *The Development of Infant Education in Ireland, 1838–1948: Epochs and Eras*, Oxford: Peter Lang.

O'Donoghue, Tom (2001), *Upholding the Faith: The Process of Education in Catholic Schools in Australia, 1922–1965*, New York: Peter Lang

O'Neill, Ciaran (2014), *Catholics of Consequence: Transnational Education, Social Mobility, and the Irish Catholic Elite, 1850–1900*, Oxford: Oxford University Press.

Ogawa, Manako (2007), "The 'White Ribbon League of Nations' Meets Japan: The Trans-Pacific Activism of the Woman's Christian Temperance Union, 1906–1930," *Diplomatic History*, 31 (1): 21–50.

Olekhnovitch, Isabelle (2007), "Les écoles protestantes en France de 1815 à 1880" (French Protestant Schools from 1815 to 1880), *Théologie évangélique*, 6 (1): 29–37. Available online: http://flte.fr/wp-content/uploads/2015/08/ThEv2007-1-Ecoles_protestantes_France_1815-1880.pdf (accessed February 14, 2019).

Olsen, Stephanie (2012), "Informal Education: Emotional Conditioning and Enculturation in British Bands of Hope 1880–1914," *Jahrbuch für Historische Bildungsforschung*, 18: 110–25.

Olsen, Stephanie (2014a), "Adolescent Empire: Moral Dangers for Boys in Britain and India, c. 1880–1914," in Heather Ellis (ed.), *Juvenile Delinquency and the Limits of Western Influence, 1850–2000*, 19–41, Basingstoke: Palgrave Macmillan.

Olsen, Stephanie (2014b), *Juvenile Nation: Youth, Emotions and the Making of the Modern British Citizen, 1880–1914*, London: Bloomsbury.

Olsen, Stephanie (2015), *Childhood, Youth, and Emotions in Modern History: National, Colonial, and Global Perspectives*, Basingstoke: Palgrave Macmillan.

Osborne, John W. (1964), "William Cobbett and English Education in the Early Nineteenth Century," *History of Education Quarterly*, 4 (1): 3–16.

Pankhurst, Richard (2018), "Learn About Ethiopia: The Pankhurst History Library," Link EthiopiaLink E. Available online: https://www.linkethiopia.org/ethiopia/learn-about-ethiopia/pankhurst-history-library/ (accessed April 20, 2020).

Papenheim, Martin (2003), "Roma o Morte: Culture Wars in Italy," in Christopher Clark and Wolfram Kaiser (eds), *Culture Wars: Secular-Catholic Conflict in Nineteenth-Century Europe*, 202–26, Cambridge: Cambridge University Press.

Parents' National Education Union (PNEU), ed. (1923), *In Memoriam, Charlotte M. Mason*, London: PNEU.

Passerini, Luisa (1987), *Fascism in Popular Memory: The Cultural Experience of the Turin Working Class*, Cambridge: Cambridge University Press.

Patriarca, Silvana (2013), *Italian Vices: Nation and Character from the Risorgimento to the Republic*, Cambridge: Cambridge University Press.

Pawlikova-Vilhanova, Viera (2007), "Christian Missions in Africa and Their Role in the Transformation of African Societies," *Asian and African Studies*, 16 (2): 249–60.

Pearson, J.D. (1830), *The British System of Instruction: As Adapted to Native Schools in India*, Calcutta: Baptist Mission Press.

Pedersen, Joyce (1987), *The Reform of Girls' Secondary and Higher Education in Victorian England: A Study of Elites and Educational Change*, New York: Garland.

Pepperman Taylor, Bob (2010), *Horace Mann's Troubling Legacy*, Lawrence: University Press of Kansas Press.

Pestalozzi, Johann Heinrich (1894), *How Gertrude Teaches Her Children: An Attempt to Help Mothers to Teach Their Own Children and an Account of the Method*, New York: Swan Sonnenschein.

Pietsch, Tamson (2013), *Empire of Scholars: Universities, Networks and the British Academic World, 1850–1939*, Manchester: Manchester University Press.

Pinckaers OP, Servais (1995), *The Sources of Christian Ethics*, Washington, DC: Catholic University of America Press.

Pinckaers OP, Servais (2001), *Morality: The Catholic View*, South Bend, IN: St Augustine's Press.

Pinoche, Auguste (1901), *Pestalozzi and the Foundations of the Modern Elementary School*, Syracuse, NY: C.W. Bardeen.

Pitman, Emma Raymond (1895), *Missionary Heroines in Eastern Lands: Woman's Work in Mission Fields*, London: S.W. Partridge.

Platt, Brian (2004), *Burning and Building: Schooling and State Formation in Japan, 1750–1890*. Cambridge, MA: Harvard University Press.

Pombo de Barros, Surya (2016), "Slaves, Freedmen, Free African Descendants, Non-Free, Blacks, Ingênuos: Education Legislation Concerning the Black Population in Nineteenth Century Brazil," *Educação e Pesquisa*, 42 (3): 591–605.

Pomfret, David M. (2014), "World Contexts," in Colin Heywood (ed.), *A Cultural History of Childhood and Family in the Age of Empire*, 189–212, London: Bloomsbury.

Pooley, Siân (2015), "Children's Writing and the Popular Press in England 1876–1914," *History Workshop Journal*, 80 (1): 75–98.

Popkewitz, Thomas S., Miguel Peyrera, and Barry M. Franklin, eds (2001), *Cultural History and Education: Critical Essays on Knowledge and Schooling*, London: RoutledgeFalmer.

Porter, Mary, Mary Woodward, and Horatia Erskine (1921), *Mary Sumner Her Life and Work and A Short History of the Mothers' Union*, Winchester: Warren and Sons.

Porter, Roy (2001), *Enlightenment: Britain and the Creation of the Modern World*, London: Penguin.

Powell, Avril (2017), "Challenging the 3Rs. Kindergarten Experiments in Colonial Madras," in Ezra Rashkow, Sanjukta Ghosh, and Upal Chakrabarti (eds), *Memory, Identity and the Colonial Encounter in India: Essays in Honour of Peter Robb*, 276–97, London: Routledge.

Pratt, Mary Louise (1992), *Imperial Eyes: Travel Writing and Transculturation*, London: Routledge.

Prevost, Elizabeth E. (2010), *The Communion of Women Missions and Gender in Colonial Africa and the British Metropole*, Oxford: Oxford University Press.

Prochaska, Frank K. (1978), "Little Vessels: Children in the Nineteenth-Century English Missionary Movement," *Journal of Imperial and Commonwealth History*, 6 (2): 103–18.

Pruess, James (1983), "The 'Koran' School, the 'Western' School, and the Transmission of Religious Knowledge: A Comparison from the Sudan," *Northeast African Studies*, 5 (2): 5–39.

Pruneri, Fabio (2006), *Oltre l'Alfabeto, L'istruzione Popolare dall'Unita d'Italia all'Età Giolittiana: il Caso di Brescia* (As well as the Alphabet, Popular Education from the Unification of Italy Until the Age of Giolitti), Milan: Vita e Pensiero.

Przystupa, Paulina F. (2018), "Nineteenth Century Institutional 'Education': A Spatial Approach to Assimilation and Resistance at Hoopa Valley Indian School," in Jane Eva Baxter and Meredith Ellis (eds), *Nineteenth Century Childhoods in Interdisciplinary and International Perspectives*, 166–78, Oxford: Oxbow Books.

Purvis, June (1985), "Reflections upon Doing Historical Documentary Research from a Feminist Perspective," in Robert G. Burgess (ed.), *Strategies of Educational Research: Qualitative Methods*, 179–205, London: Falmer.

Pycior, Julie Leininger (2013), "The History of Education in Latin America: An Overview," in *History of Education: Trends in History*, 33–48, Abingdon: Routledge.

Quiroca, Gloria (2003), "Literacy, Education and Welfare in Spain, 1893–1984," *Paedagogica Historica*, 39 (5): 599–619.

Raftery, Deirdre (2012), "Religions and the History of Education: A Historiography," *History of Education*, 41 (1): 41–56.

Raftery, Deirdre and Martina Relihan (2012), "Faith and Nationhood: Church, State and the Provision of Schooling in Ireland, 1870–1930," in Laurence Brockliss and Nicola Sheldon (eds), *Mass Education and the Limits of State Building, c. 1870–1930*, 71–88, Basingstoke: Palgrave Macmillan.

Raftery, Deirdre, Catriona Delaney, and Deirdre Bennett (2018), "The Legacy of a Pioneer of Female Education in Ireland: Tercentennial Considerations of Nano Nagle and Presentation Schooling," *History of Education*, 48 (2): 197–211.

Ramabai Association, ed. (1898), *Report of the Annual Meeting of the Ramabai Association, held March 16, 1898*, Boston: Press of George H. Ellis.

Ramirez, Francisco O. and John Boli (1987), "The Political Construction of Mass Schooling: European Origins and Worldwide Institutionalization," *Sociology of Education*, 60 (1): 2–17.

Randeria, Shalini (2009), "Entangled Histories of Uneven Modernities: Civil Society, Caste Councils, and Legal Pluralism in Postcolonial India," in Heinz-Gernhard Haupt and Jürgen Kocka (eds), *Comparative and Transnational History: Central European Approaches and New Perspectives*, 77–103, New York: Berghahn Books.

Rao, Parimala V. (2014), "Introduction: Perspectives Old and New," in Parimala V. Rao (ed.), *New Perspectives in the History of Indian Education*, 1–42, New Delhi: Orient Blackswan.

Rappaport, Erika (2004), "'The Bombay Debt': Letter Writing, Domestic Economies and Family Conflict in Colonial India," *Gender & History*, 16 (2): 233–60.

Rawick, George P. (1972), *From Sundown to Sunup: The Making of the Black Community*, Westport, CT: Greenwood.

Real Sociedad Económica de Amigos del País de Cádiz (1818), *Manual práctico del método de mutua enseñanza para las escuelas de primeras letras*, Cádiz: Imprenta de Hércules.

Reeves-Ellington, Barbara (2010), "Embracing Domesticity: Women, Mission, and Nation Building in Ottoman Europe, 1832–1872," in Barbara Reeves-Ellington,

Kathryn K. Sklar, and Connie A. Shemo (eds), *Competing Kingdoms: Women, Mission, Nation, and the American Protestant Empire, 1812–1960*, 269–92, Durham, NC: Duke University Press.

Ressler, Patrick (2010), *Nonprofit-marketing im Schulbereich: Britische Schulgesellschaften und der Erfolg des Bell-Lancaster-Systems der Unterrichtsorganisation im 19. Jahrhundert*, Frankfurt: Peter Lang.

Ressler, Patrick (2013), "Marketing Pedagogy: Nonprofit Marketing and the Diffusion of Monitorial Teaching in the Nineteenth Century," *Paedagogica Historica*, 49 (3): 297–313.

Ricardo López, A. and Barbara Weinstein, eds (2012), *The Making of the Middle Class: Toward a Transnational History*, Durham, NC: Duke University Press.

Rich, R.W. (1933), *The Training of Teachers in England and Wales During the Nineteenth Century*, Cambridge: Cambridge University Press.

Roach, John (1986), *A History of Secondary Education in England, 1800–1870*, London: Longman.

Roberts, M.J.D. (2004), *Making English Morals*, Cambridge: Cambridge University Press.

Roberts, Robert ([1971] 1990), *The Classic Slum. Salford Life in the First Quarter of the Century*, London: Penguin.

Rocca, Giancarlo (1999), "La Formazione delle Religiose Insegnanti tra Otto e Novecento" (The Formation of Teaching Sisters Between the Nineteenth and Twentieth Centuries), in Luciano Pazzaglia (ed.), *Cattolici, Educazione e Trasformazioni Socio-Culturali in Italia tra Otto e Novecento*, 419–58, Brescia: La Scuola.

Rocca, Giancarlo (2019), "Maria Montessori e i corsi di pedagogia infantile" (Maria Montessori and Courses on Child Pedagogy), *Annali di storia dell'educazione e delle istituzioni scholastiche*, 25: 74–88.

Rodwell, Grant (2000), "'Persons of lax morality': Temperance, Eugenics and Education in Australia," *Journal of Australian Studies*, 24 (64): 62–74.

Rogers, Rebecca (2005), *From the Salon to the Schoolroom Educating Girls in Nineteenth-Century France*, University Park: Pennsylvania State University Press.

Rogers, Rebecca (2011), "Teaching Morality and Religion in Nineteenth-Century Colonial Algeria: Gender and the Civilizing Mission," *History of Education*, 40 (6): 741–59.

Roldán Vera, Eugenia (1999), "The Monitorial System of Education and Civic Culture in Early Independent Mexico," *Paedagogica Historica*, 35 (2): 297–331.

Roldán Vera, Eugenia (2007), "Export as Import: James Thomson's Civilizing Mission in South America," in Eugenia Roldán Vera and Marcelo Caruso (eds), *Imported Modernity in Post-Colonial State Formation: The Appropriation of Political, Educational, and Cultural Models in Nineteenth-Century Latin America*, 231–76, Frankfurt: Peter Lang.

Roldán Vera, Eugenia (2017), *The British Book Trade and Spanish American Independence: Education and Knowledge Transmission in Transcontinental Perspective*, London: Routledge.

Roldán Vera, Eugenia and Marcelo Caruso (2007a), "Introduction: Avoiding the National, Assessing the Modern," in Eugenia Roldán Vera and Marcelo Caruso (eds), *Imported Modernity in Post-Colonial State Formation*, 7–28, Frankfurt: Peter Lang.

Roldán Vera, Eugenia and Marcelo Caruso, eds (2007b), *Imported Modernity in Post-Colonial State Formation: The Appropriation of Political, Educational, and Cultural Models in Nineteenth-Century Latin America*, Frankfurt: Peter Lang.

Roldán Vera, Eugenia and Eckhardt Fuchs (2019), "Introduction: The Transnational in the History of Education," in Eugenia Roldán Vera and Eckhardt Fuchs (eds), *The Transnational in the History of Education: Concepts and Perspectives*, 1–47, Cham: Palgrave Macmillan.

Roldán Vera, Eugenia and Thomas Schupp (2005), "Bridges Over the Atlantic: A Network Analysis of the Introduction of the Monitorial System of Education in Early-Independent Spanish America," *Comparativ*, 15 (1): 58–93.

Romanes, Ethel (1908), *Charlotte Mary Yonge: An Appreciation*, London: Mowbray.

Rose, Jonathan (2001), *The Intellectual Life of the British Working Classes*, New Haven, CT: Yale University Press.

Rose, Jonathan (2007), "The History of Education as the History of Reading," *History of Education*, 36 (4–5): 595–605.

Rousmaniere, Kate (2015), "Looking at the Man in the Principal's Office," in Sevan G. Terzian and Patrick A. Ryan (eds), *American Education in Popular Media: From the Blackboard to the Silver Screen*, 195–217, New York: Palgrave Macmillan.

Rousmaniere, Kate, Kari Dehli, and Ning de Coninck-Smith (2013), "Moral Regulation and Schooling: An Introduction," in Kate Rousmaniere, Kari Delhi and Ning de Coninck-Smith (eds), *Discipline, Moral Regulation, and Schooling: A Social History*, 3–18, Hoboken, NJ: Taylor and Francis.

Rubinger, Richard (1990), "From 'dark corners' into 'the light': Literacy Studies in Modern Japan," *History of Education Quarterly*, 30 (4): 601–12.

Rubinstein, William, Michael Jolles, and Hillary Rubinstein, eds (2011), *The Palgrave Dictionary of Anglo-Jewish History*, Basingstoke: Palgrave Macmillan.

Rudé, George (1981), *The Crowd in History, 1730–1848*, 2nd edition, London: Lawrence and Wishart.

Rudé, George (1985), *Criminal and Victim: Crime and Society in Early-Nineteenth Century England*, Oxford: Clarendon Press.

Russell, James Earl (1898), *German Higher Schools: The History, Organization and Methods of Secondary Education in Germany*, New York: Longmans, Green.

Ryan, Mary P. (1981), *The Cradle of the Middle Class: The Family in Oneida County, New York, 1790–1865*, Cambridge: Cambridge University Press.

Said, Edward W. (1993), *Culture and Imperialism*, New York: Knopf.

Sánchez-Eppler, Karen (2005), *Dependent States: The Child's Part in Nineteenth-Century American Culture*, Chicago: University of Chicago Press.

Sanderson, Michael (1991), *Education, Economic and Social Change and Society in England 1780–1870*, Basingstoke: MacMillan.

Sandin, Bengt (2014), "Education," in Colin Heywood (ed.), *A Cultural History of Childhood and Family in the Age of Empire*, 91–110, London: Bloomsbury.

Sardar, Ziauddin and Borin Van Loon (1994), *Introducing Cultural Studies*, New York: Totem Books.

Scaraffia, Lucetta (1999), "'Christianity Has Liberated her and Placed her Alongside Man in the Family': From 1850 to 1988 (*Mulieris Dignitatem* [The Dignity of Women])," in Lucetta Scaraffia and Gabriella Zarri (eds), *Women and Faith: Religious Life in Italy from Late Antiquity to the Present*, translated by Keith Botsford, 249–80, Cambridge: Cambridge University Press.

Schram, Stuart R. (1967), *Mao Tse Tung*, London: Allen Lane.

Schriewer, Jürgen, ed. (2007), *Weltkultur und kulturelle Bedeutungswelten: Zur Globalisierung von Bildungsdiskursen*, Frankfurt: Campus.

Schriewer, Jürgen and Marcelo Caruso (2005), "Globale Diffusionsdynamik und kontextspezifische Aneignung: Konzepte und Ansätze historischer Internationalisierungsforschung," *Comparativ*, 15 (1): 7–30.

Schultz, Lucille M. (1999), *The Young Composers: Composition's Beginnings in Nineteenth-Century Schools*, Carbondale: University of Illinois Press.

Scientific Temperance Federation (Boston), ed. (1923), *Der wissenschaftliche Nüchternheits-Unterricht: Begründung und Entwicklung*, in collaboration with Julie Schall-Kassowitz, Bielefeld: Zentrale f. Nüchternheits-Unterricht; Wien: Bund abstinenter Frauen.

Scott, Henry S. (1938), "The Development of the Education of the African in Relation to Western Culture," in *Yearbook of Education, 1938*, 693–739, London: Evans Bros.

Scott, Joan Wallach (1992), "Experience," in Joan Wallach Scott (ed.), *Feminists Theorise the Political*, 22–40, London: Routledge.

Seccombe, Wally (1993), *Weathering the Storm: Working-Class Families from the Industrial Revolution to the Fertility Decline*, London: Verso.

Sedra, Paul (2011), "Exposure to the Eyes of God: Monitorial Schools and Evangelicals in Early Nineteenth-Century England," *Paedagogica Historica*, 47 (3): 263–81.

Sen, Satadru (2005), *Colonial Childhoods: The Juvenile Periphery of India, 1850–1945*, London: Anthem Press.

Seth, Sanjay (2007), *Subject Lessons: The Western Education of Colonial India*, Durham, NC: Duke University Press.

Seth, Sanjay (2008), *Subject Lessons: The Western Education of Colonial India*, Delhi: Oxford University Press.

Shahidullah, Kazi (1987), *Patshalas into Schools: The Development of Indigenous Elementary Education in Bengal, 1854–1905*, Calcutta: Firma KLM.

Shapin, Steven and Barry Barnes (1976), "Head and Hand: Rhetorical Resources in British Pedagogical Writing, 1770–1850," *Oxford Review of Education*, 2 (3): 231–54.

Shefrin, Jill and Mary Hilton, eds (2009), *Educating the Child in Enlightenment Britain: Beliefs, Cultures, Practices*, 41–55, Farnham: Ashgate.

Shuttleworth, Sally (2013), *The Mind of the Child: Child Development in Literature, Science, and Medicine, 1840–1900*, Oxford: Oxford University Press.

Siegel, Alexander W. and Sheldon H. White (1982), "The Child Study Movement: Early Growth and Development of the Symbolized Child," *Advances in Child Development and Behavior*, 17: 233–85.

Silber, Kate (1960), *Pestalozzi: The Man and His Work*, London: Routledge and Kegan Paul.

Silver, Harold (1983), *Education as History*, London: Methuen.

Simon, Brian (1960), *Studies in the History of Education 1780–1870*, London: Lawrence & Wishart.

Simon, Brian (1985), "Why No Pedagogy in England?," in *Does Education Matter?* 77–105, London: Lawrence and Wishart.

Simon, Brian (2005), "Can Education Change Society?," in Gary McCulloch, *The RoutledgeFalmer Reader in the History of Education*, 139–50, London: Routledge.

Sinha, Mrinalini (1995), *Colonial Masculinity. The "Manly Englishman" and the "Effeminate Bengali" in the Late Nineteenth Century*, Manchester: Manchester University Press.

Sinn, Elizabeth (2017), *Meeting Place: Encounters across Cultures in Hong Kong, 1841–1984*, Hong Kong: Hong Kong University Press.

Sloan, Catherine (2017), "'Periodicals of an objectionable character': Peers and
    Periodicals at Croydon Friends' School, 1826–1875," *Victorian Periodicals Review*,
    50 (4): 769–86.
Smelser, Neil J. (1991), *Social Paralysis and Social Change: British Working Class
    Education in the Nineteenth Century*, Berkeley: University of California Press.
Smith, Claire and Graeme K. Ward (2000), *Indigenous Cultures in an Interconnected
    World*, Vancouver: University of British Columbia Press.
Smith, John T. (2009), "*A Victorian Class Conflict?" Schoolteaching and the Parson,
    Priest and Minister 1837–1902*, Brighton: Sussex Academic Press.
Smitley, Megan (2002), "'Inebriates', 'Heathens', Templars and Suffragists: Scotland
    and Imperial Feminism c. 1870–1914," *Women's History Review*, 11 (3): 455–80.
Smuts, Alice (2006), *Science in the Service of Children, 1893–1935*, New Haven, CT:
    Yale University Press.
Snow, Edgar (1938), *Red Star Over China*, London: Victor Gollancz.
Sobe, Noah W. (2010), "Concentration and Civilisation: Producing the Attentive Child
    in the Age of Enlightenment," *Paedagogica Historica*, 46 (1–2): 149–60.
Society of the Sacred Heart (n.d.), "Key Figures in our History." Available online:
    https://rscj.org/who-we-are/heritage/history (accessed February 14, 2019).
Soldani, Simonetta (2010), "Chequered Routes to Secondary Education: Italy," in
    Joyce Goodman, Rebecca Rogers, and James C. Albisetti (eds), *Girls' Secondary
    Education in the Western World*, 59–76, New York: Palgrave Macmillan.
Soltow, Lee and Edward Stevens (1981), *The Rise of Literacy and the Common School
    in the United States: A Socioeconomic Analysis to 1870*, Chicago: University of
    Chicago Press.
Song, Jin-Woong (2012), "When Science Met People Through Education: The
    Mechanics' Institute Movement in Nineteenth-Century Britain," *Journal of the
    Korean Association for Science Education*, 32 (3): 541–54.
"Speech Day" (1892), *Ulula*, October 1892: 136–40.
Spencer, Stephanie (2010), "'Knowledge as the Necessary Food of the Mind':
    Charlotte Mason's Philosophy of Education," in Jean Spencer, Sarah Jane Aiston,
    and Maureen M. Meikle (eds), *Women, Education, and Agency, 1600–1920*,
    105–25, London: Routledge.
Stack, V.E. (1963), *Oxford High School: Girls' Public Day School Trust, 1875–1960*,
    Abingdon: Girls' Public Day School Trust.
Stamp, Robert M. (1973), "Empire Day in the Schools of Ontario: The Training of
    Young Imperialists," *Journal of Canadian Studies*, 8 (3): 32–42.
Steedman, Carolyn (1985), "'The Mother Made Conscious': The Historical Development
    of a Primary School Pedagogy," *History Workshop Journal*, 20 (1): 149–63.
Stephens, W.B. (1987), *Education, Literacy and Society 1830–70: The Geography of
    Diversity in Provincial England*, Manchester: Manchester University Press.
Stephens, W.B. (1990), "Literacy in England, Scotland, and Wales, 1500–1900,"
    History of Education Quarterly, 30 (4): 545–71.
Stephens, W.B. (1998), *Education in Britain 1750–1914*, Basingstoke: Macmillan.
Stevens, E.W. (1995), *The Grammar of the Machine: Technical Literacy and Early
    Industrial Expansion in the United States*, New Haven, CT: Yale University Press.
Stoler, Ann Laura (2001), "Tense and Tender Ties: The Politics of Comparison in
    North American History and (Post)Colonial Studies," *Journal of American History*,
    88 (3): 829–65.
Stone, Lawrence (1969), "Literacy and Education in England, 1640–1900," *Past and
    Present*, 42: 69–139.

Street, Brian (1990), "Putting Literacies on the Political Agenda," *Research and Practice in Adult Literacy (RaPAL) Bulletin*, 13: 2–7.

Street, Brian (1994), "Struggles over the Meaning(s) of Literacy," in Mary Hamilton, David Barton, and Roz Ivanic (eds), *Worlds of Literacy*, 15–20, Clevedon: Multilingual Matters.

Sumner, George Henry (1876), *Life of C. R. Sumner, D.D., Bishop of Winchester, During a Forty Years' Episcopate*, London: John Murray.

Sumner, Mary (1881), *Our Holiday in the East*, London: Hurst & Blackett.

Sumner, Mary (1895), *Home Life*, Winchester: Warren and Son.

Sumner, Mary (1910), *Memoir of George Henry Sumner, D.D. Bishop of Guildford: Published for his Friends by Special Request*, Winchester: Warren and Sons.

Sumner, Mary (n.d.-a), "Account of her Early Life at Hope End 1828–46," *Mothers' Union Archive*, Lambeth Palace Library.

Sumner, Mary (n.d.-b), "Account of the Founding of the Mothers' Union and Parochial Work at Old Alresford," *Mothers' Union Archive*, Lambeth Palace Library.

Sutcliffe, Marcella P. (2016), "Reading at the Front: Books and Soldiers in the First World War," *Paedagogica Historica*, 52 (1–2): 104–20.

Sutherland, Gillian (2015), "Self-Education, Class and Gender in Edwardian Britain: Women in Lower Middle Class Families," *Oxford Review of Education*, 41 (4): 518–33.

Swartz, Rebecca (2019), *Education and Empire: Children, Race and Humanitarianism in the British Settler Colonies, 1833–1880*, London: Palgrave Macmillan.

Szasz, Margaret Connell (1994), "Introduction," in Margaret Connell Szasz (ed.), *Between Indian and White Worlds: The Cultural Broker*, 3–20, Norman: University of Oklahoma Press.

Tamboukou, Maria (2016), *Women Workers' Education, Life Narratives and Politics: Geographies, Histories, Pedagogies*, London: Palgrave Macmillan.

Taylor, Insup and M. Martin Taylor (2014), *Writing and Literacy in Chinese, Korean and Japanese*, Amsterdam: John Benjamins.

Thompson, E.P. (1968), *The Making of the English Working Class*, Harmondsworth: Penguin.

Thorne, Susan (2006), "Religion and Empire at Home," in Catherine Hall and Sonya O. Rose (eds), *At Home with the Empire: Metropolitan Culture and the Imperial World*, 143–65, Cambridge: Cambridge University Press.

Tipton, Elise K. (2002), *Modern Japan: A Social and Political History*, London: Routledge.

Tolstoy, Leo (1967), "Are the Peasant Children to Learn to Write from Us? Or, Are We to Learn from the Peasant Children?," in *Tolstoy On Education*, edited by R. Archambault, 191–224, Chicago: University of Chicago Press.

Tosh, John (1999), *A Man's Place: Masculinity and the Middle-Class Home in Victorian England*, New Haven, CT: Yale University Press.

Traver, Teresa Huffman (2010), "The Ship that Bears Through the Waves," *Women's Writing*, 17 (2): 255–67.

Trenkov, Martin (2014), "Reasons for the Success of American Education in Late Ottoman Bulgaria," MA diss., Central European University.

Tröhler, Daniel (2016), "Curriculum History or the Educational Construction of Europe in the Long Nineteenth Century," *European Educational Research Journal*, 15 (3): 279–97.

Tröhler, Daniel (2020), "Introduction: Learning, Progress, and the Taming of Change," *Cultural History of Education in the Enlightenment*, volume 4, 1–16, London: Bloomsbury.

Trollope, Anthony ([1875] 1994), *The Way We Live Now*, London: Penguin Classics.

Truth and Reconciliation Commission of Canada (2015), *Honouring the Truth, Reconciling for the Future: Summary of the Final Report of the Truth and Reconciliation Commission of Canada*.

Tschurenev, Jana (2014), "A Colonial Experiment in Education: Madras, 1789–1796," in Barnita Bagchi, Eckhardt Fuchs, and Kate Rousmaniere (eds), *Connecting Histories of Education: Transnational and Cross-Cultural Exchanges in (Post) Colonial Education*, 105–23, Oxford: Berghahn Books.

Tschurenev, Jana (2018), "Women and Education Reform in Colonial India: Trans-Regional and Intersectional Perspectives," in Dörte Lerp and Ulrike Lindner (eds), *New Perspectives on the History of Gender and Empire: Comparative and Global Approaches*, 241–67, London: Bloomsbury.

Tschurenev, Jana (2019), *Empire, Civil Society, and the Beginnings of Colonial Education in India*, Delhi: Cambridge University Press.

Tsujimoto, Masashi and Yoko Yamasaki, eds (2017), *The History of Education in Japan (1600–2000)*, Abingdon: Routledge.

Twells, Alison (1995), "'So Distant and Wild a Scene': Language, Domesticity and Difference in Hannah Kilham's Writing from West Africa, 1822–1832," *Women's History Review*, 4 (3): 301–18.

Twells, Alison (2006), "Missionary Domesticity, Global Reform and 'Woman's Sphere' in Early Nineteenth-Century England," *Gender & History*, 18 (2): 266–84.

Tyack, D. (1974), *One Best System: A History of American Urban Education*, Boston: Harvard University Press.

Tyack, David and Larry Cuban (1995), *Tinkering Toward Utopia*, Cambridge, MA: Harvard University Press.

Tyack, David B. and Thomas James (1985), "Moral Majorities and the School Curriculum: Historical Perspectives on the Legalization of Virtue," *Teachers College Record*, 86 (4): 513–37.

Tyrrell, Ian (1991), *Woman's World, Woman's Empire: The Woman's Christian Temperance Union in International Perspective, 1880–1930*, Chapel Hill: University of North Carolina Press.

Tyrrell, Ian (2010), *Reforming the World: The Creation of America's Moral Empire*, Princeton, NJ: Princeton University Press.

Uglow, Jenny (2002), *The Lunar Men: The Friends Who Made the Future 1730–1810*, London: Faber and Faber.

Välimaa, Jussi (2004), "Nationalization, Localization and Globalization in Finnish Higher Education," *Higher Education*, 48 (1): 27–54.

Vallgårda, Karen (2014), *Imperial Childhoods and Christian Mission: Education and Emotions in South India and Denmark*, Basingstoke: Palgrave Macmillan.

Vallgårda, Karen, Kristine Alexander, and Stephanie Olsen (2015), "Emotions and the Global Politics of Childhood," in Stephanie Olsen (ed.), *Childhood, Youth and Emotions in Modern History: National, Colonial and Global Perspectives*, 12–34, Basingstoke: Palgrave.

Van der Walt, J.L. (1992), "The Culturo-Historical and Personal Circumstances of Some 19th-Century Missionaries Teaching in South Africa," *Koers*, 57 (1): 75–85.

Veysey, Lawrence (1990), "Review of Lawrence Cremin's *American Education: The Metropolitan Experience 1876–1980*," *American Historical Review*, 95 (1): 285.

Vinard, Jean-Claude (2004), "Les ecoles protestantes du Gard et de l'Hérault" (Protestant Schools of the Gard and the Hérault), in Jean-Paul Chabrol and Laurent Gambarotto (eds), *Éclairer le Peuple: Jean-Louis Médard 1768–1841* (To Enlighten the People: Jean-Louis Médard 1768–1841), 165–80, Aix-en-Provence: Presses universitaires de Provence. Available online: http://books.openedition.org/pup/6089 (accessed January 1, 2019).

Vincent, David (1981), *Bread, Knowledge and Freedom: A Study of Nineteenth Century Working Class Autobiography*, London: Europa Publications.

Vincent, David (1989), *Literacy and Popular Culture: England 1750–1914*, Cambridge: Cambridge University Press.

Vincent, David (1997), "The Domestic and the Official Curriculum in Nineteenth-Century England," in Mary Hinton, Morag Styles, and Victor Watson (eds), *Opening the Nursery Door*, 141–79, London: Routledge.

Vincent, David (1999), "Reading Made Strange: Context and Method in Becoming Literate in Eighteenth and Nineteenth Century England," in Ian Grosvenor, Martin Lawn, and Kate Rousmaniere (eds), *Silences and Images: The Social History of the Classroom*, 180–97, New York: Peter Lang.

Vincent, David (2000), *The Rise of Mass Literacy: Reading and Writing in Modern Europe*, Cambridge: Cambridge University Press.

Vinovskis, Maris A. (1992), "Schooling and Poor Children in 19th-Century America," *American Behavioural Scientist*, 35 (3): 313–31.

Viswanathan, Gauri (1989), *Masks of Conquest: Literary Study and British Rule in India*, New York: Columbia University Press.

Vojtáš, Michal (2018), "8 Itinerari educativi: pedagogia della gioia e della festa" (8 Educational Journeys: Pedagogy of Joy and Festivals). Available online: https://www.academia.edu/36578524/8_Itinerari_educativi_Pedagogia_della_gioia_e_della_festa (accessed May 20, 2018).

Walker, Martyn (2016), *The Development of the Mechanics' Institute Movement in Britain and Beyond*, London: Routledge.

Walsh, Patrick (2008), "Education and the 'universalist' Idiom of Empire: Irish National School Books in Ireland and Ontario," *History of Education*, 37 (5): 645–60.

Walther, Daniel J. (2001), "Creating Germans Abroad: White Education in German Southwest Africa, 1894–1914," *German Studies Review*, 24 (2): 325–51.

Walton, Susan (2010), "Charlotte Yonge: Marketing the Missionary Story," *Women's Writing*, 17 (2): 236–54.

Walton, Susan (2016), "'Spinning the webs': Education and Distance Learning Through Charlotte Yonge's Monthly Packet," *Victorian Periodicals Review*, 49 (2): 278–304.

Wang Jiang, He (2010), "The Investigation of Teacher Community's Process of Modernization at the Turn of the Late Qing Dynasty and Early Republic of China," MA diss., Northwest Normal University.

Watkins, Frederick ([1845] 1969), "Report of the Committee of the Council on Education, 1845, volume 2, 164–6," in P.H.J.H. Gosden (ed.), *How They Were Taught: An Anthology of Contemporary Accounts of Learning and Teaching in England 1800–1950*, 18–20, Oxford: Blackwell.

Watts, Ruth (1998), *Gender, Power and the Unitarians in England, 1760–1860*, London: Longman.

Watts, Ruth (2009), "Education, Empire and Social Change in Nineteenth Century England," *Paedagogica Historica*, 45 (6): 773–86.

Wayland Carpenter, George (1960), "African Education and the Christian Missions," *Phi Delta Kappan*, 41 (4): 191–5.

Weaver, Jace (1998), "From I-Hermeneutics to We-Hermeneutics: Native Americans and the Post-Colonial," in Jace Weaver (ed.), *Native American Religious Identity: Unforgotten Gods*, 1–25, Maryknow, NY: Orbis Books.

Weaver, William (2004), "'A School-Boy's Story': Writing the Victorian Public Schoolboy Subject," *Victorian Studies*, 46 (3): 455–87.

Webb, Robert K. (1955), *The British Working Class Reader 1790–1848: Literacy and Social Tension*, London: George Allen and Unwin.

Whitehead, Clive (2003), *Colonial Educators. The British Indian and Colonial Education Service 1858–1983*, London: I.B. Tauris.

Whitehead, Clive (2005a), "The Historiography of British Imperial Education Policy, Part I: India," *History of Education*, 34 (3): 315–29.

Whitehead, Clive (2005b), "The Historiography of British Imperial Education Policy, Part II: Africa and the Rest of the Colonial Empire," *History of Education*, 34 (4): 441–54.

Whitehead, Kay and Lyn Wilkinson (2008), "Teachers, Policies and Practices: A Historical Review of Literacy Teaching in Australia," *Journal of Early Childhood Literacy*, 8 (1): 7–24.

Whyte, William (2003), "Building a Public School Community, 1860–1910," *History of Education*, 32 (6): 601–26.

Whyte, William (2015), *Redbrick: A Social and Architectural History of Britain's Civic Universities*, Oxford: Oxford University Press.

Wiener, Martin (1981), *English Culture and the Decline of the Industrial Spirit, 1850–1980*, Cambridge: Cambridge University Press.

Wilkinson, Mathew L.N. (2015), *A Fresh Look at Islam in a Multi-Faith World*, Abingdon: Rutledge.

Williams, Heather Andrea (2005), *Self-Taught: African American Education in Slavery and Freedom*, Chapel Hill: University of North Carolina Press.

Williams, Maria Patricia (2015), "Mobilising Mother Cabrini's Educational Practice: The Transnational Context of the London School of the Missionary Sisters of the Sacred Heart of Jesus 1898–1911," *History of Education*, 44 (5): 631–50.

Williams, Maria Patricia (2018), "The Contribution of Saint Frances Xavier Cabrini (1880–1917) to Catholic Educational Practice in the Late Nineteenth and Early Twentieth Centuries," PhD diss., University College London.

Williams, Raymond (1961), *The Long Revolution*, London: Chatto and Windus.

Williams, Raymond (1983), *Keywords: A Vocabulary of Culture and Society*, London Fontana.

Williams, Susan A., Patrick Ivin, and Caroline Morse (2001), *The Children of London: Attendance and Welfare at School, 1870–1990*, London: Institute of Education.

Winchester Diocesan Mothers' Union Committee (1886–1910), Minute Book, *Diocese of Winchester Mothers' Union*, Hampshire Record Office.

Wolf, Eric R. (1982), *Europe and a People Without History*, Berkeley: University of California Press.

Wollons, Roberta Lynn (2000a), "Introduction: On the International Diffusion, Politics, and Transformation of the Kindergarten," in Roberta Lynn Wollons (ed.), *Kindergartens and Cultures: The Global Diffusion of an Idea*, 1–15, New Haven, CT: Yale University Press.

Wollons, Roberta Lynn, ed. (2000b), *Kindergartens and Cultures: The Global Diffusion of an Idea*, New Haven, CT: Yale University Press.

Woodin, Tom (2017), "Introduction: East London History," in UCL Library Services, *East Side Stories: Londoners in Transition*, 6–7, London: UCL.

Woodin, Tom (2018), *Working Class Writing and Publishing in the Late Twentieth Century: Literature, Culture and Community*, Manchester: Manchester University Press.

Woodin, Tom, Gary McCulloch, and Steven Cowan (2013), *Secondary Education and the Raising of the School Leaving Age—Coming of Age?*, New York: Palgrave Macmillan.

Woodley, Sophia (2009), "'Oh miserable and most ruinous measure!': The Debate Between Private and Public Education in Britain, 1760–1800," in Jill Shefrin and Mary Hilton (eds), *Educating the Child in Enlightenment Britain: Beliefs, Cultures, Practices*, 21–39, Farnham: Ashgate.

Wright, Susannah (2012), "Citizenship, Moral Education and the English Elementary School," in Laurence Brockliss and Nicola Sheldon (eds), *Mass Education and the Limits of State Building, c. 1870–1930*, 21–45, London: Palgrave Macmillan.

Wright, Susannah (2018), "Educating the Secular Citizen in English Schools 1897–1938," *Cultural and Social History*, 15 (2): 215–32.

Wright, Wendy M. (2004), *Heart Speaks to Heart: The Salesian Tradition*, London: Darton, Longman and Todd.

Wu, Jialin Christina (2015), "'A Malayan Girlhood on Parade': Colonial Femininities, Transnational Mobilities, and the Girl Guide Movement in British Malaya," in Richard Jobs and David Pomfret (eds), *Transnational Histories of Youth in the Twentieth Century*, 92–112, London: Palgrave Macmillan.

Wyatt, Victoria (1994), "Female Native Teachers in Southeast Alaska: Sarah Dickinson, Tillie Paul and Frances Willard," in Margaret Connell Szasz (ed.), *Between Indian and White Worlds: The Cultural Broker*, 179–96, Norman: University of Oklahoma Press.

Wyman, Andrea (1995), "The Earliest Early Childhood Teachers: Women Teachers of America's Dame Schools," *Young Children*, 50 (2): 29–32.

Yamaguchi, Midori (2014), *Daughters of the Anglican Clergy: Religion, Gender and Identity in Victorian England*, Basingstoke: Palgrave Macmillan.

Yonge, Charlotte Mary (1854), "To Mary Anne Dyson, 9 June," in Charlotte Mitchell, Ellen Jordan, and Helen Schinske (eds), *The Letters of Charlotte Mary Yonge (1823–1901)*. Available online: https://c21ch.newcastle.edu.au/yonge/3048/to-mary-anne-dyson-19 (accessed February 2, 2019).

Yonge, Charlotte Mary ([1856] 1899), *The Daisy Chain*, London: Macmillan.

Yonge, Charlotte Mary ([1868] 2006), *New Ground*. Available online: https://play.google.com/books/reader?id=_BICAAAAQAAJ&printsec=frontcover&pg=GBS.PP1 (accessed April 21, 2020).

Yonge, Charlotte Mary ([1871] 2015), *Pioneers and Founders, or, Recent Workers in the Mission Field*, Hastings: Delphi. Kindle edition.

Yonge, Charlotte Mary (1875), *Life of John Coleridge Patteson, Missionary Bishop of the Melanesian Islands*, 2 volumes, London: Macmillan. Kindle edition.

Yonge, Charlotte Mary (2015), *The Making of a Missionary*. Available online: https://ia800501.us.archive.org/16/items/makingofmissiona00yong/makingofmissiona00yong.pdf (accessed March 15, 2019).

Youmans, Charles D. (2003), "The Development of Richard Strauss's Worldview," in Mark-Daniel Schmid, *The Richard Strauss Companion*, 63–100, Westport, CT: Praeger.

Yu, Tingjie (2013), "Teacher Education in China: Current Situation & Related Issues." Zhejiang Normal University, April 26. Available online:A https://www.uta.fi/cerec/

educationandresearch/ChinaEduLecture/TeacherEducationinChina.pdf (accessed April 20, 2020).

Yun Casalilla, Bartolomé (2014), "Transnational History: What Lies Behind the Label? Some Reflections from the Early Modernist's Point of View," *Culture & History Digital Journal*, 3 (2): 25.

Zeldin, Theodore (1977), *A History of French Passions 1848–1945*, volume 2, *Intellect Taste and Anxiety*, Oxford: Oxford University Press.

Zeldin, Theodore (1980a), *A History of French Passions 1848–1945*, volume 3, *Intellect and Pride*, Oxford: Oxford University Press.

Zeldin, Theodore (1980b), *A History of French Passions 1848–1945*, volume 4, *Taste and Corruption*, Oxford: Oxford University Press.

Zimmerman, Jonathan (1992), "'The Queen of the Lobby': Mary Hunt, Scientific Temperance, and the Dilemma of Democratic Education in America, 1879–1906," *History of Education Quarterly*, 32 (1): 1–30.

Zimmerman, Jonathan (1999), *Distilling Democracy: Alcohol Education in America's Public Schools, 1880–1925*, Lawrence: University Press of Kansas.

Zoraida Vázquez, Josefina (2019), "Education: Latin America," *Encyclopedia Brittanica*. Available online: https://www.britannica.com/topic/education/Migration-and-the-brain-drain#ref47729 (accessed April 20, 2020).

CONTRIBUTORS

Sue Anderson-Faithful is a senior lecturer at the University of Winchester and a member of the university's Centre for the History of Women's Education. She is author of *Mary Sumner, Mission, Education and Motherhood: Thinking a Life with Bourdieu* (2018). Her research focus is on Anglican women's philanthropic and educational activism in the Victorian and Edwardian eras, in particular the Mothers' Union and Girls' Friendly Society. Sue is the editor of the Sybil Campbell Collection newsletter and a joint editor of *History of Education Researcher*.

Alys Blakeway is an independent researcher and lifelong Charlotte Yonge enthusiast. Formerly the Local Studies Librarian for Hampshire County Libraries, she is now Secretary of the Charlotte Mary Yonge Fellowship and has presented papers on Yonge in numerous fora, including the History of Education Society (UK) and Winchester University's Centre for the History of Women's Education.

Maxine Burton is a freelance researcher and consultant, based in Sheffield. Her doctoral research examined attitudes to illiteracy in nineteenth-century England, drawing on the documentary sources of Parliamentary Papers and Victorian novels. She has many years' experience of adult literacy and linguistics teaching, and worked as a Research Fellow at the University of Sheffield on a major ESF-funded project on adult literacy.

Heather Ellis teaches and researches history of education at the University of Sheffield. She has recently completed a project exploring the history of British students' study abroad funded by the Society for Educational Studies. She is the author of two books: *Generational Conflict and University Reform: Oxford in* *the Age of Revolution* (2012), which was jointly awarded the Kevin Brehony Prize by the History of Education Society UK and *Masculinity and Science in Britain, 1831–1918* (2017). She is currently a coeditor of the journal *History of Education.*

Joyce Goodman is Professor of History of Education at the University of Winchester and chercheure associée at CERLIS.eu. Her research explores the intersection of women's work in and for education with internationalism and empire. She is working on a biography of artist Rosa Branson. Her previous books include *Girls' Secondary Education in the Western World* (2014), with James Albisetti and Rebecca Rogers; and *Women and Education: Major Themes in Education* (2011, four volumes), with Jane Martin. Joyce is an honorary member of ISCHE and Network 17 of EERA. For her publications see www. joycegoodman.org.uk.

Marianne A. Larsen is Professor in the Faculty of Education, Western University in London, Canada. Her first book, *The Making and Shaping of the Victorian Teacher* (2011) presented a comparative, new cultural history of teachers in North America and Europe. While her early research focused specifically on teachers, over the past fifteen years she has studied a wide range of international education topics, including global citizenship education, international service learning, and academic mobility. Her 2016 book, *Internationalization of Higher Education: An Analysis through Spatial, Network and Mobilities Theories* demonstrated her ability to theorize "outside of the box."

Gary McCulloch is Brian Simon Professor of the History of Education at UCL Institute of Education London. He is currently Editor of the *British Journal of Educational Studies* and previously Editor of *History of Education,* and is a past president of the UK History of Education Society and the British Educational Research Association. His recent publications include *Transnational Perspectives on Curriculum History* and *A Social History of Educational Studies and Research,* which won the 2019 Society for Educational Studies book award.

Stephanie Olsen is Senior Researcher at the Centre of Excellence in the History of Experiences, Tampere University. The author/coauthor of *Juvenile Nation: Youth, Emotions and the Making of the Modern British Citizen* (2014) and *Learning How to Feel: Children's Literature and the History of Emotional Socialization* (2014), and the editor of *Childhood, Youth and Emotions in Modern History* (2015), Olsen is the coeditor of the forthcoming six-volume *Cultural History of Youth* and the four-volume *Children, Childhood and Youth in the Long Nineteenth Century.* She coedits the journal *History of Education.*

Catherine Sloan is Fellow of Hertford College, Oxford, UK, where she divides her time between her own research and designing and delivering academic skills support. Her research interests include childhood, youth, education, periodical culture, and children's cultures in modern Britain. She is currently writing a monograph on youth cultures in nineteenth-century English schools.

Stephanie Spencer is Professor of the History of Women's Education at the University of Winchester. She has published on formal and informal approaches to girls' education and convenes the Centre for the History of Women's Education at the University of Winchester.

Jana Tschurenev is Lecturer at the Institute of Asian and African Studies, at the Humboldt University of Berlin. She is the author of *Empire, Civil Society, and the Beginnings of Colonial Education in India* (2019). Her research focuses on the global history of education systems, childcare institutions, and the professionalization of teaching and care. Moreover, she is interested in questions of colonialism, postcolonial institution building, social inequality, and intersectionality in modern education.

Maria Patricia Williams completed her PhD at UCL Institute of Education in 2018. Her doctoral research explored the progressive educational practice of Saint Frances Xavier Cabrini (1850–1917) and her Missionary Sisters of the Sacred Heart of Jesus (1880–1917). Her current research focuses on the history of migrant education. She was a principal investigator on "A Pedagogy of Peace: The Theory and Practice of Catholic Teaching Sisters in Educating Migrants," a project led by the Cushwa Centre, University of Notre Dame.

Tom Woodin is a reader in the social history of education at the UCL Institute of Education. He is the author of *Working-class Writing and Publishing in the Late Twentieth Century* (2018). He led an ESRC-funded project that resulted in a book, with Gary McCulloch and Steve Cowan, *Secondary Education and the Raising of the School Leaving Age—Coming of Age?* (2013). He edited *Learning for a Co-operative World* (2019) and *Co-operation, Learning and Co-operative Values* (2014). His current projects include updating the history of the Institute of Education and writing a history of the Co-operative College.

Index